Gathering Years

Gathering Years

A novel by
Robert Nicholson

SUNACUMEN
PRESS

Cover art: W. B. Allen
Interior formatting: Sunacumen Press
Set in Adobe Garamond Pro

Publisher's Cataloging-In-Publication Data
(Prepared by The Donohue Group, Inc.)

Names: Nicholson, Robert, 1949- author.
Title: Gathering years : a novel / by Robert Nicholson.
Description: Palm Springs, CA : Sunacumen Press, [2020] | Includes
bibliographical references.
Identifiers: ISBN 9781734564303
Subjects: LCSH: Widows--United States--History--19th century--Fic-
tion. | Reconstruction (U.S. history, 1865-1877)--Fiction. | Diaries--Au-
thorship--Fiction. | Soldiers--United States--History--19th centu-
ry--Fiction. | Man-woman relationships--United States--History--19th
century--Fiction. | LCGFT: Historical fiction.
Classification: LCC PS3614.I35346 G38 2020 | DDC 813/.6--dc23

Library of Congress Control Number: 2020901956

Published by Sunacumen Press
Palm Springs, CA
Printed in the United States of America

For Karen

To think of time … to think through the retrospection,
To think of today … and the ages continued henceforward.

— Walt Whitman

1. 1866

Tuesday, February 13th

It has been an unusually wet winter, one gray, misty day following another in a seemingly endless succession. A light rain is falling this afternoon, one that promises to continue through the night. I really do not mind such days—they are conducive to reflection, and it is comforting to sit by the fire and watch the small droplets rap upon the windowpanes. Then, too, my artist's eye takes a certain delight in the way the rain transforms the scene outside, compelling us to view the houses, trees, and passing wagons as if through a shimmering film. And yet, there is one aspect of these somber days that disconcerts me: the poor, frail quality of the light. The house always seems dark now, and I had to light the lamp to write my letters even though my writing table is right beside the window. Even then, however, my hand cast long shadows on the page and the effort strained my eyes.

All the same, it has been rather warm and we shall probably have an early spring. On my walk this morning I noticed a few blades of crocus pushing up through the damp earth along the river bank. We must be patient and let everything come of its own accord.

Friday, February 16th

Another dull, gray day. I returned home about a quarter past twelve, as soon as the last of my classes was finished. Alicia had luncheon ready (some cold ham and pickled onions to go with her freshly made bread), which I shared with her at the long table in the kitchen. It is the warmest room in the house and on dark days one of the brightest, and this afternoon it was suffused with the smells of the dishes she was preparing for the weekend.

Although I am home two other afternoons a week, Fridays have always been special—the time when I set aside day-to-day concerns and attempt to take the measure of my week's work. As often as not, I come into the library and make a lengthy entry in this journal. It seems important to set it all down, even though my external life is so commonplace and my thoughts seldom attain real depth. It is as if the ordinary acquires significance by being recorded in this way.

Of the last few days, however, there is not much to say. Life at the Academy has taken on the same lethargy it has everywhere else this dreary month, as if our intellects too were awaiting renewal with the spring. Only the drawing exercises rouse any interest in the girls—these, at least, afford them a little activity, unlike passively attending to a lecture on the masters of the Quattrocento or the troubadour poets. I suppose, too, that after more than twenty years my lectures have lost some of their edge, that the passion I felt upon returning from Europe (when I was nineteen and breathless with so many new ideas) has waned. It is a sad thought, and so I shall put it off for a while. It will have to be taken up eventually, I know, but I prefer to believe that the time has not yet come.

Sunday, February 18th

Wet snow and a strong, northerly wind this morning. To my great relief, Judge Halston sent his carriage round to take me to church. He is such a dear man and has been so kind to me since John's death.

It was a fine, inspirational service, a needed tonic for the somber mood in which we have found ourselves these last few weeks. Mr. Williams spoke on the theme of reconciliation, taking as his text the story of Jacob and Esau. There was, he said, a new spirit of malevolence in the North, a desire to have our pound of flesh for the sufferings we had endured. And yet, had we not, through these same sufferings, prevailed in a righteous cause? Would we not leave a lasting memorial to all the generations to come? Aggrieved as we were, it was now our part to be magnanimous, to extend the hand of friendship to our countrymen. And he reminded us of that admonition of our late President, to let "the better angels of our nature" govern us at such difficult times.

I lingered a while after church, talking with a number of people, and then accepted a lift home. The house was quiet, as Alicia was away visiting her family and would not return until nightfall. I made myself a simple luncheon, read for a while in the library, and then, giving in to the lethargy of the day and the season, lay down to rest.

Friday, February 23rd

A pleasant week, graced by a couple of bright days. My classes were more successful (the girls seemed less restive and their fortnightly essays showed more focus and inspiration), and yesterday afternoon I managed to get in a long walk, the first since last autumn.

This afternoon I indulged in another rare luxury—a long, leisurely bath in the solitude of my dressing room. Alicia and I prepared it together, heating the water in kettles on the stove in the kitchen and then carrying it upstairs. At first I was reluctant to take her from her work, but she assured me that it would be no trouble—she would just assist me with my hair and then leave me to myself. I lay there quite a long while, lulled into a sort of trance by the warmth and softness enveloping me and the delicate touch of the steam on my temples. I may even have fallen asleep for a few moments.

An even more delightful sensation awaited me on stepping out of the bath—the sight of my own body in the full-length mirror adjacent to my wardrobe. Only on rare occasions have I looked at myself in this way, consciously and without hurry. Though not overly puritanical, my upbringing frowned upon vanity and the frivolous use of time, and with all the pressing concerns of life such an act would ordinarily have seemed extravagant. For some reason, however, I could not pull myself away. I lingered there before the mirror, intrigued by the image it presented: a woman forty years of age, a little taller than usual, with light brown hair and alert green eyes; pleasant in appearance, but with an intensity that makes her seem handsome rather than pretty; well proportioned, with the subtle feminine contours of the figures in the *Primavera*. I have resolved to look at myself more often, perhaps even to do my own portrait when the warm weather returns.

Tuesday, February 27th

I spent the afternoon settling the household accounts, as I am accustomed to doing towards the end of the month. Although it is no great accomplishment to look over the bills that have come in and write out a few drafts, I have always found it very satisfying to have my affairs in good order.

The house, of course, has been my responsibility since the time of my marriage, when my grandfather formally deeded it to me. Though large, its economy has been so perfected over the years that it almost seems to run itself. Alicia prepares the meals and does most of the cleaning (though I usually assist her with these tasks as my time permits); the laundry is sent out; a boy from several streets over furnishes our firewood, stacking it neatly on the porch by the kitchen door; various mechanics see to the repairs. The one change that I have made since my husband's death was to part with the carriage. In a village as small as ours there is really no need for one, and I usually prefer to walk anyway.

My income is diminished, of course, but remains comfortable. In addition to my shares in the company and some other investments, I have my teacher's salary and the fees from the drawing lessons that I give. With due care, I shall probably not want. Though I am very grateful for my good fortune, I am humbled by it too, knowing how many war widows have been reduced to charity. Every few weeks, it seems, we hear of a new subscription, to which I contribute as generously as I can.

Thursday, March 1st

This afternoon's post brought a letter from Judge Halston inquiring whether Thursday the 22nd would be an acceptable date for his lecture on the history of the village. With his customary modesty, he added that he hoped so ordinary a topic "would not be unworthy of our little lyceum." On the contrary, it seems fitting that we render some account of the past at this particular time, as we are probably on the threshold of a new era. Then, too, though we have occasionally managed to get a renowned lecturer, our "little lyceum" has been a largely homespun affair—which may well be one reason for its success.

There was also a note from Meredith Sims asking me to serve on a committee to arrange a day of commemoration for those who fell in the war. I wrote back to her saying that, of course, I would be very pleased to. Though committee work tends to be tedious, it is really my duty as wife of the regimental commander and it will enable me to honor him in a more public way than I have heretofore.

At these thoughts, however, I became profoundly sad. For the first time in months, the reality of my husband's death overcame me, and I slumped down in my chair (the same one in which I would sit beside him in the evening) and let my tears pour out. Alicia, hearing me in the hall, came in and put her arm around my shoulder. I pulled her to me and held her close for a long time, more grateful than ever that she is here.

Saturday, March 3rd

I have been thinking of John a great deal the last two days, but with fond remembrance rather than sadness. This morning, as Alicia and I were working in the kitchen, I thought about how pleasant our Saturdays had been. He would usually go to his office for a few hours in the morning, "just to tie up the loose ends," but return in time for luncheon. As often as not he would come in the side door, greeting us as lightheartedly as a boy just let out of school. After Alicia left we would have a quiet luncheon together and talk over the events of the week. In the afternoon, we might go for a drive (if the weather was nice and we felt like getting out) or just sit together and read. Occasionally we would have an engagement in the evening but were always content simply to be at home. It was a simple life but a rich one in its way, and though I miss him greatly I have many years of happiness to look back on.

Tuesday, March 6th

Mr. Williams paid me a pastoral visit this afternoon, as he does every month or so. We had tea in the parlor and conversed for perhaps an hour, first about church matters and then, in a rare and delightful turn of events, about Mr. Emerson's essay on experience. I had recently been reading this essay and the book was open on the table beside him. He noticed it and remarked what a profound piece of work it was. I replied, a bit hesitantly, that I had had some difficulty with it, that there was a passage that was still obscure after several readings. "Show me," he said. I found the passage and read it to him:

> It is very unhappy, but too late to be helped, the discovery we have made that we exist. That discovery is called the Fall of Man. Ever afterwards we suspect our instruments. We have learned that we do not see directly, but mediately, and that we have no means of correcting these colored and distorting lenses which we are, or of computing the amount of their errors. Perhaps these subject-lenses have a creative power; perhaps there are no objects.

Taking the volume from me, he reread the passage in silence, then scanned the next two or three pages. At that point a knowing look came over him and he nodded slightly as if in recognition of my difficulty. "It *is* a demanding section," he said, looking up at me. "In it Mr. Emerson gives us the whole problem of modern philosophy." He paused for a second, as if taking a deep breath, then went on: "The ancient philosophers assumed, without ever really questioning the idea, that there is an objective reality that our minds grasp more or less directly. It is a quite natural belief, and it held sway until the 17th century. Then it was almost completely overturned by the opposite notion—that all we can really know are our own perceptions, to which, to a large extent, we ourselves give form." He paused a moment to let this register, then added, "When Mr. Emerson says 'we exist,' I believe he means in this very subjective way—that we are alone and uncertain, without …" (here he glanced down at the pages that were open in his lap) "the assurance of a benevolent deity or a firm moral code."

I asked whether such a bleak vision could possibly be such a renowned author's final statement on the matter. Mr. Williams thought for a moment, then said in a measured tone, "It is difficult to say. He seems to present the problem and then to pass on without attempting to resolve it. But he does counsel us to show courage in the face of it." Here he ran his finger down the page until he found the passage he was looking for:

> We must hold hard to this poverty, however scandalous, and by more vigorous self-recoveries … possess our axis more firmly.

In response I merely nodded, not with complete understanding but with the feeling that I had a new key to this essay. As Mr. Williams was leaving he offered to lend me some works of philosophy, which I readily accepted.

Thursday, March 8th

There are definite signs of spring now. The days are markedly longer and many touches of green are starting to appear. For me, though, the most irrefutable sign is the change in the light. Unhindered by leaves on the trees or moisture in the air, it is remarkably intense—and the objects suffused in it sharp and almost praeternaturally real. I'm not certain that any of our painters have truly captured this sensation, this particular quality in the spring light.

I had these thoughts as I was coming down Academy Hill this afternoon, whence I could see the whole village at once. Though it is a view with which I am intimately familiar (having seen it countless times over many years), it always seems to hold something new.

Monday, March 12th

I went by the dressmaker's this afternoon with some things to be mended. Having been raised for the most part by my grandfather, I never really learned to sew. Nor have I ever had much inclination in that direction, though I have had Alicia show me a few simple stitches for use in emergencies.

I dress rather conservatively, of course, as befits one of Puritan stock. I have never gone in for the hoops and bustles that are so much *à la mode* these days—such things seem vain and frivolous to me, like the sculpted ices we serve at Christmas. It is not that I am indifferent to my clothes—I want them to be well made and I take considerable pleasure in their quiet elegance. But I want them to have a practical air as well, to proclaim that their wearer is a person with important work to do.

Friday, March 16th

I spent the afternoon checking on the arrangements for the Judge's lecture. Everything seems to be in order: the town clerk assures me that he will have the hall ready before he leaves for the day at half past five (there being no public business that day, this should present no real difficulty). Cynthia Edwards has spoken to the manager of the hotel about the refreshments to be served in the entryway afterwards. And a notice is set to appear in the *Clarion* tomorrow. The editor says that he will run the entire text in the next issue if we will secure him a copy. I imagine that the Judge will be agreeable to this but will have to discuss it with him.

Friday, March 23rd

The lecture was a great success. Any number of people came up to me afterwards to say how informative (and even inspiring) they had found it, and already I have had several notes of congratulation. The Judge himself appeared very pleased, warmly shaking hands and talking affably with those crowded around the refreshment table.

I was, I admit, rather anxious about the attendance on my

way to the hall, as it was a cold, blustery night, not the sort
to encourage going out of doors. But the room was nearly filled
when I got there and the mood seemed almost festive. No doubt
this warm and brightly illuminated place, with its tidy rows of walnut benches, appeared cheerful and reassuring on such a raw night.

The Judge declined an introduction, and simply took his
place at the podium at the appointed time. A large man with rather
stern features, he looked very imposing as he stood there waiting
for the audience to give him its full attention. When the room was
quiet, he began reading from the sheaf of papers in front of him
in that strong, pleasing voice that is so familiar to us. He went rather slowly, enunciating his words with care and pausing from time
to time to let his statements register. Though not a solemn address
(his wry sense of humor came through at any number of points),
it was clearly a serious one: in the simple history of our village one
could discern larger truths.

He began by saying that the muse of history had always been
strong in him, that even as a child the past had been very much
alive in his mind. Over the years his experience had only strength-
ened the conviction that a knowledge of "precedents" was as necessary to life as it was to the law. Now that nearly four decades had
passed since the first settlers had come here, it was time for those
who remembered the early years to render some account of them.

Of the history of this region prior to settlement we know
very little, he said. Its favorable situation and the large number of
arrowheads we have uncovered strongly suggest that the Shawnee inhabited the valley for a time. However, the early explorers,
who as a rule were very meticulous in recording their observations, make no mention of this. So if there ever was a permanent
encampment here it must have been abandoned well beforehand.

The first occupation by a member of our own race occurred
around 1810, when a trapper built a crude cabin along the river
opposite Academy Hill. He took out no patent to the land, however, and within a few years had moved on, leaving virtually no
trace of himself, not even his name. The cabin was subsequently
damaged by a flood and was torn down.

The present village was founded by settlers from the general
area of Springfield, Massachusetts, the first party arriving in the

summer of 1827 after an arduous overland journey. Though part of the general westward migration of the times, the settlement of this area was singular in one important respect: it was spearheaded by a small group of businessmen, including members of the most distinguished families in Springfield. (Here the Judge mentioned several names, among them that of my grandfather.) Their express purpose was to establish a manufactory for the making of optical instruments. To this end, they recruited master craftsmen from Europe as well as the manufacturing centers of New England and set about looking for a suitable site in the newer regions of the country. The high quality of the sand along the river and in its bed (judged to be perfect for lenses), along with the relative accessibility of the valley, led to its selection as the site of the enterprise. Though the fact undoubtedly played no role in the discussions, it is an area of some natural beauty as well, its gently flowing river and the rounded hills in the distance clearly offering a balm to the soul.

As it happened, the decision to look westward had a religious element also. For some years the Congregationalist Church had been racked by controversy between modern and traditional views, with much division and bitterness. Like the Puritans from whom so many of them were descended, the first settlers were a devout people, patient and long-suffering but determined to follow their own consciences. Accordingly, one of their first acts was to organize a church along liberal lines and call a minister—with the stipulation that he be a member of the Unitarian Association. In time that radical term would become part of the church's name as well.

The early years were difficult, as always in new settlements. That first summer was spent clearing land, laying out the principal streets, and erecting rude houses. A second party arrived in the autumn, bringing with them much-needed provisions—unlike their ancestors, these colonists would have no "starving time." Over the winter the company established a sawmill, cleared a plot of ground on the north side of the river for the factory, and erected a bridge. The following spring there were more settlers and the pace of activity quickened. It was a time of restless energy and clear purpose, a time when the surveyor and the architect, the stone mason and the joiner, had charge of things.

Within a few years a village distinctly reminiscent of those from which the settlers had come took shape. Indeed, seen from Academy Hill in the fullness of summer it could easily be mistaken for a town in the more thinly settled parts of New England. There is the same common, the same white clapboard houses, the same old-fashioned church with its simple steeple rising above the tops of the trees. It is an altogether worthy monument, both to our heritage and to our present purpose.

Much thought was given to the name by which they were to call the village. There are no natural features that especially distinguish the site, nor had prior occupants left us any sort of appellation. Although it might have been natural to name the village after a place from which the settlers had come, they were in fact from so many different places that agreement on one would have been difficult. At length they settled on the rather unusual name by which it is now known: Westerly. The literal meaning of this term, drawn from its old English roots, is "western meadow." The settlers, however, seem to have taken it in its adverbial sense, as an indication of the direction in which they had come and, more importantly, as a signal of the bright future that it appeared to promise them. For the direction of progress—and perhaps that of civilization itself—always seems to be westward.

In keeping with their hopes if not their expectations, the company that spawned our community has prospered greatly, enabling us to enjoy a number of the amenities of life—most importantly, the leisure to indulge in thought and the arts. It is not, as in many other places, all drudgery with us. In 1837, the village became the seat of government for the county, and a courthouse was erected along the west side of the common. Two years later came what is perhaps our richest adornment, the academy for girls whose overarching buildings in the classical style form a sort of Acropolis. A lending library and this lyceum (here he paused and looked around the room) were formed shortly thereafter. In 1850 the railroad came through, and the following year the telegraph.

Of our more recent history it was unnecessary to speak—it was a vivid memory for virtually all. Suffice it to say that we had acquitted ourselves honorably throughout the great difficulties that had beset our nation in the last two decades and thereby had earned a lasting place in the hearts of our countrymen. The Judge then closed with the hope that in some future year another would stand in his place, recounting for the people of that time the things he had said and adding those that were then necessary. In that way our village would have a continuous archive to guide and uplift all those to come.

Sunday, March 25th

The Judge's lecture prompts me to set down something of my own history, if only to leave a complete record. It is improbable, of course, that anyone else will ever see these lines: John and I did not have children and I have only distant relations in the next generation. Still, I feel compelled to paint my portrait in full.

I was born into an old commercial family in Springfield, Massachusetts, on the 11th of August 1825. Tradition has it that my forebears came from England in the early 1640s—the first years of that country's civil war—but of this I cannot be certain. I have only indistinct memories of my parents (they were to die of smallpox when I was nine), but I imagine that our life was pleasant and comfortable. My father, I have been told, was a compassionate man with an easy-going nature and an interest in the arts. My mother was more reserved, particularly in company, but I believe that her inner fires burned brightly. I recall the intensity with which she read scripture during our family devotions, an intensity born both of her precise mind and her strong moral sense. I probably take after my mother more, though certain elements of my father's character are pronounced in me as well.

Each of us, it is said, retains certain images from early childhood, images that epitomize our experience of that time. Mine are simple: a large brick house on a fashionable street, climbing into a carriage with my parents to go to church, studying piano in the front parlor, a particular dress that I was fond of. The vestiges, I suppose, of the relatively uneventful life of a successful merchant's daughter in good times.

But it was not to last. In the summer of 1834 there was an outbreak of smallpox in Massachusetts, caused, it was thought, by a returning seaman. I was sent away immediately—to my cousin Elizabeth's in Lenox—but my parents remained in Springfield, my mother even assisting in the hospitals. In September word came that they had both fallen ill and passed away within a few days of one another.

I was not allowed to attend the funeral—the risk of contagion was still too great, and it was thought that such a ceremony would be too unsettling for a child. I seem to recall my aunt taking me into her arms and telling me that it was God's will, that I would still be loved and cared for and that I had to be courageous in the face of suffering. But I don't believe that I felt real grief for very long. However painful initially, death tends not to be an enduring reality for children and it had all come about so suddenly.

I remained with Elizabeth's family until after Thanksgiving, when my grandfather came for me. It had been decided that I would return to Ohio with him. Though the frontier was perhaps not the best place for a young girl, he wanted me to be with him and believed that he could give me a proper upbringing.

We spent the winter in Springfield, settling my father's business affairs and preparing for the move west. My only distinct memory of that period is of our visits to my parents' graves. They are in the new cemetery east of town, where a rise in the ground affords a fine view of the valley. Unlike the old burying ground with its crumbling slate headstones (so emblematic of the Puritans' belief in the transitoriness of all earthly things), it is a richly landscaped park with pleasant drives and shaded benches on which to rest. It makes for a nice excursion, and I believe my grandfather found it very soothing. On the way back he would be given to reminiscing about his first years in Springfield, when he was just getting started in business. It must have been a painful leave-taking for him: though his restless energy had taken him west, his heart remained in New England and he cherished the hope of spending his last days at home with his son, secure in the knowledge that all of the ventures he had launched were thriving. Now many were to be in other hands entirely.

We left for Ohio around the first of May, taking the easiest route: by train and coach to Buffalo, along the shore of Lake Erie by steamer, and then overland by coach and wagon. It must have been a fairly arduous journey but to me it was pure adventure. I had never travelled with my parents and Ohio still seemed wild in those days—heavily wooded, with narrow, rutted roads along which things were quickly lost to view.

Westerly had a more settled look, but even so its newness was evident in the fields still full of stumps, the constant hammering, and the smell of fresh paint. And as it happened, it was a marvelous place in which to grow up. There was a handful of girls about my own age, and we soon formed our own knot. Our elders' preoccupation with establishing an entirely new community, along with the general optimism of the times, afforded us a great deal of freedom and we took full advantage of it. On some days we roamed the hills and woods like little savages, shouting at the top of our lungs and sending the small forest animals scurrying for cover. On others we put on our finery and held "salons," sipping tea and talking in the exalted tones of the landed gentry. And, as always with girls of that age, we were much taken with the notion of romance. Looking back, I am certain that chores and lessons formed the largest part of our young lives; but it is the carefree moments, the moments of wonder and indulgence, that I remember most clearly.

My education was thorough but largely conventional, seldom going beyond the subjects thought suitable for a girl of my age. History, modern literature, and the arts formed the core of my studies, with small excursions into mathematics and the sciences. My grandfather took a great deal of interest in what I was learning, however. Each night at dinner he would ask what I had done in class that day as well as what I made of it. Though I did not realize it at the time, these conversations were an important part of the formation of my mind. They forced me to review—and more importantly, to assess—the content of my lessons, to form actual judgments about them and to find in them some meaning of my own. He also encouraged me to study in the library (this room in which I now write) rather than in my bedchamber. The solemn air of the room and the presence of his books would lend seriousness to my purpose, he believed. We would sometimes go there together after dinner, I to sit at the large desk and work on my lessons, he to sit by the fire and peruse a favorite author or perhaps just a newspaper.

My one regret is that I am not more proficient at the classical languages. I have had a bit of Latin, of course, and can read it well enough to get the general meaning. But the subtleties are lost on me, I'm afraid—the solemnity of Virgil and the sarcasm of Cicero I must take largely on faith.

At eighteen, I went to Europe to study art. Though by no means displeased with my education, my grandfather wanted me to have a firsthand acquaintance with the world's cultural and intellectual achievements. We left here in early summer and spent eight weeks or so taking in the sights in England, France, and Germany. I have a few distinct memories of those travels (Napoleon's tomb and Goethe's house in Weimar, the latter of which my grandfather was particularly anxious to visit), but mostly it is a blur—too many unfamiliar things crowded into too small a period of time.

We arrived in Rome, where I was to spend the coming year, on the first of September. My grandfather got me settled into my lodgings, concluded the arrangements with the studio where I was to study, and then left for home. Although it took me a little while to get my bearings, my new surroundings could not have been nicer. My lodgings were located on a side street near the Piazza di Spagna with its famous steps. The neighborhood had been favored by artists for more than two centuries, and there were numerous studios and galleries in addition to its major attractions: the Villa Borghese with its vast gardens, ornate churches from the sixteenth and seventeenth centuries, and an abundance of ancient columns and arches. It has connections with literature as well—Goethe and Shelley lived nearby and the house in which Keats died is right on the square. If Rome were no more than this one section of the city, it would still offer a very full education.

The house in which I was staying was a small palazzo owned by an affable English woman who let rooms to students and seasonal visitors. Though probably no more than two hundred years old, it had an air of timeless antiquity, as so many things in Italy do. The interior was quiet and cool, a welcome relief from the noise and bustle of the street. And in the back was a large walled garden, a bit overgrown but filled with secluded spots where I could go on nice afternoons to sketch or read—or simply to breathe in the luxuriant air of this ancient land.

The studio was about twenty minutes away, through a sequence of narrow streets. It was not an especially pleasant walk, but I was generally so engrossed in conversation with the other students from the house as not to notice. The studio itself was a large, open room with white walls, which would have seemed cavernous had it not been for the light admitted by a row of windows just beneath the ceiling. The focal point of the room was a small platform surrounded by an untidy array of stiff-backed chairs and easels. Various sketches, oils, and copies of famous paintings hung from the walls.

The classes, which were largely devoted to the fine points of technique, lasted only until midday. In the afternoon we were supposed to work on our assignments, visit galleries, and roam the city with our sketch pads, cultivating those powers of observation so essential to the artist. Of all my memories of that period, the most vivid is that of the drawing master, Signor' Antonelli. He would come around behind me as I sat at my easel, put his hand on the back of my chair, and leaning forward, study my work in silence for a few moments. Then he would take the sliver of charcoal from my hand and, holding it just off the paper, sketch out in the air the correction he had in mind. Only then would he look at me and, smiling politely, ask if I had understood. His own drawings were exquisite—graceful, precise lines that nonetheless had something transcendental about them. A drawing must have *spiritu*, he would say—a soul.

But it was not a year devoted to art alone. As my grandfather had urged me, I visited the ancient monuments, took in concerts, and attended lectures on current topics, recording my observations in long letters home. There was also something of a social season among the Americans residing in Rome. Through the Harrisons, an elderly couple from Richmond whom I met at the Protestant chapel, I gained admission to several dinners as well as a diplomatic reception. I also took long carriage rides through the city with them.

With the coming of spring there was great interest in getting up excursions into the countryside. Sometimes the object would be a chapel with a famous fresco or some ruins from antiquity, at others the delightful Italian countryside itself. Whatever their purpose, they remain among the most vivid memories of my year abroad—little villages that seemed to transcend time, hillsides bathed in the intense light of early spring, finely etched cypresses along the roads, the air dry and aromatic as if scented with herbs. Though I made a number of sketches on these excursions, no sketch could ever truly capture all the subtleties of such a scene or the exquisite emotions they engendered. I always returned in a sort of trance, like one who has undergone a religious conversion.

Around the first of May I received a letter from my grandfather saying that he had arranged for me to sail directly from Ostia so that I could see something of the western Mediterranean. He also mentioned that the headmistress of the Academy wished to take me on as an art instructor in the autumn. Up 'til then I had given little thought to a profession, so this came as a complete surprise. I was a little frightened at the prospect and wrote back that I would have to think about it. But without really intending to I began formulating a sequence of lessons in my mind.

Six weeks later I bid my acquaintances in Rome a rather tearful farewell and set out for home. Though it was to be some time before we passed through the strait at Gibraltar and into the open ocean, my thoughts turned to America almost immediately. To be sure, I had acquired a great deal of culture and a sense of refinement that I could not have gotten at home. But I was also very conscious of the Old World's failings: its rigidities of class and custom; its lack of seriousness, even about the most significant things; and (perhaps the most disturbing for one used to democratic government) the repression of dissent. Indeed, throughout Europe political unrest seemed to be seething just below the surface, and one had the feeling that it could erupt at any time—as it did only four years later.

Realizing these things, I began to understand the forces drawing people to the New World as well as the unique forms that our social and political life has assumed. But the voyage was not entirely taken up with such weighty reflections. I also found time to draw, to read (I had gotten a copy of Irving's Sketch Book just for the trip and found it thoroughly delightful), and to engage in pleasant conversations with the other passengers. And by the time we landed in New York, my thoughts had turned entirely to Westerly and the direction that my future life would take.

That autumn I began teaching at the Academy. It was only a single drawing class—two hours, three times a week—but it became clear almost immediately that this was my calling. I seemed to have a natural rapport with the girls (who were not that far from me in age and who were very impressed by my European education) and their enthusiasm proved contagious. At Thanksgiving the headmistress suggested adding a course of lectures on art history in the second term and I accepted without hesitation. Thus, with no real effort or even a clear purpose, my career was launched.

The other question hanging over me that autumn was that of my marriage. To this, too, I had not given much thought apart from recognizing that I probably would marry and that my husband would most likely come from our own circle of acquaintance in Westerly. I had known John since childhood and owing to the close ties between our families had even been paired with him in some minds. But it had been at least a couple of years since I had even seen him, as he had been away studying law, and we were certainly not promised to each other in any sense. All the same, we found ourselves together a great deal that autumn in an informal sort of courtship. We became engaged at Christmastime and were married Sunday evening, the 25th of May 1845, one of the loveliest days of that entire year.

Nowadays it is common to marry for love, and that alone. In my generation, however, it was considered sufficient if the couple were persons of good character and had a certain measure of respect and affection for each other. Though based on the modest expectations of the times, ours was a good union. John was always very kind and devoted to me, and I believe that in time we forged a love that was deeper and richer than even the ideal of this current age.

Though my grandfather continued to live with us, he made a point of not being obtrusive. He removed his bedchamber to a small room at the back of the house, gave me complete charge of the household, and retired early in the evening. Of course, he was beginning to decline then and within a couple of years would need an attendant at all hours. He died the 18th of November 1850, at age seventy-eight, and (as he had requested) was returned to

Springfield for burial. Though greatly saddened, I took comfort in the fact that he was a great man who had lived a full life and whose legacy would endure.

The only other thing to disturb the placidity of those years was the fact that we could not have children (I only conceived twice, and miscarried early both times.) This may have been all for the best, however. Though I am fond of children, I am not certain that I have the patience to be a mother and might have resented the overwhelming demand on my time.

Throughout that decade, of course, there was increasing turmoil in the country, but it seemed so remote from our day-to-day concerns that we only occasionally gave it any serious thought. When the war came, we found it hard to believe that matters had taken so extreme a turn. But come the war did, bringing our charmed life to an end. That winter John helped organize the regiment and was elected captain of a company; they left to join the Army of the Potomac in late spring. I saw him only twice after that, at Christmastime that year and then the following November when he was made regimental commander. He was killed at Spotsylvania on the 12th of May 1864.

Thus my history. What the future may hold, I cannot say: few things endure, and most are beyond our knowing. My best years are past in any case, and I must be grateful that they were as good as they were.

Friday, March 30th

A rather somber day. Probably nothing more than being overly tired from the week, but as I have had periods of melancholy in the past I am always a little guarded about such moods.

Alicia was out when I got home, so I made myself some tea and got into bed. At first I attempted to read (a light novel, nothing very demanding) but could not hold onto the thread. At length I put out the lamp and simply lay there with my eyes closed, hoping to induce sleep to come. For some time, however, it would not; try as I might to clear my mind or concentrate on some simple, innocuous image, ragged, half-formed thoughts kept passing through my brain. Finally, after perhaps an hour, my fatigue overcame me and I drifted off. I was awakened several hours later by Alicia's knock at the door.

We had a simple dinner in the kitchen and afterwards I wrote letters, still feeling a bit subdued but better than I had.

Monday, April 2nd

First meeting of the Commemoration Day committee, at Lucy Thornton's house. After some wrangling we agreed on a program that indeed seems a fitting tribute to those whom we wish to honor. At ten there will be a parade along Main Street, from the cemetery at the eastern edge of town to the square. At eleven, after a prayer and remarks by several dignitaries, Colonel Thornton will recount the history of the regiment. Following this, members of the committee will read the names of the fallen for each year of the war. (Considerate as ever, Meredith Sims suggested that I read the names for 1863; without saying so, she wanted to be certain that I would not have to read my own husband's name.) This ceremony concluded, we shall adjourn to the open field along the river for an afternoon of picnicking and games. In the evening there will be a band concert, followed by fireworks. It will be a truly grand event, saddened only by the absence of those for whom it is being held.

Thursday, April 5th

This afternoon I received a letter from my cousin Elizabeth inviting me to spend the summer with her in the Berkshires. Ordinary as such an invitation might be, it caught me completely unawares (John and I did not travel a great deal and were seldom away for more than a few weeks at a time). Still, I shall have to give it serious consideration—there is really no reason why I should not go away and the diversion might be salutary.

Monday, April 9th

This afternoon, about half past four, the sexton rang the steeple bell in observance of the anniversary of Lee's surrender. It was a solemn, largely private occasion: we simply put aside whatever we were doing for a few minutes and listened as the clear notes reverberated through the soft spring air.

How vividly I recall the events of a year ago. We did not receive the news until after ten in the evening the following day. I was undressing for bed when I heard the bell being rung—loudly and insistently but not in the frenetic way in which it is rung for a fire. By the time I reached the square there was a large crowd, everyone anxiously milling about in cloaks hastily thrown over night-clothes or huddled together under umbrellas to ward off the light rain that was falling. After a few minutes the mayor ascended the courthouse steps and, in the light from a lamp held by the station master, read us the telegram. It was quite brief, no more than that the previous afternoon General Lee had surrendered the Army of Northern Virginia to General Grant at a place called Appomattox Court House, on generous terms.

For several seconds there was no reaction, as if the news were not to be believed. Then a huzzah from someone at the back of the crowd brought forth a torrent of shouts and tears and embraces, as if all the anxieties and hopes and sorrows of the last four years were finding release in that one moment. Overcome by my own emotions, I began to tremble, turning from one person to another and weeping uncontrollably. I do not know how long I remained in that state, but when I regained my composure Judge and Julia Halston were at my side, quietly attempting to comfort me. "It is over now, isn't it?" I recall saying to them. "Yes, dear Ellen, it is," the Judge replied, and folded me into his great arms.

At length the mayor called for quiet and asked Mr. Williams if he would lead us in prayer. In measured but joyful tones, our minister proffered humble thanks to God for vouchsafing us this victory and called upon Him to be mindful of all those who had suffered in His righteous cause. Then, after pausing a moment, he added, "We pray also for our former enemies, asking that you comfort them in this time of sorrow and restore the natural bonds of friendship between us. Amen."

The crowd then began to break up, many heading over to the lobby of the hotel, too happy and excited to go to bed just then. Though invited to accompany the Halstons, I went home instead, feeling the need to be alone with my thoughts. It was, indeed, quite an emotional moment for me. As long as the war was going on it was possible for me to imagine that John was still alive, that he would eventually return. Now, I knew, that illusion was gone forever.

Sunday, April 15th

The first truly warm day that we have had since last autumn. To take full advantage of it, I went for a long walk along the river in the afternoon (as far as the point where the road veers off to the south). Apart from a few solitary travelers the route was deserted, and once away from the village I was alone with my thoughts and the rich sensations of this lovely spring day.

The soul, of course, seems to expand on such days, as if drawn out by the warmth of the sun or the softness of the air. And yet, what delighted me the most, what gave me the greatest sense of peace and renewal, was the intensity of the sunlight. Strange to say, we now have as much daylight as we will in late summer, but coming after a long winter and without many leaves on the trees the April sun seems very much brighter. Certainly it has brought forth a profusion of early-season flowers, delicate bluets and spring beauties, along with the bolder marsh marigold. (Though it seemed a sacrilege, I picked one of these buttery blossoms as a companion for my walk.)

Toward evening the wind picked up and it began to grow cold. Once again I was reminded that for all her grace and charm, spring is a fickle lover.

Saturday, April 21st

I have spent the morning gardening, or rather preparing to garden—cleaning out the flower beds around the house and loosening the soil. At first I wasn't sure that I would be able to get out today, as it was cool and there was a light rain when I looked out just after dawn. By eight, however, the rain had let up and the man I'd engaged to turn over the vegetable garden had arrived with his horse. So, putting on an old woolen coat, I decided to press ahead with my plans.

As it happens, it is the tasks that come earliest in the gardener's year that I find the most satisfying. For I love the pungent odor of moist soil, love running my hands through it as one might with a piece of velvet. It seems so full of promise then, as if nothing that we might plant in it could possibly fail. But then, beginnings have always had a strong attraction for me. The sight of carpenters framing a house, the yard all strewn with stone and loosely stacked boards, gives me a sense of comfort that the finished structure, however pleasing its appearance, simply cannot. It is the difference between possibles and actuals, I believe—between the perfection we imagine and the necessarily flawed reality.

Of course, every time that I work outside I am reminded of the care with which my grandfather laid out the grounds. They are not large (at least in comparison with the house), but they provide shade and seclusion and a certain artistic interest. The front is small and relatively formal, mainly shrubs and brick walkways surrounded by a low picket fence. To the right is a narrow lane that leads to the carriage entrance on the side of the house, to the left a row of hemlocks. Immediately behind the house is a small area of lawn we have come to call the "piazza," where we sometimes entertain or have our meals in the warm weather. It is separated from the rest of the yard by a bed of rose bushes. Past that point the grounds have the look of a country estate—a broad expanse of lawn relieved by a massive oak and judiciously placed shrubs and flower beds. It is altogether a peaceful, tranquil spot, lovely to look at even in winter.

Beyond the road we have a small orchard with several varieties of apples and my grandfather's beloved plum trees, and beyond that a large vegetable garden. At that point the ground begins to rise and it is all woods. Indeed, in that direction there are no signs of a human presence for several miles.

Wednesday, April 25th

Continued wet and cool; I find myself longing for summer. I have written to my cousin saying that I shall accept her invitation and leave here shortly after the term ends on the 12th of June.

Tuesday, May 1st

I suppose committees have their place, but they can be endlessly frustrating as well. We have just spent an hour arguing over whether or not to solicit funds for a monument to the regiment in conjunction with our day of commemoration. Cynthia Edwards raised the question, saying that we should "strike while the iron was hot." With several others nodding in agreement, things became rather awkward. Though no one is opposed to a monument, most of us felt that we had our hands full as it was and that it would be best to defer the idea. Meredith tried to voice this view, suggesting that we sound out public opinion over the summer and approach the town council in the autumn. But Cynthia would not have it—her hackles were up, and she insisted on bringing the question to a vote. So Lucy (who had every appearance of wanting to table the matter for now) was forced to open the floor for discussion. In the end the motion was defeated six to four, but not without wasted time and a good deal of ill feeling. Cynthia, in fact, was rather cold to me as we were leaving, and I suspect it will be a while before we are on good terms again.

On the plus side of the ledger, however, the arrangements for the event appear to be going well. A date (Friday, the 8th of June) has been set, the speakers have been confirmed, and the other details are being attended to. I have written to John's father in Chicago asking him if he would like to attend, though it is probable that his health will not permit him to.

Saturday, May 5th

To Sentinel Hill for a day of sketching. I left early—just a little after dawn—Alicia having prepared a simple lunch for me and laid out my "field dress" (a plain linen frock fraying at the sleeves that I often wear to garden) the night before.

Though the day would later turn warm, it was cool and fresh as I set out, taking the path through the orchard up to the ridge behind the house. I have always loved the woods in the early morning, when the light is still subdued and they are filled with birdsong and the scurryings of little creatures in the litter. As I walked along I fell into a sort of reverie, conscious of my surroundings and my purpose yet somehow lifted above them.

It was going on eleven when I reached the summit. Though it is not that far away, the last mile or so is strenuous and toward the end there is much scrambling over rocks. As I had hoped, the spring was much less advanced up there and there were excellent views of the valley. I worked for several hours, comfortably perched on a large boulder, striving to record with my sliver of charcoal all the many details of the scene—the fields, farmhouses, woodlots, roads, and in the distance, portions of the village. Trying, too, to capture the serenity one feels in looking out over this valley. For though it is a settled place, filled with the hubbub of human activity, from this distance it is almost idyllic, so quiet and peaceful does it seem.

Landscapes, of course, have always held a special attraction for me, and it is here, I believe, that American art truly excels. For who can look at our painters' scenes of the Hudson River valley without a surge of emotion? And even in the *Lackawanna Valley,* purportedly a celebration of progress and the mechanical age, the sublimity of the setting largely eclipses the hideous tree stumps and intruding locomotive. It is as if, in a country so new, the instinct for primal nature cannot but predominate.

It must have been nearly three when I started back. The woods were almost entirely quiet, and I walked briskly, too bent on getting home to pay much attention to my surroundings. I arrived at half past five, tired but very satisfied with the day. Alicia, of course, had gone but left me a cold supper and a note wishing me a pleasant Sunday.

Wednesday, May 9th

This afternoon, after classes were over, there was a meeting at the Academy to plan the ceremonies marking the end of the school year. As always, I am to present the awards for drawing and the best essay on art. It is a task that gives me great satisfaction: in honoring individual girls we implicitly recognize the achievements of all, and more importantly, pay homage to the educational mission itself.

Saturday, May 12th

Our annual spring cleaning. Alicia and I were up early in order to have things ready for those who were coming to help us—her brother, two of her sisters, and several cousins, along with the boy who brings the firewood and one of his older brothers. After a hasty breakfast, we gathered up the pails, mops and brooms, dust cloths, carpet beaters, and so forth, and put them in the center hall (just beneath the stairs) where they would be easy to find but not in the way. Then, while I worked on the list of things to be done, Alicia made a large pot of coffee and prepared a table with several loaves of bread, butter, cornmeal muffins, and preserves.

By eight everyone was here and we set to work. Alicia and one of her sisters took charge of the kitchen, not to be seen again for several hours. The men took down the drapes (to be either laundered or shaken out), moved all but the largest pieces of furniture out into the yard, and put up lines on which to beat the carpets. The women (myself included) scrubbed walls and floors, cleaned windows, and polished furniture. It all went like clockwork, each one seeming to know just what to do next and how his own tasks had to mesh with those of the others. The comparison is trite, but it resembled nothing so much as a beehive—industry in every direction, perfectly harmonized. (I did, however, have to admonish one of the cousins to be careful in moving a mirror.)

At noon we broke for lunch: lamb stew and biscuits and apple cobbler that I had arranged to have sent over from the hotel. It must have been a fairly comic scene, people in work clothes lounging on sofas and chairs strewn haphazardly about the lawn, with much laughing and joking and horseplay. But after our morning's work it felt good to be a bit silly, and I joined in the fun with a will.

By four we were done. I paid everyone and said goodbye to Alicia, who was going to stay with her family until Monday evening. As I walked back through the now quiet rooms, so clean and fresh in appearance, I had a sense of immense satisfaction. There is a certain comfort, of course, in putting one's dwelling in order, particularly after the ravages of winter. But beyond that, I had the feeling of having kept a promise to this house, a promise first made by my grandfather when he built it, namely, to care for and preserve it to the best of our ability. For as he said on many occasions, we do not truly own our houses—we may possess them for a time, but ultimately we have to pass them on to others. As with so many other things of value—our learning, our mores, our institutions—we are stewards only.

My grandfather, of course, designed this house, and took great pleasure in it. It is a white clapboard structure in what might be called the Federalist style—balanced, with relatively simple lines but possessing a certain studied elegance. The front door, a large square of black walnut with narrow pilasters on either side and a bit of scrollwork above, is its most distinguished feature. In terms of layout it is what my grandfather called a "four poster," that is, four rooms on each floor with central hallways and the kitchen (which is brick, though painted white so as not to stand out) at the rear. There is also a short hallway on the main floor that leads to the side entrance.

The house faces northwest, and to take advantage of the afternoon light my grandfather put the library in that corner, just to the right of the door. It was his favorite room, the one where he spent most of his time when he was at home and the one on which he lavished the most care and attention. It is the only room in the house that is paneled, and though more solemn than the others offers a greater sense of repose. I always enter it as I might a chapel—reverently, and careful not to disturb its mysteries.

Opposite the library is a small, formal parlor where we receive our guests, and behind that is the dining room—a large, cheerful room done mainly in various shades of yellow. The last room on the main floor was intended to be a family parlor but was mainly used for storage during my grandfather's time and is now Alicia's bedchamber.

My own bedchamber is directly above the parlor, where it catches the morning light. It is my own favorite, of course, and much thought has gone into its decoration. The walls are painted a sort of grayish blue, a light shade that sets off the cherrywood furnishings and the rich ruby color of the Persian carpet very nicely. The counterpane is cream-colored, as are the lace curtains. Along with my bed and bureau, there is a small writing table beneath one of the east windows and a sitting area (sofa, ladies' rocker, and tea table) along the front wall. With so many comforts in this room, I have often spent entire mornings in this room or passed the evening here rather than in the library or parlor.

The small room adjacent to my bedchamber is now used

as a dressing room. The two across the hall are reserved for guests. Though attractively furnished, they are seldom used.

Thursday, May 17th

The arrangements for spending the summer away are coming along nicely. Alicia has agreed to spend two days a week here and generally see to things (instead of being with her family all summer), and a neighbor boy will look after the grounds. I have advanced money to the various merchants from whom things may be needed and given Mr. Sims a special power of attorney to act in my behalf should the need arise. Both he and Alicia, of course, will know how to reach me in Massachusetts. Finally, I have seen the station master and arranged for my ticket. I am to leave Monday the 18th of June, at eight-thirty in the morning.

Sunday, May 20th

Dinner at the Halstons' this afternoon. It was a small, quiet gathering (the only other guests were the Thorntons and Elisha Caldwell, the president of the company and an old friend of my grandfather's) but, as always, perfectly delightful. I have always enjoyed being in their house. It has a slightly old-fashioned air, a grace and calm that one associates more with the eighteenth century than with our own times. (The Judge, in fact, sometimes refers to himself as a latter-day "Augustan," as the leading lights of the first part of that century were known.) The dining room, in particular, is light and airy, and today they had opened the double doors leading to the garden so that we could see the different flowers, shrubs, and trees in bloom and feel the breeze. The fare, as always, was relatively simple—roast beef, new potatoes, and fresh asparagus, along with the Judge's favorite Burgundy—but exquisitely prepared.

What I shall remember most, however, is the conversation, which was about what the future might hold for us now that the war is over. It was Julia who first raised this question—in that casual way in which hostesses attempt to engage their guests in table talk. But to judge from the serious turn that things took it was clearly a matter that was weighing on all our minds.

Mr. Caldwell expressed the hope that the coming years would be good for business, recalling how difficult things had been during the panic that occurred just before the war. The company had done well in the war years, he said, owing to the contracts it had received from the government for binoculars and telescopes in particular. Now our hopes would have to be placed on an increase in scientific work, particularly in the universities. It was to that quarter that the company was directing its drummers.

To this Henry Thornton (who became vice president of the company this past January) replied that the state of trade was certainly a concern but that he had good reason to be sanguine about it. It was, he thought, to be an age of unparalleled expansion and progress, one in which commerce would flourish as never before. The company, moreover, was in a good position to profit from this. It had an excellent reputation and only a few competitors of any note. "One may be able to erect a sawmill overnight," he said, "but grinding lenses and making finely machined parts are another matter entirely." In response Mr. Caldwell nodded, saying he supposed that Henry was right but that long experience had taught him never to take anything completely for granted.

After a brief silence, Julia proffered the thought that apparently lay behind her question: her hope that the coming years would bring a respite from the turmoil that had plagued us for nearly half a century. As long as she could remember, she said, the country had been torn by the question of slavery and other sectional differences. Now that those had been settled, now that the great challenge of our times had been met, had we not a right to expect a period of calm and tranquility? "Of course," she added, "this may only be an aging woman's desire to live out the rest of her life in peace."

Lucy was quick to agree, saying that after all her war work (she had spent countless hours folding bandages for the Sanitary Commission and trying to raise money for the families of the dead and wounded), she would be glad to turn most of her attention to the needs of her own family.

My turn having come, I said that I could not imagine what the future might bring but that I thought many people shared the desire for calmer times. I then added, rather weakly, that there seemed to be grounds for optimism about this. (In truth, this was a question to which I had not given much thought. I have never been much inclined to such speculations, and the loss of my husband made them rather painful for me.)

Everyone then turned to the Judge, as if expecting him to render a verdict on the matter. "Well," he said with a knowing smile, "it appears the poet is right in his contention that

> 'Tis with our judgments as our watches, none
> Go just-alike, yet each believes his own.

There was a round of laughter (the Judge, of course, is renowned for his ability to quote Alexander Pope to effect), then he added, with some seriousness, "I should like to think that Mrs. Halston's wish will be granted—and, indeed, there is a certain element of progress in human affairs. But I would also urge caution in our expectations, as history seems to be mainly a matter of trading one set of troubles for another—and though there are not many clouds on the horizon now, it is very difficult to say how things might stand even a year from now."

The wisdom of this was generally accepted and the conversation turned to lighter matters. I returned home about five-thirty and started getting things ready for the week.

Thursday, May 24th

This afternoon I met with Mr. Sims at the bank to go over my investments. I do this periodically, of course, but there was a special urgency this time because I am going away for the summer. As it happens, he does not believe that any action will be required of us. There are some interest and dividends due, which he will receive and place on deposit for me; but he is satisfied with my holdings and will only make changes "if there is a favorable opportunity to exchange my 'greenbacks' for gold." He added that with the war now over he hoped the Treasury would retire "that damned scrip" as soon as possible, for it could only be a drag on commerce. In response I merely nodded—though I trust his judgment, I have only a limited understanding of these matters. I was pleased by the state of my affairs, however, not least because now I can put them out of my mind for the summer.

On my way home, I ran into Mr. Hoffmann, the master lens maker at the firm who was brought over from Germany some years ago to perfect the skills of our artisans. He greeted me kindly, cupping my small hands in his large, heavy ones with evident pleasure. Of course, I have been something of a favorite of his since I was a girl. We chatted amiably for a few minutes (an avid gardener, he was eager to know how my roses were coming along), and then, bidding me a good day, he hastened off. To my mind, he is one of this world's truly good souls. I have always marveled how such a simple, unassuming man can be so precise and passionate in the pursuit of his craft.

Sunday, May 27th

Last evening I watched the sun set from the piazza. It had been a lovely spring day—bright and clear, with that softness in the air that both soothes and invigorates the soul. I had gone outside with the intention of reading but was soon caught up in the sensations of the oncoming night—the stillness, a certain increase in the wind, the hum of the insects in the growing shadows. Looking up through the trees, I watched as the sky was transformed from a transparent blue to an opaque hue resembling pearl, and then, in the space of a few minutes, become suffused with the darkness. A few high clouds, catching the last rays of the sun, momentarily shone a delicate shade of pink, then faded into shadow.

I lingered there until it was completely dark, then went in feeling an immense sense of calm. It is sad that we must always be *doing*, seldom allowing ourselves the luxury of simply contemplating things in silence. Our activity has a purpose, of course, and gives our lives a richness that they would not otherwise have. But there are times when we would do well not to try to "improve" the day but simply to be in it—to yield to it and let it take us wherever it will. To study sunsets, and the flow of water in a stream, and insects maneuvering along leaves. Ultimately, to recall that we are part of a larger universe, of things both seen and unseen.

Tuesday, May 29th

This afternoon Meredith and I finished putting together the lists of names to be read at the Commemoration Day ceremonies; there are 596 in all. Because the official casualty lists are not considered reliable, we have had to cross-check them against the regiment's own records and the lists published in the newspaper (along with, in some cases, contacting the families themselves). It has been tedious work but it would be awful to omit a name or even to get the engagement wrong.

Tuesday, June 5th

All is a frenzy of preparations for Friday. The speakers' platform and reviewing stand have been erected, the square hung with patriotic bunting, and the park (where the games, concert, and fireworks are to be held) freshly mowed and the different sections marked off. The growing excitement is evident even in the way people don't linger to talk but have to rush off to tend to something or other. All that is wanting, it seems, is favorable weather— but that, of course, we must leave to Providence.

Saturday, June 9th

Our day of commemoration was a great success. Everything went smoothly, and any number of people remarked to me that it had just the right tone—dignified and respectful but with an air of triumph and celebration. I know the other members of the committee were very pleased as well.

There had been rain during the night but it was clear by dawn, with everything fresh and glistening in the morning light. I got up early and after a quiet breakfast on the piazza came upstairs to dress. By nine (an hour before the procession was to begin), I could hear a distinct commotion from the direction of Main Street, as if there were a large crowd there already. Alicia's family came for her shortly thereafter, all excitement and nervous chatter, and together they set off for the square right away.

I left the house about a quarter to ten, carefully locking the door and, figuratively at least, taking a deep breath. Beyond my natural excitement and concern that everything come off all right, I knew that it would be a long and perhaps emotional day—and I wasn't certain how well I would bear up under it. As I walked the few blocks to Main Street, however, the bells from the Unitarian church began to ring as if calling people to worship. Comforted by this familiar sound, I began to feel more sure of myself and, coming in sight of the crowd, was soon caught up in its festive mood.

The procession began a few minutes after ten. As the members of the regiment had wanted, it was led by the drummer boy whose steady tapping had taken them into battle time after time. Then came the color guard, followed by Colonel Thornton on his large, black horse and the regiment's ten companies in order, the men marching six abreast with the company commanders to one side. Those who were unable to walk had already been taken to the place reserved for them in the square.

The procession itself was solemn, almost somber. The only sounds were the slow, steady beating of the drum and the heavy tread of hundreds of feet. As I watched them pass, row after row of torn and faded uniforms, taut and hardened limbs, and faces filled with what can only be called quiet determination, I realized more than ever before that this was no parade ground regiment but one that had seen hard service and suffered much. It was fitting, then, that we hold our huzzahs for a while and reflect on the enormity of their sacrifice.

The mood changed abruptly as the regiment began to enter the square and draw up in formation on the east side, opposite to the crowd. Our silent homage paid, the band struck up a sprightly military march and those in the crowd began to applaud and cheer wildly, scarcely able to contain themselves.

The ceremonies themselves opened with a prayer by Mr. Williams. With his customary simplicity, he gave thanks to the Almighty for allowing us to see this day and called upon Him to comfort those still in distress. The war, he said, "would cast a long shadow, and there are those who will need our aid and succor long after we shall be inclined to forget them."

The speeches by the invited dignitaries that followed, though fitting and no doubt sincere, were not memorable. There was much talk of "valor" and "honor" and "duty unstintingly done," but the words lacked real authority, as if those who spoke them had never known such things first-hand.

Not so Colonel Thornton's account of the regiment's history. Every sentence of his had the stamp of authenticity, and there was not so much as a cough as he related the hardships the regiment had endured, their courage and perseverance, and their ultimate triumph. He made a point of mentioning all the engagements in which they had fought, from the great battles whose names were familiar to all to the minor skirmishes remembered only by those who were involved in or otherwise directly touched by them. Toward the end, he drew a moral of sorts: in four years of war, he said, we had gone from innocence to bitterest experience, from a strategy of cautious maneuvering to one of relentless hammering, from casualty lists of half a column to ones taking up several pages. The victory we were celebrating had come at a great price. To the end of our days, we must remember this fact. The bright future lying before us was in great measure purchased for us by others—and purchased dear. Then, turning to the men whom he had commanded and addressing them particularly, he added that no words of gratitude were adequate or even necessary: they knew what they had accomplished, and he was only thankful to have had the privilege of leading them.

After allowing an appropriate interval, Lucy rose and took her husband's place at the podium to begin reading the names. We had agreed early on that they were to be read alphabetically by engagement without regard to rank. A drum roll would come right after the announcement of each engagement. Those who had died of disease would be named at the end of the year.

In her clear, rich voice, Lucy then announced that she would read "the names of all those members of the regiment who were killed, wounded, or died of disease in the year 1862." There were not a great many. The regiment joined the Army of the Potomac too late to participate in the Peninsula campaign. At the second battle of Bull Run it occupied defensive positions only, and at both Antietam and Fredericksburg it was held in reserve and did not come under fire. By the time she finished, however, a reverent silence had fallen over the crowd, and many heads were lowered as if in prayer.

For 1863 there were 185 names, the regiment having seen hard fighting at both Chancellorsville and Gettysburg. Most of the names were English, Scottish, or Welsh, a few German or other nationalities. Many were also familiar—one would undoubtedly know the family if not the particular individual. As I read them I became acutely aware of the cadence of the syllables, an irregular but steady drumbeat of two-two-three, two-three-two, one-two-two. At times I largely lost consciousness of the names themselves (though I am certain that I gave them correctly), so entranced had I become with their sound. When I finished I lingered at the podium for a few moments, looking out over the crowd. Though I cannot say why, it just seemed inappropriate to sit down right away, that there was a need for further communication between me and the audience, even if unspoken. Many of the eyes that I met were moist, but they seemed to harbor deep gratitude as well as sadness.

I passed Meredith as I was returning to my chair, and she patted my arm lightly as if to thank me for a task well done. Her own task was by far the most difficult: there were nearly 300 names for 1864, the bloodiest year of the war. The regiment came through the battle in the Wilderness with only moderate casualties but was hit hard at Spotsylvania Court House just a few days later. As Meredith began to recite those names, my apprehension grew markedly. I had tried to prepare myself for this moment, going so far as to learn the three or four names immediately preceding John's so that I would know exactly when to expect it and imagining Meredith pronouncing it in her quiet, precise way. But now all these preparations seemed useless, and I was certain that I would succumb to whatever emotions took hold of me. When the moment actually came, however, I felt only a momentary shock followed by an immense sense of well-being. To hear my husband's name spoken so, publicly and in company with those of the others with whom he had served, filled me with pride and even a certain sense of joy. It was as if his death had at last been put into its true perspective and had no further need of our grief.

There were many names yet to be read, however. From Spotsylvania the fighting moved to the North Anna River, then to Cold Harbor, and finally to Petersburg. Grant kept pressing the attack and with each advance the "butcher's bill" mounted. The war had entered its last phase, but it was to be the most terrible of all. It seemed to me that Meredith read the names with increasing rapidity as she moved through the list, an unconscious reflection of the growing intensity of the war itself. There was a noticeable sense of relief when she reached the end and, gathering up the sheets of paper, returned to her seat.

Cynthia Edwards then read the few remaining names from 1865, and the regimental bugler played "Taps" from his place at the rear of the formation. The ceremonies then closed with another short prayer.

A holiday mood took over as the crowd began to break up and head toward the picnic grounds. I made my way slowly through the mêlée as the men from the regiment sought out their families and the children ran around madly, teasing and chasing one another and even playing catch over the heads of the adults. At length I spotted the Halstons (who had asked me to join them for luncheon) sitting on camp stools beneath a large oak and worked my way over to them. "Well done, Ellen, well done!" said the Judge, rising and embracing me warmly. "Yes, indeed," Julia added, "that was just a magnificent ceremony—it couldn't possibly have been more fitting." I, too, was very pleased with it, but always being a little uncomfortable with such lavish praise, I simply thanked them and asked if I could assist with the luncheon. "By all means," said the Judge, "We'll all lend a hand."

It was then that the one unlooked-for event of the day occurred. As I was helping their girl spread the cloth I noticed a young man with captain's insignia standing nearby, apparently waiting for an opportunity to speak with me. "Excuse me," he said, coming forward at last and addressing me in a voice both firm and deferential. "I just wanted to tell you what a pleasure it was to have served under your husband." Then, with a slight bow, he added, "My name is Matthew Carey." The last name, of course, was a familiar one, as the Careys are a prominent family in town, but I had no distinct memory of this person. (The Judge said afterwards that he thought Matthew was the youngest son, who had gone east for college and then worked at a firm in Philadelphia until the war began.)

I took his hand, saying that it was very kind of him to contact me. "Well," he replied, "your husband was always so considerate of those under his command … and his cool head kept us out of trouble any number of times." In response I simply nodded and said that I could well believe it. He then said that he would have liked to call on me sooner but that he had been in Washington for the past year assisting with the military administration of the South. The Judge remarked that it was quite commendable of him to stay on, to which he replied that it seemed to be his duty, since he had a certain talent for organization. "All the same, young man," the Judge rejoined, "it was a great service to your country."

"Well," he said at length, "I really mustn't keep you. I hope all of you will enjoy the rest of the day's events." Then, turning to me, he added that the ceremonies had been very touching and the committee was to be congratulated. I thanked him and then, offhandedly and without really giving it any thought, added that perhaps we could talk further, that there were things about the war that I would like to know. "Certainly," he said, "it would be a pleasure." Then, with a final bow, he turned and took his leave.

When lunch was over, the Halstons went home, the Judge saying that he needed to "retire to his chambers … and take a nap!" I spent the rest of the afternoon going about the picnic grounds, talking with old acquaintances and enjoying the general merriment. Around six I joined the other members of the committee and their families for dinner at the hotel, then went with them to the concert and fireworks. It was a little after ten when I finally got home, tired but very satisfied with the way it had all gone.

This afternoon I am to visit John's father at the home of one of his old friends (I understand that he was too ill to attend more than a small part of the ceremonies). I have a few things to finish up at the Academy next week, and then I shall be free for the entire summer. I am already counting the hours.

Thursday, September 6th

I have had a glorious summer—ten weeks of ease and leisure, of living mostly according to my own desires and giving myself over to the many pleasures, large and small, of the season. It has been altogether restorative: I return to my duties rested, with a new sense of purpose.

The journey out was long and tiring, as I had anticipated it would be. Of course, traveling any distance is always a bit arduous for me, as the motion of the train tends to make me nauseous if I attempt to read or write letters and I have great difficulty sleeping as well. That leaves long hours staring out the window, watching the landscape slowly change.

The first leg of my journey took me to Pittsburgh, where we arrived in late afternoon. As my connection wasn't due until eight-thirty, I had dinner at the station restaurant and then walked around a little. The downtown was bustling and filled with signs of prosperity, but all the same it rather depressed my spirits. The air was heavy with noise and smoke and everywhere I turned there was the impression of grime, which only intensified as the night came on. To be sure, the night was sultry and I was tired from traveling—still, I had the sense that Pittsburgh is paying dearly for its progress. Even the rural areas of Pennsylvania had a rather hard-scrabble look, as if the towns had been literally hacked out of the rugged hillsides. One senses that it is only with immense effort that people manage to wrest a living from this harsh landscape—which they are compelled to deface in the process.

We spent much of the night in the mountains, the train slowly chugging over one ridge after another. Though I could see but little, I was aware of the changes in the grade and the laboring of the engine. We made several brief stops, but I did not get the names of the towns. By mid-morning of the following day we had crossed into New York and the gentler terrain west of the Catskills. I felt a certain sense of relief, as if we had emerged from a wild and uncharted territory, and even managed to sleep for an hour or so. By four in the afternoon we had reached Albany, where I took a hotel room near the station and got my first solid night's rest in two days.

The next morning I boarded the small train to Lenox. We proceeded down the Hudson Valley a ways, then turned eastward toward the uplands of western Massachusetts. Elizabeth had arranged for a carriage to meet me at the station and we were soon on a quiet country road heading up into the soft, green Berkshire hills. It was a heaven-sent day, clear and pleasantly warm, and I felt my soul expand as we passed the picturesque farmhouses with their newly verdant orchards and tidy fields bordered by early summer flowers. At length we turned into a narrow lane through a more extensive woods and I sensed that we were close. We climbed for perhaps a quarter of a mile alongside a small stream, and then the country became open again. In the distance I could see a white farmhouse with dark green shutters and figures in front waving excitedly. As we drove up the entire household rushed to greet me in an absolute frenzy of kisses and embraces and excited chatter. Before allowing myself to be ushered inside, however, I took a deep breath and looked around. The setting was perfect; I could not imagine a more delightful place in which to spend the summer.

The house that my cousin's family had taken for the season was large and comfortable, though a bit more rustic than I would have imagined. The oldest portion, a simple, one-story structure that now serves as the kitchen, was apparently built just after the Revolution. It has all the hallmarks of a frontier home: a large, open room with an immense hearth at one end and a sleeping loft that is reached by a narrow set of stairs. The main house, which stands at right angles to the first, was built early in this century. Though elegant in appearance (one senses a new-found prosperity in the region as a whole), it is simple country construction all the same. Instead of cutting a door between the two structures, for instance, the workmen merely removed the sashes from an attic window in the old house—forcing one to step over a rather high sill to reach the small bedchamber above the kitchen. But perhaps it is well that we live with a bit less luxury for part of the year. And my room, on the second floor of the main house, suited me quite nicely. Large and airy and situated so as to receive the morning sun, it was also somewhat removed from the hubbub in the rest of the house. I often found occasion to retire there.

The real virtue of the house, however, was the views that it offered. To the south, a broad, open landscape of fields and orchards gradually descending to the Housatonic River in the far distance. To the north, a succession of heavily wooded hills that reminded me of the folds in some plush fabric. In one direction, companionship and the familiar world of affairs; in the other, solitude and the "forest primeval." Over the course of the summer I was to make many excursions in both directions, as mood and mission dictated.

Besides myself and Elizabeth, there were her two sons, George and Henry, aged twelve and eight, respectively; her husband, George Sr., who joined us on weekends; and two servants (plus a groundskeeper hired by the landlord who came by every few days). There was also a good deal of company, both acquaintances from town who were invited to dinner or stopped by for an afternoon and visitors from further away who stayed for several days at a time. I was never hampered by the presence of these others, however. Indeed, Elizabeth was very insistent that I not be, that they were her guests and I need not socialize with them if I did not wish to. To be sure, I often did so, either to avoid giving offense or because I found them genuinely interesting. But there were also many times when I went my own way, glad to be free of social duties for a while.

My days quickly fell into a routine: I would get up early, usually right at sunrise, and while the rest of the household was still asleep go for a short walk along some farm lane or the road leading toward the river. I have always felt a special affinity with the early morning, a delight in the way in which the first rays of light gradually dispel the shadows, restoring the joys of the visual world to us. Even on rainy mornings I would walk in the garden a bit, anxious to be out in the day and to feel its freshness. On one occasion I was so taken by the sight of the raindrops collecting on the petals of a black-eyed Susan—that rich yellow almost luminescent beneath the transparent little globes—that I actually made a quick sketch of it, bracing my umbrella over one shoulder.

On returning from my walks I would have coffee on the porch while waiting for the others to come down to breakfast. It usually wasn't long before one of the boys came bounding down, followed by the rest of the household shortly after. Breakfast was usually a lively affair, with George and Henry eagerly informing us of what they wanted to do that day. That is to say, that afternoon, as Elizabeth insisted that they spend most mornings on lessons of some sort, which she would carefully outline to them before they left the table. As a rule, these lessons were less demanding than regular schoolwork (I recall Henry being assigned to read a story about life in early New England and George, who had had a couple of years of Latin, to learn the scientific names of various types of butterfly), but my cousin held her sons to them. She would not allow their minds to be idle simply because they were out of school, she said.

After breakfast I would generally go up to my room to read or write letters. This was the contemplative portion of the day, the time when I would do my own modest "lessons." Afternoon was the time for activity, for long walks and excursions to places of interest, sketching, botanizing, and playing the endless games the boys devised. Their inventiveness and energy never failed to amaze me, but that, I suppose, is the essence of children left to their own devices. As the days grew warmer, swimming became their principal passion. They had discovered a pond about a half mile away, and from the middle of July on spent most of their afternoons there. As often as not I accompanied them; and though I never went into the water, I took immense pleasure in watching them splashing about, so utterly carefree. Nothing seems to liberate the spirit so readily as being enveloped by that gentle liquid.

Unless we had company, dinner was usually a rather simple affair. There was no need to put the servants to a lot of work, Elizabeth said, when none of us wished to remain at the table for very long anyway. She was, however, particular about having the best of the season's produce—melons, berries, and even some early apples, along with peas, green beans, corn, and other vegetables fresh from our garden or nearby farms. From the market in Lenox on Saturday mornings we procured fresh trout and rabbits and other game. And a farm just down the road supplied us with milk, eggs, a coarse, pungent cheese that I particularly relished, and occasional baked goods. There were times when I would go into the kitchen to find the side table piled high with all sorts of such delectables, much like a still life from the seventeenth century. It is one of the joys of summer that it affords us such a rich and varied diet. Though other seasons have their own delicacies to offer (asparagus in the spring and walnuts in the autumn, for instance), for most of the year our fare is rather limited. We can preserve only so much from the summer, and even then there is little comparison.

Dinner over, the boys would play in the yard until dark, chasing fireflies, inventing ghost stories, and so forth. Elizabeth and I would sit on the porch, perhaps talking quietly, perhaps just watching the fading light. As often as not she would do a little sewing or cross-stitch until it was too dark to see clearly. We would generally retire about ten, with protests from George and Henry if there was even a sliver of light still in the sky. I slept well there, more peacefully than I generally do at home, lulled by the gentle night-sounds: the soughing of the breeze, the humming of the insects, and perhaps the lowing of a cow in the distance.

Another marked feature of my days, one that became increasingly regular as the weeks wore on, was spending time with Henry. I cannot really say why, but we got to be good friends. Perhaps he saw in me a sympathetic adult who offered all the attentions of a mother without the strictures. I know that I delighted in his innocence, his boundless energy and insatiable curiosity. In any case, every morning when his lessons were over, he would come quietly up the stairs and stand by my door; he would not interrupt me, just patiently wait for me to notice him. When I looked up (either because I had heard him or because I knew that it must be about time), he would smile broadly and ask what we were to do that day. I would always feign uncertainty: "Oh, I don't know. Perhaps we could …"—and then mention something that I knew would delight him. With that, he would race downstairs to inform his mother.

He was particularly fond of walking, or rather of scouring the countryside for interesting objects that he might find—hawk feathers, stones with unusual coloration, a pen-knife dropped by some passer-by, even a cigar wrapper. He kept these treasures in a tin box beneath his bed and by summer's end had amassed quite a collection.

Around the Fourth of July he became keen on the idea of looking for arrowheads. His brother immediately cast cold water on this, saying that the area had been settled for so long that there couldn't be very many left to be found. All the same, I asked George where the best places to look would be. "Well," he said, "you have to find a place where the Indians would have lost an arrow. Maybe go along some of the old trails up there (pointing to a nearby hillside); that's where they would have hunted, I guess. There wouldn't be any down there (indicating the valley) because that's where they would have had their settlements and fields. Besides, it's already been ploughed up a lot."

It took several weeks—and no small amount of good fortune—but we did actually find one. It was in just the sort of place George had suggested, along a little-used trail bordered by a small stream. We had stopped to rest and were sitting on a log. Henry, restless as always, was shuffling his feet through the leaves when I noticed a dull glint. It took shape a second or two later, and I told Henry to stop and see what it was. For a few moments he wasn't certain what I meant; then the image jelled in his mind, and reaching down he let out a loud shriek. The arrowhead was small and one edge was chipped, but it didn't matter: he had found one and it soon became his proudest possession.

My little companion was also anxious to have me show him how to draw. I was hesitant at first, fearing that he would be too restless. But he proved to be a diligent pupil, meticulously doing his exercises at the small table that we set up for him on the porch. And it soon became clear to me that he had a certain gift for art—seldom have I seen such grace and sensitivity to detail in one so young. Toward the end of the summer I took him sketching with me. We would sit close together, working on the same subject. At first he would look over at my sketch pad every few minutes, trying to get the lines exactly as I had them. Before long, however, he would go off in his own direction, realizing that he couldn't replicate my drawing (and perhaps sensing, though very faintly, that each artist's vision must be his own).

Though I had intended to leave the school room behind me for the summer, having this pupil turned out to be one of the delights of the vacation. For my birthday he presented me with a drawing of his arrowhead, which he must have worked on in his room or at times when I was not around, as I had no prior inkling of it. It was a bit crude, to be sure, but the outline was sharp and the shading of the irregular surface quite nicely done.

In only one other respect did scholastics intrude on my summer. I had decided to give more attention to the North German masters in my lectures on the history of art, and had brought along some critical essays to read (along with my own notes and sketches from my year in Europe). Working steadily but in a rather leisurely way, by early August I had completed two full lectures with which I was very pleased. Though they had a slightly scholarly tone, I believed they were right for my audience, with emphasis on the salient points and just enough detail to give it all life. In the weeks that remained I made neat copies of them, polishing the language a bit as I went. I do not ordinarily read my lectures (at least not in *toto*) but wanted to have a finished version in front of me the first time that I gave them.

For the most part, my summer's reading was not demanding—a few novels, some popular essays, and an account of an overland journey to California. I also spent some enjoyable hours with a little volume entitled *Berkshire Echoes* that I found in the house. Such collections of poetry and vignettes by local authors are common, of course, but this one was unusually fine. Printed on heavy stock and bound in a fine red cloth, with an excellent etching of Mount Greylock on the frontispiece, it had every appearance of being the work of some cultured gentlemen from the early part of the century. Nor was it lacking in literary quality, containing as it did some fine nature poems and charming portraits of country life. Sentimental, to be sure, and by no means original or even true to life, it now seems very old-fashioned. Even before the war our serious literature was becoming more rough-hewn and authentic. Yet books such as this have their place, if only as reminders of more innocent times.

We went to church only a few times, as it was some distance away and the pulpit was mainly being filled by a junior minister until the autumn. I did hear one memorable sermon, however, by a visiting minister, the Reverend John Newhouse of Albany, speaking on the nature of the soul. It was highly ironic, he said, that few of us have a distinct notion of this concept even though it is such a critical element of our faith… "to the point of our holding it to be immortal." It was also remarkable that apart from the Hindus, only Christians professed a belief in the soul. There was no such thing as soul in the Hebrew tradition, and even the ancient philosophers (so prescient in other ways) made no room for it. Plato, for instance, recognized only three dimensions to man—the body, the intellect, and what he called the "spirited element," which at its best took the form of courage, at its worst mere emotion. The widespread notion of *anima*, often translated as "soul," was merely the force or principle of life itself.

What, then, was this soul that we were so sure of? He proffered several definitions that have been given over the ages, showing the insufficiency of each in turn. Only then, when the riddle seemed beyond solution, did he present his own conception. The soul, he said, was that part of us "which perceives God directly." It was our innermost self, where the Almighty manifests Himself most purely and unambiguously. Our senses, of course, cannot lead us to God; and our reason, for all its powers, cannot give us full certainty. But the soul apprehends Him instinctively, and has no doubts about His presence. I have thought of these words many times since I first heard them. I do not pretend to understand the argument in its entirety, but I find it vaguely unsettling, relying as it does entirely on our intuition of God. It is as if in attempting to put the divine on a firm footing this minister only succeeded in removing the last pillar of support for it. I shall have to return to this question when I can give it more attention.

Summer's end seemed to come quite suddenly—indeed, it almost astonished us. The reason, I believe, is that we lose something of our time sense during this season. Delighting in the long days of early summer, we imagine that they will go on indefinitely and become entirely oblivious to the subtle changes that are taking place day by day. By the middle of August, however, there is enough alteration in the light (dawn comes noticeably later, the shadows at midday are clearly longer) that we can no longer delude ourselves. Then the days seem to advance quite rapidly, as if time, having lingered earlier, were trying to catch up.

It was late in my stay, however, that I experienced what I have come to think of as the peak moment of the summer—the one that seemed to epitomize all the sensations and good feelings I associate with this season while raising them to a new height. I was returning from a walk in the late afternoon, following an old logging road through the woods, when I came upon a small meadow I had not seen before. It was now a tangled mass of late-summer growth, the white and golden flower heads interspersed with the tall grasses, some of which had already taken on the dry and withered look of autumn. It was a pretty scene, to be sure, but what most caught my eye was the ethereal quality of the light. Though each detail was sharp, the sun was at such an angle that the entire meadow seemed to be bathed in a sort of mist. It was as if a divine aura had settled over things.

I cannot say why, but this sight gave me an immense sense of calm, even of transcendence. In the beauty and stillness of that moment, I felt that life had attained a sort of perfection, that after many false starts things had at last come together almost without effort. This was clearly one of those "spots of time" of which Wordsworth speaks, in which our thoughts and sensations so surpass the ordinary that we seem to have entered another realm altogether. I lingered there a while, knowing that this could not last but resolved to savor it fully and to carry it with me throughout the coming months. And indeed, I have thought of that afternoon many times since.

The journey home was tedious, but I seemed to mind it less than the one out. My thoughts, of course, were largely taken up with the events of the past ten weeks. At one point, however, the scattered memories gave way to a reflection on leisure itself—that is, on the theme underlying them all. As a descendent of the Puritans, I am instinctively drawn to work as the purpose of life. And rightly so, for it is well said that "a life without duties is obscene." Still, it is good to have times when we have no particular obligations. They give us space to draw breath in, the chance to reflect on the ground we have covered and where we ought to go from there. In order to take stock, we must abandon our routine. Then too, a season such as summer offers us so many sensuous delights. The world itself seems to take on more color and texture, to acquire a depth and intensity that it has at no other time. In many ways we are most alive, most truly ourselves, during these months. Several of the ancient writers have left us essays on leisure; perhaps someday I will organize these thoughts into my own *De Otio*.

Now I am back, preparing for the year ahead. It is still very warm but it is the dry heat of September, which I do not mind as much. Indeed, it is almost pleasant to stand in the sun with my eyes closed and let the warmth of its rays spread over my face. All too soon it will be cold, and such indulgent moments will seem a distant luxury.

Monday, September 10th

The first day of class. The scene is invariably the same, the girls all milling about excitedly in their new frocks and neatly combed hair, recounting their summers and sharing their expectations for the coming school year. I confess that I always feel a little trepidation when I first see them in front of Chandler Hall, doubting whether I am up to the task of imparting anything of value to such restless and inquisitive minds. This invariably passes quickly, however, and so it was today: the accustomed surroundings and the sight of so many familiar faces eased my apprehensions markedly, and I was even more heartened by a group of girls from last year who had gathered at my door, eager to resume their study of art. By mid-morning, I felt entirely comfortable once again.

There were several innovations with respect to the opening ceremonies this year. They were held outdoors, beneath the large oaks on the bluff overlooking the river. And Mrs. Marshall spoke less about the duties of the scholar than about the joys of scholarship. Though she was careful to note the seriousness of our purpose, the burden of her remarks was that for each pupil there was a world waiting to unfold, a world rich beyond their imaginations. In coming to know "the best that has been thought and said" throughout the ages, they would acquire full citizenship in that world. Diligence in their studies would therefore pay very large dividends.

The ceremonies over, I headed off to my classroom. As I would not have any classes until the following day, I spent the afternoon tidying things up and otherwise getting ready.

Friday, September 14th

There is much agitation about the upcoming election. The great issue, of course, is the terms under which the Southern states are to be readmitted to the Union (whether strict or lenient) and the legal status of the freedmen. But the immediate questions are whether the states will approve the Fourteenth Amendment and whether the "Radicals" will gain control of Congress. Sadly, they stand every chance of doing so: already they are "waving the bloody shirt" with a fury and stirring up an implacable hatred of the South. The newspapers, of course, are full of vitriol; but even among those persons whose opinions I respect there is little consensus. Ohio, it is feared, with its large contingent of "Copperheads" who were staunchly opposed to the war, will side with the President in failing to provide either full citizenship or basic protections to the former slaves.

After being blissfully unaware of these matters all summer, their importance was suddenly brought home to me in an urgent note from Judge Halston, delivered the day after I returned home. He wanted the lyceum to devote its first meeting to a debate on the election issues. Robert Sanborn, a well-known abolitionist and chairman of the Judiciary Committee of the state Senate, would argue for the Radicals' position; he himself would take the opposing position. Time was of the essence because the election was less than two months off. The lyceum committee, of course, quickly gave its assent to the debate; it is set for Wednesday the 26th of this month.

Sunday, September 16th

This afternoon I experienced one of those rare moments of revelation when the familiar takes on a whole other significance. I was out in the orchard, doing a series of water-colors of the changing tints in the leaves. As I was painting the veins, carefully drawing the tip of the brush along fine, straight lines, it struck me what a marvelous instrument the human hand is. Though it can act with great force, it is also able to perform the most delicate and exacting tasks, can wield the sewing needle and scalpel as well as the mallet and ax. As I continued to work, I made a point of observing the different positions that my fingers assumed, the subtle shifts in the angle of the brush that were needed to achieve the effects I wanted. Most astounding of all, these shifts seemed to be accomplished without conscious direction, as if my hand instinctively knew where to go on its own.

Perhaps it was just such an experience as this that led Michelangelo to portray the creation of man as he did—with the hand of God reaching across the heavens, the forefinger extended as if giving a command yet nearly touching the almost equally gifted hand of His creation.

I must give greater attention to hands in my own painting as well as having my pupils practice drawing them more.

Thursday, September 20th

I ran into Captain Carey in the square this afternoon, on my way home from the Academy. He greeted me pleasantly and inquired how I was, then asked if I still wished to talk with him about the war. To be honest, I had forgotten making that request—so much had happened that day of the commemoration, and I had not really thought about it all summer—but I replied that I would and suggested that he come for tea some afternoon. He said that that would be fine, but he wasn't certain when he would be free: having recently been named assistant treasurer at the firm, he had "a lot of ropes" to learn. We talked for several more minutes, then went our separate ways.

Friday, September 21st

I have been reflecting on my mission as a teacher a good deal in the last few days. Clearly, it is to give my pupils a good "grounding" in art—the techniques and the salient features of the various schools, along with some sense of the particular genius of each master. And yet, ideally, I would give them something else as well, namely, an intuitive notion of the *function* of art in our lives (and here I mean all of the arts—literature and music and drama as well as painting and sculpture).

This, of course, is no mean task. By its very nature, there is something ineffable about art, something that transcends all efforts at explanation. Even so, there is much that we can say, and the point that I try to impress upon my pupils is that art "takes us out of ourselves." That is, it allows us to see our lives in terms of much broader, if not universal, themes.

In my first years of teaching I had a great deal of difficulty in getting this idea across. It is a fairly abstract one for young minds, and asking the students to reflect on their reactions to a particularly sublime image (a Raphael Madonna, say, or a Vermeer interior) helped only a little. They would nod as if to acknowledge having heard me, but there was little of the light of comprehension in their eyes.

At length, however, I hit upon a device that seems to serve my purpose much better. Shortly after beginning at the Academy, I did a series of paintings portraying the day-to-day goings-on there. One of these shows the headmistress conversing with two girls on the steps of Chandler Hall. It is early in the fall term: the afternoon light is still very bright, the figures are lightly dressed, and the lilacs bordering the steps are as yet quite green. The headmistress, of course, is Mrs. Marshall, though so much younger and positioned at such an angle as not to be recognized immediately. The girls, too, were painted from life, but the originals have long since been graduated. Thus, there are some familiar elements to this painting along with many that are not.

At the beginning of my lecture on the function of art, I unveil this painting and ask the girls to study it for a few moments. All of them appear to recognize the setting and a few, perhaps, the headmistress. The signature, too, often elicits a knowing smile. But it is so different from the great works of art that I usually present to them that they naturally wonder why I have done so. I then explain that the scene depicted in the painting is quite ordinary—they themselves will undoubtedly observe it any number of times during their years at the Academy. And yet, the fact that it has been committed to canvas gives it a significance it would not otherwise have. The interchange between the headmistress and the two girls is no longer merely a conversation, but a conversation of some importance. We sense that some needed counsel is being given or some timeless wisdom handed down. It might even conjure up an image of Socrates, standing beside similar pillars so many centuries ago.

Art thus acts by calling our attention to essential things, things that we would probably not notice if we were to encounter them in the ordinary run of life. By providing a "frame," it enables us to see the familiar in a new and richer light.

I end the lecture by asking the pupils to suggest titles for the painting. Their suggestions invariably reflect the more profound way in which they now view it. I myself have never been able to settle on one, however—it has too many dimensions for that to be possible.

Wednesday, September 26th

It is late, but I want to record my impressions of the election debate while they are still vivid in my mind.

A record number of people, women as well as men, turned out for the event—at least, I cannot recall such a large crowd on any similar occasion. By a quarter past seven the hall was filled, and those who came later were compelled to stand in the entryway or outside beneath the windows. There also appeared to be a good deal more tension in the air than on previous occasions, with the crowd as a whole seeming unusually agitated and heated conversations breaking out in numerous quarters.

Shortly before eight I gaveled the meeting to order, introduced the speakers, and outlined the rules of the debate. Each speaker would have one hour to present his case, then fifteen minutes to answer his opponent. Applause or other demonstrations of approval would be counted against the speaker's allotted time; interruptions by the other side would not.

Senator Sanborn, having the affirmative as it were, went first. A tall, distinguished-looking man in his early sixties, he seemed the very model of a statesman. Though he spoke forthrightly, he did so in calm, measured tones that completely belied the designation radical. Indeed, listening to his carefully constructed arguments, it was virtually impossible to see him in the same camp as more prominent Radicals such as Thaddeus Stevens or our own Senator Wade.

He began his remarks by saying that seldom did a mid-term election present an issue of such incalculable importance. That issue, of course, was the Fourteenth Amendment, which Congress had passed and sent to the states in June over the intense opposition of President Johnson. It was not, however, simply a question of adding certain language to the Constitution; it was a matter of ensuring, with respect to the freedmen, that the Southern states would not entirely nullify the results of the war. Already they were well on their way towards doing so, as a brief recounting of recent events would make clear.

As a result of the President's leniency—by his proclamation, all that the rebellious states had to do to obtain readmission to the Union was to rescind their ordinances of secession and amend their constitutions to prohibit slavery—civil administrations had been restored in all but one of those states by the beginning of the year. One of them, his own state of Tennessee, had even been readmitted in July, a little over a year after the last Confederate soldiers laid down their arms. With few restrictions on the right of those who had participated in the rebellion to exercise the franchise or hold office, the new governments bore a distinct resemblance to those that had existed before the war. Indeed, at all levels of authority there were former Confederate officers—even in the delegations that the states sent to Congress at the opening of its session last December. As far as civil government was concerned, the status quo had been restored down to the smallest detail.

The same, sadly, was increasingly true with respect to the freedmen as well. Among the first laws passed by the new Southern legislatures were the by now infamous "black codes." Under these acts, the Negro was denied the right to vote, to serve on juries, and to testify against whites; to own or rent land in rural areas; to pursue an occupation other than domestic servant or field hand without paying a fee as high as one-hundred dollars; to possess firearms or alcohol; to preach without a license; and to appear in certain towns without the permission of his employer or after a specified hour. Fines were imposed for "insolence" or the use of "insulting gestures" toward whites, offenses that were purposely left vague. Orphans and children deemed not properly cared for by their parents could be bound over to a planter to serve an "apprenticeship" without pay.

Most grievous of all were the vagrancy laws. In Mississippi, for instance, any Negro who could not show evidence of employment for the coming year was subject to a fine of fifty dollars. If he could not pay this, he would be hired out to a person chosen by the court. A Negro who abandoned his employment before the year was out forfeited all his wages and—just as in former times— was subject to arrest by any white citizen. The clear intent of these laws was to resurrect slavery in all but name. At least, Senator Sanborn said, he could conceive of no other reason.

Nor were these restrictions the limit of Southern oppression. Last May, a collision between two carriages, one driven by a Negro and one by a white ("no more than that," he noted with apparent chagrin), led to two days of indiscriminate violence against Negroes in Memphis. By the time it came to an end, forty-six Negroes had been killed and more than eighty injured—as against one white—and four Negro churches and twelve schools lay in ashes. A pregnant woman had been raped repeatedly by a group of lawless whites. Not three months later, mob violence in New Orleans led to the death of thirty-four Negroes and the injury of more than 200 others, with few if any white casualties. In both cases, the civil authorities had not only not acted to quell the violence but had actually abetted and participated in it. With such evidence before us, Senator Sanborn asked, could we reasonably expect the Southern states to protect the lives and property of the freedmen? Could they themselves place any trust in their own governments—something that we (and white Southerners, for that matter)—take entirely for granted?

And so we have the Fourteenth Amendment, a measure intended to preserve the most fundamental liberties and provide for the equal protection of the laws. (Here he paused and looked around the room, as if to allow time for this crucial point to register.) Now, he continued, some have questioned the need for amending the Constitution to address these problems. That, too, becomes clear when one looks at recent developments: early this year, Congress passed and sent to the President two bills pertaining to the freedmen. The first simply reauthorized the Freedmen's Bureau, which was created to assist the former slaves and which, in its short life, has done immeasurable good. The second—a bill for civil rights—was more revolutionary, providing the protections now embodied in the amendment itself. Both bills were promptly vetoed. A stunned Congress immediately overrode the veto of the civil rights bill but narrowly failed in its attempt to restore the other one. Another reauthorization bill was passed subsequently, and again vetoed. This time, however, Congress managed to muster the two-thirds majority needed to enact it.

One might draw two conclusions from these events. First,

that the President was irredeemably hostile toward the freedmen and would do nothing to protect them or assist in their advancement. Second—and this was the crucial point—that ordinary legislation, which might easily be changed or even repealed, was too thin a reed on which to rest the freedmen's rights and hope of a better life. The President, of course, would be gone in a few years; but the freedmen's place in American society was a question that would haunt us for many years if not firmly settled now. Nothing would settle it more definitively than adoption of the Fourteenth Amendment.

The Senator closed by noting that the position he had advocated is commonly known as the "radical" view. "But there is only one real sense in which that is true, namely, that it seeks to eradicate a deeply rooted evil."

There was a lengthy round of applause as he returned to his seat; his remarks had clearly struck a chord in many quarters. When the hall was again quiet, Judge Halston rose and slowly advanced toward the podium. He began by congratulating Senator Sanborn on his excellent presentation of the case for the Fourteenth Amendment. He himself, he said, had found it compelling in a number of respects and would be hard put to refute it point by point. But that was not his purpose. He had agreed to take the negative in this debate not because he necessarily opposed the amendment but because it raised large and important questions—questions that we would do well to ponder carefully before embarking on this course. It was these that he now wished to lay out before us.

At this point the Judge stepped out from behind the podium; he would deliver the rest of his remarks informally, pacing back and forth much as a lawyer before a jury would do and pausing occasionally to look at one or another of his townsmen directly. He had no notes, only a page from the *Clarion* containing the text of the amendment.

There were three sections of the proposed amendment that concerned us. "Section 1… No State shall make or enforce any law which shall abridge the privileges or immunities of citizens of the United States; nor shall any State deprive any person of life, liberty, or property, without due process of law; nor deny to any person within its jurisdiction the equal protection of the laws."

This provision, he said, was understandable enough in light of the abuses so ably enumerated by Senator Sanborn. Enforcing it, however, would necessarily entail a marked expansion of the powers of the federal government, making it—and not, as always hitherto, the states—the final guarantor of individual liberties. This same objection had been raised with respect to the Freedmen's Bureau (which had the authority to void labor contracts that it found objectionable) and the civil rights bill (which gave powers of enforcement to the federal courts). True, he said, action of some sort was needed to protect the freedmen. But it would be wiser to grant federal authorities emergency powers for this purpose than to alter the fundamental relationship between the federal government and the states—unless the people themselves fully understood and wished to make that change.

"Section 2. Representatives shall be apportioned among the several States according to their respective numbers ... But when the *right* to vote at any election ... is denied to any of the male inhabitants ... or in any way abridged, except for participation in rebellion, or other crime, the basis of representation therein shall be reduced in the proportion which the number of such male citizens shall bear to the whole number of male citizens twenty-one years of age in such State." This provision, of course, was intended to give the freedmen access to the ballot box. But its formulation was problematical: it conferred no absolute right to suffrage, merely imposing penalties for its denial. It was possible that some Southern states would choose to incur the penalty rather than allow the freedmen a voice in their governance. More likely, those states would contrive to restrict the former slave's exercise of his right to vote without denying it outright. In all probability, the Judge said, "we shall soon find ourselves having to add another amendment to correct the failure of this one." *Sotto voce*, he added that he wondered how many of the Northern states were prepared to grant such full citizenship to the Negro.

It was, however, the third section of the amendment that raised the most concerns in his mind: "No person shall be a Senator or representative in Congress, or elector of President and Vice President, or hold any office, civil or military, under the United States, or under any State, who, having previously taken an oath ... to support the Constitution of the United States, shall have engaged in insurrection or rebellion against the same, or given aid or comfort to the enemies thereof." On its face, he said, this provision was intended to ensure the loyalty of Southern officials. But in reality, it was a spiteful and punitive measure that would have the effect of denying to the South its natural leaders. "For what person of character, his community under assault, would refuse it his support?" Here he reminded us that there were many in the South who had neither condoned slavery nor desired secession but who nonetheless took up arms when their homeland was invaded. And with a bit of sarcasm, he added that as a jurist he wasn't certain how to interpret the stipulation about giving "aid or comfort" to the rebellion—though a strict reading would probably bar everyone who had so much as sold a bushel of wheat to the Confederate army from holding office.

The temper of the Judge's remarks then changed markedly. Laying aside the page from the newspaper, he advanced to the first row of the audience, hands folded and head bowed slightly. After a few moments of silence, he resumed quietly but in great earnest: "Only a few short months ago, we celebrated the successful conclusion of a war fought for the noblest of reasons, namely, the freedom of certain of our fellows and, in a larger sense, freedom itself. Yet welcome as that victory was, it has presented us with some very difficult problems—among them the need to integrate the Negro into our society. This, I need not remind you, is no mean task. It entails a complete revolution in social relations, a revolution that will meet with much resistance in the North as well as in the South. It cannot be accomplished overnight—indeed, it will probably require a generation or more of patient effort. Nor can it be brought about solely by the legislator's pen. Where the will of the people is lacking, the law is largely powerless.

"For the reasons I have given, the amendment that is now before us seems a very blunt instrument with which to effect the change we desire. In all probability, it will merely harden the South's natural reluctance to accept the freedmen on fair and decent terms. If so, it will set back the cause of equality for a long time. What, then, ought we to do? Clearly, we need to prevent the worst abuses, and the responsibility for this must lie with the federal government. Beyond that, however, we must help to prepare the freedmen for full participation in the society—through education primarily, but also through relief where necessary. Above all, we must be patient, and accept the inevitable setbacks with a good grace."

After a brief pause, he added, "I realize that this is asking a great deal. We who have spent decades opposing the evil of slavery naturally feel justified in forcing the issue of full equality right now. But we cannot, the times will simply not bear it. To be faithful to our ideal, we must now return to the vineyard, assiduously tending the vines until the harvest is ready. Fourteenth Amendment or no, it will only come in its own time."

The Judge's remarks were greeted with applause and some nodding of heads, but on the whole it seemed to me that the audience's response was rather subdued, as if his sober assessment of the situation had given us all pause. Senator Sanborn then rose and thanked the Judge for his "wise and useful" comments, adding that although he himself still favored adoption of the amendment, it was clearly no panacea. He then said that as it had been an evening of "earnest discussion" rather than debate, and as the main points of difference were now clearly laid out, he would yield the remainder of his rebuttal time. Nodding appreciatively in his old friend's direction, the Judge signaled to me that he would do likewise and I gaveled the meeting to a close.

I left shortly thereafter, staying only long enough to thank the participants and exchange a few words with another member of the committee. The audience, of course, was on its feet immediately, intently if not passionately discussing all of the issues that had been raised. From the fragments that I overheard as I made my way through the crowd, it would be hard to say which, if either, view had prevailed. Indeed, there seemed to be a real uncertainty about the whole question of Reconstruction, as if it were vastly more complex than those of slavery and the Union. Nor can I myself really say where I stand. I shall have to think about it, of course, as it is of the utmost importance; but perhaps this is one occasion when I shall be glad to be spared the necessity of casting a ballot.

Monday, October 1st

The *Clarion* has come out in favor of the Fourteenth Amend-ment. Notwithstanding Judge Halston's "excellent" arguments, the editor feels that decisive action is required and failure to adopt the amendment would do irreparable harm to the freedmen's cause:

> While it is true that the Congress might have passed a more conciliatory measure, and that on the whole such a measure may have been wiser, it is this particular amendment that is now before the states—and whatev-er its flaws, to reject it would be to signal the weakness of our resolve regarding equality for the freedmen, of which the South will take full advantage.

There is no doubt truth in this view, and yet I cannot but feel that we have tossed a certain amount of caution to the winds and are being guided by events rather than guiding them. But perhaps matters are so far advanced that that would be unavoidable in any case.

Tuesday, October 9th

First meeting of the committee to consider revisions to the Acad-emy's curriculum. Besides myself and several other members of the faculty, it includes George Sims, who (as one of the trustees) oversees the Academy's finances, and Rev. Williams, a long-time friend of the Academy and the most distinguished scholar in our community.

After offering us tea and thanking us for our willingness to serve on the committee, Mrs. Marshall came right to the point: she wished to "modernize" the Academy's system of instruction to reflect both the advances in learning and the changes in society that were now taking place. The present curriculum, she said, was largely rooted in the perceptions and mores of the early part of the century. Its aim was to give young ladies a certain "gentility," that is, a nodding acquaintance with culture and the things of the mind but not a deep understanding of them. It did not prepare

them for full participation in the life of the world or enable them
to take advantage of the opportunities that were now opening up
for them. Scholarship, too, had changed markedly over the last
few decades, becoming much more rigorous and analytical. This
was certainly the case with the sciences ("witness Mr. Darwin"),
but it was true of many other areas of inquiry as well—and here
she alluded to the Biblical studies currently being carried out in
Germany.

Her notion was to add certain courses to the curriculum
(principally in the physical sciences and the newly emerging sciences of society) as well as to make the traditional offerings more
truly academic in character. She would like, for instance, to have
the girls learn physics and astronomy, along with something about
political economy. And she thought that a subject such as botany
would do well to go beyond the details of classification to the
principles of biological life itself ("insofar as we now understand
them"). Even in the study of letters, she said, there was room for
new perspectives: we had a tendency to treat the great authors
as sacrosanct, seldom questioning the wisdom that they have to
impart or inquiring into the origins of their ideas. And yet, each
writer saw the problems of life in his own light, nor was there necessarily agreement among them. ("Cicero's view of things is very
different from Horace's, even though they were very close in time,
for example.") Thus, it might behoove us to read such authors in a
more critical way, with due attention to their individual visions and
what it all might mean in our own times.

In barest outline, these were the issues that she wanted the
committee to address. She would give us as free a hand as possible,
and although she would like to have a specific proposal to present
to the Board of Trustees when it met in the spring, we were not
to rush our deliberations. She then invited us to offer any initial
thoughts that we might have.

As might be expected, several members of the committee immediately voiced concern about the "denigration" of the
traditional curriculum, arguing that letters could never become a
"clockwork business." Nodding knowingly, as if she had anticipated this objection, Mrs. Marshall replied that she envisioned
the liberal arts remaining the core of the curriculum for some

time to come—only she "wanted the students to have a deeper appreciation of them." This they would acquire by giving the great masterpieces a more scholarly scrutiny, by getting more "into Shakespeare's mind," as it were.

Mr. Sims then inquired whether she intended to increase the number of faculty, adding that he did not believe the Academy's finances would permit more than modest changes. To this Mrs. Marshall replied that she might want to take on one or two new teachers, but that most of the changes she envisioned could probably be effected with the current ones. With a slight smile she added that if there was anything the trustees had taught her over the years, it was the virtue of economy.

A more anarchic discussion then ensued, with everyone offering ideas just as they occurred to them and frequently interrupting one another. Ordinarily this would have annoyed me, but in this case I took it as a sign of the general enthusiasm for the project.

There was one sour note, however, sounded by Susan Wright, a young woman who teaches mathematics. She said that while she applauded the changes being considered, she was concerned lest we set the girls up for a great disappointment. "After all, as females, they will necessarily have a very limited role in the world's affairs—and a precise mind is almost a liability in a drawing room."

The room became very quiet, and Mrs. Marshall turned unusually serious if not somber. She had thought of this, she said, and it had given her pause with respect to reforming the curriculum. But then she had remembered that even in her own generation women of ability and conviction had managed to do great things. And she was confident that the state of affairs would be very different in another generation or so, even suggesting that women would have the right to vote by the end of the century. The important thing, for those now in school, was to prepare adequately for the changes to come.

Mr. Williams then said that he believed we all shared these sentiments and were committed to bringing about an "orderly revolution" in the education of young women. Though Miss Wright's concerns were well placed, by our actions we should be working to render them irrelevant.

This being heartily approved all around, the committee agreed to meet in a week's time, select a chairman, and set to work. As we were leaving, Mrs. Marshall took me aside and asked me to use the general respect that I enjoy to keep things on an even keel. "Your level-headedness will be very important to making any of these reforms practicable," she said. I thanked her and said that I would do my best. Indeed, I am very excited about this whole undertaking.

Friday, October 12th

It is distinctly autumnal now. Though the days are quite pleasant, there is a noticeable chill in the air in the mornings that causes me to quicken my pace as I walk to the Academy. The world is rapidly putting on its autumn dress as well, the varied greens of summer giving way to the browns and yellows of the maturing year. In this part of the country, of course, the reds tend to be fairly subdued; but here and there a dogwood, sumac, or sugar maple gives us a splash of that hue, sometimes tinged with orange and sometimes with purple.

As many delights as the season offers to the eye, it does not neglect the other senses. I am particularly struck by the almost praeternatural stillness of the afternoons: apart from the occasional clattering of acorns on the dried leaves that cover the ground, there is almost no sound, as if the earth itself were resting quietly, its gentle breaths entirely imperceptible to us. Then too, there is a slightly musty smell in the air, no doubt due to the decaying leaves, that I find particularly pleasant.

And as on many autumn afternoons, there is a distinct haze in the distance. I cannot account for this (it having been very dry of late), so perhaps it means that some old woods deity is quietly warming himself at his fire beneath the ancient oaks. On days such as these, one can as easily imagine that here as in the vales of Thessaly.

Tuesday, October 16th

The curriculum committee has selected Mr. Williams as its chairman, a natural enough choice given his position in the community and long association with the school. We have also decided that our first order of business will be to interview all the teachers regarding the current content of their courses and any changes that they deem beneficial. This will take time, of course, but is thought to be an essential step. By dividing the task up among the members of the committee, we hope to conclude it by the start of the Christmas holidays.

Friday, October 19th

This afternoon Alicia and I performed one of our annual rituals: dusting the shelves in the library. It is a rather tedious task, of course, but we soon fell into a rhythm that made the work seem to go quickly. I, being the tallest, would hand a shelf-full of books down to her and then polish the shelf with an oiled cloth; she, meanwhile, would arrange the books on an old trestle table that we had moved into the library just for that purpose, dust them with her feather duster, and hand them back to me in the same order.

We chatted for a while as we worked, mostly about a cousin of hers who is getting married next month, then lapsed into a studious silence. At that point my thoughts naturally turned to this room and its contents. My grandfather was very particular about his library. He would not allow the workmen who built the house to construct the shelves but brought in an experienced cabinet maker from Columbus. They are indeed a work of art, being made of a rich black walnut and lining one entire wall and the better part of the two adjacent ones. The room is also more luxuriously furnished than the others in the house, with a leather settee and wingback chairs, mahogany desk and tables, and thick Turkish carpet.

My grandfather, of course, was a great reader, and even now (some sixteen years after his death) most of the books that one finds on these shelves were his. Nicely bound editions of many of the world's classics, carefully arranged by general category such as history, philosophy, literature, and science. There is a shelf devoted to his beloved Goethe with editions of that master's works in German as well as English, along with several biographies and critical studies. And in a place of honor above the fireplace is his "American pantheon"—Emerson, of course, but also Bryant, Bancroft, Irving, and a number of others. He was a great champion of our native letters, often referring to the injunction that Emerson ("the sage of Concord") made to that effect in his oration "The American Scholar."

My husband, by contrast, did little in the way of pleasure reading, probably because he spent his days immersed in the records of court decisions and the briefs he was writing. He was fond of essays, however (over the years I gave him several collections of these as gifts, which are now over by the desk), and found much to occupy his exacting mind in the newspaper. Indeed, he put more care into reading the latter than anyone else I have ever known, occasionally pausing to make some noteworthy remark about an article.

My own reading is rather limited, no more than eight or ten books a year. Nor is it at all systematic, the particular selections usually being made according to the inspiration of the moment. In a way this is regrettable, and yet there is truth in Dr. Johnson's dictum that "a man ought to read exactly as inclination leads him, for what he reads as a task will do him little good." Then, too, I read things quite closely, often copying out lengthy excerpts into my notebooks and adding my own comments. No one can say that I am not serious about this aspect of my life.

I remained in the library for a while after we had finished, going from shelf to shelf and finding no small satisfaction in their clean and orderly appearance. As I scanned the titles (occasionally taking down a volume and perusing its opening pages), I was struck by the immense amount of human knowledge that had been collected in this room. Indeed, one could obtain a very full education from these books. In the most literal sense, books such as these are the guardians of civilization, the means through which our greatest achievements are transmitted from one generation to another—and thus deserving of our utmost care. And yet, my attraction to books has never been purely intellectual, they have always had a distinctly sensuous quality for me. I love the feel of them, their weight and the way one can rifle the pages with one's thumb. I am also quite fond of the smell of aged paper and will put my nose right down on an opened page. Whence this fondness comes I cannot say, though it occurs to me that there is a similarity between the musty odor of these "leaves" and that of those now quietly dropping to the ground outside.

It occurs to me also that I should make special provisions for the disposition of these books in my will. It is too valuable a collection to be treated simply as other household goods.

Sunday, October 21st

This morning at church I found myself staring at Captain Carey. He was seated to my right, one pew ahead of me, his head turned to the left so that he was in full profile. It is quite a handsome head, and though his features are distinctly masculine there is a softness to them that suggests a gentle nature. Indeed, as I observed him thoughtfully listening to the sermon, his head slightly elevated and his clear eyes fixed on the pulpit, I sensed a real nobility about him.

In recent weeks he has begun growing a beard, which should make him fairly distinguished looking as well as somewhat less youthful in appearance (I do not know his age but would judge him to be some seven or eight years younger than me). That will no doubt be an asset to his career and perhaps give him somewhat greater standing in the community as well.

I really should make a point of having him for tea. Perhaps I can also persuade him to allow me to draw him sometime.

Thursday, October 25th

There is a real hunter's moon tonight. It is perhaps one day shy of being full but is already giving off a brilliant light and the irregularities on its surface are sharp and distinct.

I am always somewhat at a loss in describing the scene that such a moon paints. Though some objects are illuminated more clearly than at other times, others are cast into deep shadow—much the effect that is produced by having a single candle in a room. The result is that we look at the world through a sort of scrim, a fine cloth that softens the objects in our view and gives them a marked bluish tint.

Not that there is not a spiritual quality to this ghostly scene. On the contrary, it is easy to imagine spirits being abroad on such a night— if not a certain transfiguration of reality itself. Many a time, in fact, I have looked up toward the ridge beyond the orchard and pictured Shawnee hunters moving noiselessly through the darkened woods.

Sunday, October 28th

These days, it seems, our world is all leaves. Despite repeated rakings, they litter the ground and one cannot go anywhere without having to shuffle through them. The shrubbery, too, is festooned with them and some of the smaller plants are completely covered. By the amount of sky that is visible through the trees, I would judge that more than half the leaves are now down.

The eye, of course, delights in this annual "threshing" of nature's, in the richly varied colors and textures of the autumn landscape. I experienced this pleasure myself this afternoon on a short walk up to the ridge. The path is lined with tulip poplars, and the intense yellow of their leaves, almost luminescent in the brilliant sunlight, was so perfectly set off against the azure sky that it could have taken my breath away. It was as though I were walking beneath some exquisite canopy of otherworldly origin. One of our writers has compared the autumn woods to an illuminated manuscript, and I can think of no image so apt, particularly where a stand of evergreens abuts deciduous trees in full fall dress.

Included in the delights of the autumn woods, of course, is the motion of the leaves—now fluttering quietly above our heads, now twirling gently to the ground, now descending in torrents in response to a sudden gust. Falling leaves, it seems, are like rain in this respect, that they can have many different moods.

This evening it is blustery, and the wind is driving the leaves against the windowpanes. Their sharp edges scrape the glass for a moment or two, then they casually slide away. This happens over and over, the intensity of the assault varying with the strength of the wind. It is a sound one could easily find annoying and yet I take a certain comfort in it. The changing of the seasons goes on night and day—Nature has her own designs, not all of which she shares with us.

Saturday, November 3rd

I have decided to give a small dinner party in a couple of weeks and spent part of the afternoon writing out the invitations. This is a more significant step for me than it might seem: though I have always liked entertaining, I have done very little of it since the war began—and none since my husband's death. In some sense, then, this gathering represents a return to a more normal condition of life.

The guests will include the Halstons, the Williamses, and Thomas Barlow (who teaches European history at the Academy and whose conversation I have always found interesting) and his wife. To round out the number, I am taking the bold step of asking Matthew Carey.

Friday, November 9th

The indications are that the Republicans have swept the election, and will have a substantial majority in the next Congress. In our own state they and the War Democrats (running under the banner of the Union Party) have won sixteen of the nineteen seats in the House of Representatives. This, of course, is a larger margin than one would have expected in a state that elected a moderate governor just twelve months before.

What it signifies is not altogether clear, however. Judge Halston feels that there was no small amount of duplicity in the campaign, with the victors appealing to a crude, unthinking patriotism and soft-pedaling the issue of Negro suffrage. He senses a fundamental conservatism in Ohio voters (and indeed, in those of other Northern states) that will make them reluctant to accept any significant changes. But be that as it may, these are the men who have been elected and who will chart our course over the next two years.

Monday, November 12th

Tonight we held our annual leaf-burning. Bonfires were visible all across the town and, I imagine, throughout the valley as well. Someone who was unfamiliar with the custom would no doubt have concluded that he had stumbled upon some vast pagan ritual of former times.

There is never an appointed date for this event, it simply happens of its own accord. Of course, it always occurs at a logical time, namely, a damp, windless night after all the leaves are down. And yet I sense a certain quiet conspiracy on this matter, a common instinct among my fellow citizens that such-and-such a day is the right one.

The preparations begin several days before. On Saturday, for instance, I had some neighbor boys rake up all the leaves and pile them at the far end of the vegetable garden. To this they added several wagons-full of leaves from their own yards. Just before dark tonight they neatened up the pile and dampened the area around it with buckets of water. Then, about eight o'clock, we gathered around as they tossed some kerosene on the pile and set it on fire.

It kindled quickly, the flames seeming to leap upwards; we instinctively drew back, with some of the smaller children ducking behind their parents while screaming in delight. After a few minutes, however, the more aggressive flames receded and the fire began to burn at a slow, steady rate. In the soft glow of the firelight, the children then led us in some "witches' songs" and, joining hands, skipped around the pyre. As the pile burned down, this merriment gave way to quiet conversation and even silence, as we watched the bright sparks rise into the blackness and contemplated the ancient mystery of fire, the ever-changing colors of those incandescent vapors lit from within. When the flames died out completely, the boys doused the remnants of the pile with water, sending up a cloud of pungent steam. Then I had everyone into the kitchen for hot cider and corn muffins.

Although it did not seem especially cold while we were outside, it looks to be a very raw night. My bedchamber is uncommonly chilly and there are little ice crystals forming on the insides of the windowpanes. I shall be glad to finish up and get under the covers.

Thursday, November 15th

Things are shaping up nicely for my dinner party on Saturday.

After checking with the various provisioners, I have settled on the following menu: cold trout with dill, followed by French onion soup, followed by roast goose with a Madeira sauce, a mêlée of roasted potatoes, turnips, and rutabaga with herbs, Brussels sprouts, and light dinner rolls. For dessert we shall have spice cake with a lemon glaze; it is not particularly fancy, but seems to complement an autumn meal quite well. As to the wine, I have pulled several bottles of a nice Rhône rouge from the little cellar that John put together so assiduously.

Alicia has agreed to stay over until Sunday and take charge of the preparations. She will iron the table linens and polish the silver tomorrow, leaving only the cooking and setting up for Saturday. I will assist her with that, of course, but only as she directs— as always, she will be the *chef de la cuisine.*

Sunday, November 18th

I am very pleased with my little dinner party. All of the dishes turned out well, the company was thoroughly congenial, and even the conversation proved to be somewhat out of the ordinary.

I have always been a little nervous about entertaining, worried that some dish will fail or some crucial task will not be completed on time. But as I saw the various pieces fall into place—the table set, the fires lit, the warm dishes coming out of the oven— my anxieties abated and I began to look forward to a pleasant evening. Indeed, I felt a genuine rush of satisfaction as we sat down to dinner, with the first course neatly arranged on the plates, the silver and glassware gleaming in the candlelight, and a large bouquet of yellow and brown chrysanthemums at the center of the table. And it was with real pleasure that I watched my guests set to, commenting on the excellence of the trout amid the clatter of knives and forks on the plates.

As Alicia was serving the main course, I retrieved a decanter of wine from the sideboard and, purely from instinct (this was always John's function), asked Captain Carey to pour it. He appeared a bit surprised at first but graciously took the decanter and made the rounds of the glasses. The wine met with general approval, Mr. Williams remarking that I had clearly not "saved the best for last" and the Judge pursing his lips with evident satisfaction.

At first the conversation was unexceptional, casual remarks about the war, the recent election, and various town matters. At some point, however (I am not sure how, as I was getting more rolls from the kitchen at the time), it turned to the subject of courage and became distinctly philosophical in character. The Judge, eagerly assuming the role of his beloved Socrates, was just in the process of asking the others how they would define the term when I reentered the dining room.

There appeared to be some initial puzzlement at this question, but at length Julia responded by asking whether it could mean anything other than "fearlessness." At that point a slightly mischievous smile spread over the Judge's features, as if he had just caught a witness in a obvious fabrication. That, indeed, was the common conception, he said, but there were at least two reasons why it was not fully adequate. First, a fearless person might be merely reckless, and if so we would probably not call him courageous—or at least not find anything to admire in his actions. Second, and more importantly, it was questionable whether one who had no fear at all could be said to show courage.

Mr. Barlow then suggested that perhaps courage consisted in overcoming one's fears, that was to say, in acting in spite of them. The Judge nodded approvingly, saying that he thought that was much closer to the mark, and the others seemed to agree. The question then, he went on, was how one came to possess courage, whether it was inherent in one's nature or something one could acquire. It was at that point, however, that Elizabeth Williams raised the discussion to another level altogether. "Perhaps," she said, "we should ask Captain Carey that question. Of all of us, he undoubtedly has the most real experience in this matter."

All eyes then turned to Matthew. He was silent for a few moments, apparently taking the time to consider his answer. When at last he spoke it was in a cautious tone: "When we speak of courage in battle, say, we usually mean confronting a danger headlong, without flinching. I have seen this on a few occasions, to be sure." He then went on to relate an incident that occurred at the Battle of the Wilderness. The ground there consists of a dense thicket in which visibility can be quite limited, such that it is difficult to maintain coherent battle lines. The regiment was advancing, and emerging into a relatively open area his company met heavy fire and instinctively took cover. Realizing that if they remained there they would leave the rest of the regiment exposed, he ordered the men to reload, fix bayonets, and advance toward the enemy's position at a run, holding their fire until they were almost upon them. His hope was to overwhelm the enemy by concentrating his force in one blow. The stratagem succeeded and the Confederates were forced back (though later in the day the tide turned and his entire division had to retreat).

But there was another sort of courage that he had observed, one that was actually much more common. He didn't know what to call it other than a "quiet determination." It was the courage one needed to carry on in the face of exhaustion and the immense confusion of battle, to overcome the feeling of having fallen into a maelstrom and being rapidly drawn down. Asked how one accomplished that, he replied that it was by finding things on which to focus—the drummer boy's tapping, the faces of the other members of the company, the line of trees that marked the enemy's position—and holding on to them at all cost. Though, to be sure, he added, "inner qualities" undoubtedly mattered a great deal as well.

No one spoke for several moments, then Susanna Barlow suggested that perhaps this second form of courage was to be found in many other undertakings as well. Indeed, she thought that everyday life itself required the sort of courage that Matthew had spoken of, though we did not usually recognize it as such. There was general agreement with this, and then—as if the evening could bear only so much intensity—the conversation moved on to more mundane matters. Because it had been so interesting, however, I served coffee right at the table instead of in the parlor, which would have tended to break things up.

My guests began to leave around eleven o'clock. The Williamses were first, Mr. Williams saying that he had important "chores" to attend to in the morning. As it had turned very cold, Matthew accepted a ride home from the Halstons. Before leaving, however, he thanked me profusely for including him, saying that it had been a thoroughly delightful evening.

Tuesday, November 20th

I have been thinking about John a lot the last two days, no doubt because of my dinner party. It was an occasion on which he would naturally have had a commanding presence, occupying the head of the table and seeing that all of the guests were well provided for. Yet he was not: I myself sat in that place, playing both of our customary roles. And successful as the evening was, it now seems a little hollow to me, a fond attempt to recover a gaiety and innocence that is no longer possible.

Then too, an event such as this symbolizes the intent to "get on with life," to set the past aside and focus on the present. For whatever reason, I am not completely ready to do that.

Monday, November 26th

The cold weather has seemingly settled in at last. It has come about quite suddenly: yesterday was bright and warm, a perfect Indian summer day; this morning the sky is leaden and an icy rain is falling. Twenty-four hours ago we felt the exhilaration of being en plein air, now we just want to hunker down by the fire.

Nature, of course, does not shut the door on the season so neatly. We will undoubtedly have some mild days between now and New Year's, maybe even a warm spell in January or February. But the mind draws lines of its own, preferring sharp demarcations to irresolution and ambiguity. To all intents and purposes it is now winter, time to gather in our more sublime feelings and brace ourselves against the elements.

Saturday, December 1st

I spent most of the day helping to put the garden to bed. As the cold has held on, I was afraid that the ground would be too hard to work if we waited much longer.

With assistance from a hired man, I cut back or uprooted last season's growth, turned over the beds, and generally straightened up the grounds. It was a larger task than I had envisioned (we created quite a mound of debris at the far end of the property), but it gives me great satisfaction to have everything so neat and ready for spring.

Wednesday, December 12th

The first snowfall of the season. It was quite wet and did not even cover the ground completely, leaving a patchwork of dark blotches. And by the time I left the Academy this afternoon it had melted in all but the most sheltered places.

Tuesday, December 18th

For the last week or so virtually all our spare moments have been taken up with preparations for Christmas. There seems to be unusual excitement about the holidays this year, probably because it is the first year since 1860 that our minds have not been preoccupied with war.

As always, my own preparations will be rather simple. Over the weekend Alicia and I put out some greenery—a wreath made of hemlock and juniper on the front door, some feathery white pine garlands over the mantles in the parlor and dining room, and sprigs of holly around festive candles on the table in the front hall. There are also dishes of nuts and dried fruits for those who drop by.

I have sent out only a few cards, mainly to people who live elsewhere and whom I shall not see during the season. Although it is increasingly common to send them to everyone in your acquaintance, I find that practice rather forced and have resisted it.

As for gifts, I have had a nice dress made for Alicia that I will present to her along with a twenty-dollar gold piece and a turkey for her family. For Judge Halston I have a new biography of John Marshall, and for Julia a silk shawl. My other gifts will be small, principally fruitcakes and other fancy foods.

It should be a quiet week, what with the Academy out of session and Alicia away. The Thorntons have invited me for dinner on Christmas Day, but otherwise I have no social engagements. It will be good to have some time alone, to pause briefly at this midpoint in the working year.

Sunday, December 23rd

Last night brought another of our annual rituals, the Halstons' tree-trimming party. I enjoyed myself immensely—there is probably no other event of the season that is so festive or that stands out so much in my memories of Christmas over the years.

The tree itself was magnificent, a large fir with stout branches and an almost perfectly conical shape. (The Judge would not say where he had gotten it, only that "he had had someone scouting the woods since last summer.") Brightly illuminated by dozens of small candles, it cast a warm, almost magical glow over the room.

As it was already richly festooned with ornaments when I arrived, I lost no time in adding my own contribution: a brightly painted carving of a child on a rocking horse that has been in our family since my grandfather's time.

The conversation, of course, was for the most part light and amiable. I did, however, enjoy chatting with Meredith about Mr. Hawthorne's *Marble Faun*, which appeared several years ago but which she had only now gotten around to reading. Though it is clearly a romance, and in that sense divorced from actual life, she feels that it raises a profound moral question, namely, the amount of sway that we ought to allow our sensuous side. Donatello, of course, gives it virtually free rein but is utterly incapable of moral judgment—to the point of committing a murder almost from whim. The Americans in the novel are more circumspect, though they, too, seem to be unable to come to terms with this part of themselves. "We are such a practical, sober-minded people that it is difficult for us," she has concluded. We agreed to talk further after I have had a chance to reread the book. It will be a good winter pastime because, whatever the book's moral dimensions, it is filled with the sun and color of Italy.

About half past nine a group of carolers appeared in front of the house and treated us to a couple of old carols. When they were done the Judge invited them in, "as they would clearly not be able to complete their rounds without some refreshment." Before leaving, they led us in a rousing chorus of "Good King Wenceslas," accompanied by Julia at the piano.

It was nearly midnight before I left to come home. The night had turned very cold, but all along the way I was warmed by the sight of lighted candles in windows and the sound of merry-making within.

Tuesday, December 25th

Christmas Day. Bright but very cold in the morning, with a hard frost that gave everything a crystalline appearance. The air too seemed almost brittle, and I found it a bit difficult to breathe as I walked to church, my lungs seeming to close up rather than admit it. And when I exhaled, of course, it was in great clouds of vapor, as if my body were trying to generate its own steam. It was unusually cold inside the church as well, so much so that I kept my coat buttoned and my gloves on.

The sermon was good though not terribly original. Mr. Williams began by asking what it was that had brought us there that morning. Our Puritan ancestors, after all, had refused to celebrate Christmas, finding the ritual too idolatrous. And, as Unitarians, we did not recognize the divinity of Christ—the seeming *sine qua non* for observing this day. The answer, of course, was that we had come to celebrate the birth of a great and good teacher—indeed, the most profound teacher in the entire history of the world. Though not divine himself (neither reason nor Scripture would support that contention), he had nonetheless shown us a clear path to God. There might be other paths, and our understanding of God had certainly become more refined over the years; yet one had to wonder where the world would be without this carpenter from Nazareth, who had made radical goodness conceivable. Then too, his message of brotherhood had a special relevance for those in the United States this Christmas of 1866.

I lingered at church for quite a while after the service was over, having so many people to say hello to and enjoying the general holiday mood. At length, however, the Thorntons collared me and took me away to dinner, which was quiet but quite pleasant. I returned home about half past five. As the house was very chilly and I would probably retire early, I decided to light only the fire in my bedchamber. I am now comfortably holed up here in my nightclothes, another indulgence of this special day.

Saturday, December 29th

We have reached the end of another year. Though tumultuous politically, in most other respects it has been very tranquil. Indeed, life in our village has become much as it was before 1850: untroubled but largely insular, our concerns not extending much beyond the horizon. I suppose that this is natural—one can stand only so much intensity, after all. And yet it would seem that after the ordeal we have gone through our lives ought to have more purpose, that things ought to be different in some fundamental way. Certainly there are many whose lives *have* been irrevocably altered by the war and for whom the future looms uncertainly if not darkly.

My own situation, of course, is blessed by comparison. Yet I have lost my life's companion, and although the initial pain is gone I now face long years alone. I try to console myself with the thought that death is ever present and that John might have been taken from me at any point, but it is of only so much use. The fact remains that this war has cost me dearly, and good as my life is it can never be complete.

II. 1868

Saturday, January 11th

My first entry for the new year. A year, of course, is an arbitrary designation, and although it would be comforting to "close the books" on the old one and start afresh, that is seldom possible. And no more so, it seems, than this year—there is too much unfinished business from 1867, too many of the processes set in motion then have yet to run their full course.

Our national life, of course, has become increasingly tumultuous. The discord between the President and Congress has hardened into a bitter contest of wills, with the Radicals employing every device at their disposal to circumscribe Mr. Johnson's power. In March, for instance, Congress took direct control of the reconstruction of the Southern states, setting aside the existing governments and imposing military rule. Apart from keeping order, the commanders' principal task is to supervise the election of delegates to new constitutional conventions. As this anticipates the rapid reestablishment of civil authority, it cannot really be viewed as a gross abuse of power. But the law goes to extraordinary lengths to influence the form of the new constitutions by excluding "disloyal" persons from the process altogether. Thus, although the Fourteenth Amendment has not as yet actually been adopted, persons disqualified from office under it may not elect or serve as delegates.

The President, of course, vetoed the bill when it was present-ed to him, citing its unprecedented expansion of federal authority. By most accounts, he did so in mild and conciliatory language, striving to avoid a worsening of the situation. But Congress was in no mood to bargain and summarily brushed aside his objections. The same day that it passed the Reconstruction Act it enacted two other measures aimed at hemming him in. One of these, the Tenure of Office Act, forbids the President from dismissing a pre-viously appointed official without the approval of Congress; the other requires him to issue all military orders through the General of the Army (that is, General Grant). At one point things got so bad that the House of Representatives actually began an impeach-ment inquiry. It was only with difficulty that the Judiciary Commit-tee could find any grounds for this, however, and the full House had the wisdom to reject it out of hand.

As to what to make of all this, I am afraid that I am at some-thing of a loss. To some extent, each of the contenders has princi-ple on its side—and yet each is clearly governed by its own interests and prejudices as well. The President is undoubtedly right in resist-ing Congress's usurpation of power, both with respect to his own office and with respect to the Southern states themselves. Yet it is clear that he would condemn the freedmen to virtual slavery—his incessant pleas to the country not to "Africanize" our political life are ample evidence of that. And while his opponents appear to have a genuine concern for the black man, it is a fact that their po-litical fortunes depend on him: readmission of the Southern states on anything like the old terms would soon lead to a radical diminu-tion of their power. Nor can one entirely discount the spitefulness and petty rivalries that characterize so many human endeavors.

Life in Westerly remains quite placid, of course, little affect-ed by distant events however momentous they may be. Indeed, it seems to have lost the intensity that it had even before the war, when each new development was greeted with such anxious con-cern. In many ways we have turned inward. It is business and family affairs that occupy us at present, we have little time for larger questions. This, I suppose, is only natural. Our generation has been hard at it for some years now, and the desire for peace is very strong.

The one exception to the prevailing spirit of conservatism is the Academy, which is attempting to introduce some major reforms. We have taken on two new teachers: a young man recently graduated from Amherst College to instruct the girls in the physical sciences, and one who studied at Heidelberg to teach them German and what is known as philology (humane letters, but from a distinctly philosophical point of view). Susan Wright, who has an interest in the science of political economy, has been asked to develop a course in that subject and Thomas Barlow to put together one on the theory and practice of government. And throughout the curriculum there is a new emphasis on the cultivation of critical thinking. That is, the girls are being asked not merely to grasp certain facts and opinions (though that element is still fairly strong, to be sure) but also to form judgments with respect to them. As my own classes have long sought to develop the critical faculty (through, for instance, comparing the predominant concerns of artists at different times), I have not had to make great changes to accommodate the Academy's new philosophy. Still, it is very exciting, and I shall be eager to see what becomes of the girls who are educated in this fashion.

The one development of note in my own life is my growing friendship with Matthew Carey. It has come about quite gradually since our first encounter at the commemoration for the regiment. At first, it was mostly chance meetings on the street or brief conversations after church. Then I began inviting him for tea on Saturday afternoons from time to time, which he reciprocated by asking me to luncheon at the hotel. At present, we occasionally have dinner there on Sunday (either alone or in the company of others) or take long walks into the countryside. He has even acted as my escort on several occasions, though in so small a village and with my social standing I certainly do not require one.

There is no mystery as to why I am so fond of his company: He is perhaps the most thoughtful person I have ever known, in both senses of that term. Though no better read than many others, he brings unusual care and insight to intellectual matters, so that his views are invariably both refined and compelling. Yet he is never overbearing about this; there is a fundamental humility to his character (one might almost say a diffidence) as well as great regard for others. As a result, he often exerts a calming influence, defusing the tensions inherent in difficult situations. Indeed, it is virtually impossible to be in his presence and not feel a certain sense of tranquility.

I suppose, too, that I am flattered by the attentions of this handsome and gracious man. Friends, of course, have asked whether we shall ever be "involved" romantically. Though the thought has crossed my mind, I have never really given it serious consideration. We are simply friends, and though society cannot readily accommodate such friendships, there it will remain.

Thursday, January 16th

I find that as time goes on I am writing in this journal less often, that whereas I once made an entry virtually every day I now do so only once a week on the average. Its purpose, too, has changed markedly over the years. When I first began keeping it, shortly before my marriage, it was essentially a day-book in which I would record all the household details—the dates on which the bed linen was changed or the cleaning done, the names of visitors, and so forth. This, of course, was largely owing to my grandfather, who was very particular about such matters and who, as his memory failed, was ever more desirous of having precise "accounts." Even then, however, I would record memorable passages from my reading in a section at the back that I reserved for this purpose. And by the beginning of the war it had become a true journal, that is, a running transcript of my thoughts.

This change in the journal's character is reflected in its physical nature as well. Early on it was kept in printed ledgers, with rows and columns that facilitated the recording of household expenses and other routine items. For a time I tried to use bound volumes of blank pages, but writing in them proved to be too awkward. At present I make my entries on individual sheets of good-quality paper and have them bound into annual volumes every January. The entire set, in their proper order, is kept in a large safe in the library.

I refer to my "thoughts" as though they were particularly weighty or would be of interest to anyone other than myself, neither of which is really the case. And yet I have found it useful to set them down formally, in precise and well-considered language. This forces me to be clear in my thinking, it will not permit me to be content with vague and preliminary musings. As often as not I draw a moral from an event or perception, a precept that I can put into practice. In this way my entries in this journal take on the character of little *essais*. And having a continuous record, of course, enables me to see how my views have unfolded over time—in other words, what progress I have made. Occasionally, I even begin an entry by referring to a previous one; I might say, for instance, "Several years ago, I expressed my belief that....A recent event has given me another perspective on this matter, however."

To be sure, my literary style is rather plain, at least by the standards of the age. Even in writing for others, I avoid the long introductory clauses and circumlocutions that seem to be the hallmarks of contemporary writing. Nor have I much use for inflated words—"animadversion," say, where "criticism" will do. Judge Halston says that to avoid the excesses of the times he attempts to stay current with the writers of the last century. I do not believe that we have to go so far afield, however. Several of our contemporaries, including our late President, have given us fine examples of directness, simplicity, and grace in expression. They have the added virtue of being distinctly American voices, addressing our own concerns in the idiom that is most natural to us.

Saturday, January 18th

My entry two days ago has prompted another observation, namely, the delight that I take in my own handwriting. Though not truly calligraphic, it has a grace and precision akin to those of fine filigree, the delicate, almost perfectly shaped letters amounting to a work of art in themselves. Indeed, I derive much the same pleasure from wielding a pen as I do from wielding a paintbrush.

Friday, January 24th

The heavens have awarded us a snow holiday, the first in several years.

The snow began sometime after midnight. By dawn over a foot had fallen and it was coming down so heavily that we could see no more than a rod or so beyond the house. It was also unusually cold, 18 degrees by the thermometer outside the library window when I looked out just after daylight. At half past seven the church bell rang. Three times, widely spaced—the customary signal that activities were suspended and that everyone was advised to remain indoors. This tocsin (as the Judge calls it) having sounded, we settled in for a long and perhaps dull day of being confined to our quarters. Though there would be little things to occupy us, our principal task would be simply to keep ourselves safe from the elements.

To simplify matters, Alicia and I decided that we would maintain only two fires, one in the kitchen stove and the other in the parlor, where we would spend the day and where we could sleep if necessary. After breakfast, we got in a large quantity of wood, stacking part of it in the kitchen and part in the hallway adjacent to the parlor. As the day promised to be dark, we also assembled some extra lamps as well as a good supply of oil. By ten o'clock we were comfortably ensconced in our "cabin," Alicia on the sofa with some mending and I in a large wing chair with note paper and pen and a volume of poetry. As Alicia gets cold easily when not actively engaged in work, she wrapped herself up in a comforter with only her head and hands exposed. I was able to make do with a heavy shawl, but only by getting up frequently to stir the fire or pour tea from the kettle that we kept going much of the morning.

For all the hardships that they entail, I love the insularity of such days, the way they bring everything to a standstill and force us out of our routine so completely. Then too, there is something infinitely soothing about the falling of snow, a sense of calm and wonder that comes over us as we watch the feathery flakes emerge from an opaque sky and drift softly to the ground, sometimes with greater urgency and sometimes with less, but always silently and with perfect grace. Even the crescents of snow forming at the bottoms of the window panes delight us, for they remind us that we are safe and warm within our houses. From time to time I found myself looking up from my work and staring out the window at the ethereal scene just beyond it.

By afternoon, however, the ethereal mood of the morning hours had given way to one of festivity. Shortly after one o'clock the snowfall became noticeably lighter; by two it had stopped altogether and a little sunlight was managing to work its way through the clouds. Our village then took on something of the aspect of a Brueghel painting. First, a veritable brigade of men and boys armed with shovels came to dig us out; immediately the air was filled with the sounds of scraping and heaving and, of course, loud and friendly banter. Then, when enough passageways had been opened, all of the other shut-ins emerged from their houses, anxious for company as much as fresh air. While the adults traded stories, the children sledded or threw snowballs at one another. Though there had been no provocation, at one point Alicia and I came under attack from the "Fourth Cavalry." We held our ground against a heavy barrage of snowballs as long as we could, but finally, outnumbered and attacked in force on our flank, we were compelled to surrender. Our captors let us go, however, in exchange for some slices of candied orange left over from Christmas.

By nightfall it was completely clear and a strong wind had come up. Little by little we were forced back into our houses … and into the daily round.

Tuesday, January 28th

This afternoon I sent a note to Matthew inviting him to tea a week from Saturday and saying that I would like him to tell me about Spotsylvania. The question has remained in suspension for too long, it is time that I put it to rest.

Sunday, February 9th

I have had a most interesting conversation with Matthew. The truth is sadder than I had realized, but it is well that I am aware of it.

We took tea on the sofa. He sat beside me, a bit stiffly I

thought and dressed rather formally for a Saturday. As his narrative unfolded, however, I came to appreciate these marks of respect as well as the quiet, precise manner in which he addressed me. He also dispensed with much of the preliminary chitchat that would ordinarily have attended such an occasion, asking me if we might begin as soon as I had poured the tea. When I bid him do so, he drew out a map that he had prepared (with some care, it appeared) and commenced:

"The campaign opened on the 4th of May, with the army's crossing of the Rapidan River at Germanna Ford," he said, pointing out the spot. "Now, below the river is a vast thicket known as the Wilderness. It was Grant's intention to move through this area as rapidly as possible so as to meet the Army of Northern Virginia on open ground, where our advantage in numbers would tell. Lee, of course, had every reason to try to thwart our advance and immediately went on the offensive. There followed two days of intense but inconclusive fighting. On the morning of the 7th, Grant resolved to break the impasse by a night march around Lee's army ("by the left flank," as he put it) to Spotsylvania Court House, which is located on the main road to Richmond. If we could secure that point, Lee would be forced either to retreat or to meet us on unfavorable ground.

"The 5th Corps ('our own corps,' he said with emphasis) would form the vanguard, advancing along this road as soon as the cavalry had secured it against the Confederates. In doing so, we were to swing behind the 2nd Corps, being screened by them until we were well down the road; they were then supposed to fall into line behind us. The remaining two corps were to circle around behind us, approaching Spotsylvania Court House along a different road." He paused while I fixed in my mind the dispositions of the various units on the map as well as the routes by which they were to advance. The 5th Corps, it appeared, had to proceed some eight or nine miles down a thoroughfare called Brock Road, which ran to the southeast. There were no major Confederate units in the vicinity, and from the configuration of the roads it appeared that interception would be difficult. "It was unquestionably a masterful strategy," Matthew said, "designed to put our forces into an advantageous position in a short time while holding the enemy at bay."

"Yet it did not succeed?" I inquired.

"No. The movements were not well coordinated, with the result that things quickly fell behind schedule. And even worse, the cavalry failed to clear Brock Road. Only with the arrival of the first regiments from our own corps were the defenders dislodged from the barricades that they had erected along the road, and by then some of the Confederate infantry had dug in at Laurel Hill." He pointed out the spot on the map, and then, apparently recalling its significance for me, lapsed into an awkward silence. The name had indeed given me a momentary shock, but I asked him to go on, which he did with evident relief.

"We made two assaults against them on the morning of the 8th, but without success—as we were to learn to our sorrow, the position would remain impregnable throughout the engagement. By late morning, the Confederates were frantically trying to extend their lines eastward to stem the columns of bluecoats that were converging on the area. As a result, they were well entrenched along their principal line of defense by the afternoon of the 9th." I studied the map for a moment, recognizing the peculiar loop extending out from the Confederate line that had figured so prominently in the newspaper accounts; I remarked on it to Matthew. He replied that it was indeed a very odd line of battle, as it would leave the men positioned there exposed on three sides. But Lee's engineers had evidently concluded that the "salient" occupied high enough ground that it had to be held.

"Over the next three days," he continued, "there was only sporadic and inconclusive fighting. Although a general assault had been ordered for five o'clock on the afternoon of the 10th, it quickly disintegrated, including our own attempt at Laurel Hill. A select brigade did manage to briefly penetrate the salient, however, convincing Grant that he could take it if he brought enough force to bear at a single point. Accordingly, he decided to send the 2nd and 6th Corps against it before dawn on the 12th; the other two corps would either support the assault against the salient or attack other points of the line, depending on how the battle developed."

I must have flinched slightly at Matthew's mention of "the 12th," for he turned to me and asked whether he should continue. I nodded and he agreed to do so, but with the caveat that I was to tell him if it became too painful for me. It did not, however; on the contrary, it gave me an odd sense of comfort to learn the details of my husband's death, to know what he had experienced on that day.

"Until that point, the 2nd Corps had been positioned on our right. To attack the salient, it would have to move some three miles over largely roadless terrain, if at all possible without being detected. The maneuver was to take place after dark, and as the 2nd Corps pulled out we were to extend our own line to secure the army's right wing. As it happened, a cold, heavy rain came to our aid in concealing these movements. It slowed them considerably, however, and it was midnight before the first units of the 2nd Corps got into position for the assault, which was scheduled for half past four.

"At first, the attack on the salient was successful beyond all imagination—the 2nd Corps easily overran it, taking several thousand prisoners and forcing many of the other defenders to flee. Apparently, in the darkness and rain we had taken the Confederates completely by surprise. Then too, it is said that Lee had withdrawn his artillery from the salient, anticipating that Grant was going to retreat to Fredericksburg. The initial success was to be short-lived, however. By six o'clock the Confederates had mounted a vigorous counterattack and forced us back. From then on it was to be a death struggle, with more and more units thrown into the fray and the casualties mounting beyond all imagining. I did not witness it myself, of course, but was told by several officers who were there that it was the worst carnage they had seen at any time during the war."

I recalled the accounts that had appeared in the newspapers: the vicious, at times hand-to-hand fighting, with whole companies being cut down by canister fired at close range, bodies piling up in front of the breastworks, and the trenches running red with blood. Even now I find such slaughter difficult to imagine—and it is a fact attested to beyond all doubt. Turning to Matthew, I asked whether it was at that point that the 5th Corps was ordered to advance against Laurel Hill.

"Yes," he said softly. "Grant apparently believed that Lee had been compelled to withdraw troops from that position in order to hold the salient—either that or he wished to prevent him from doing so. In any event, the order to advance came through about eight o'clock. At first, the corps commander, General Warren, objected, arguing that Laurel Hill simply could not be taken. But under pressure from General Meade, he at length gave the command to advance. Many of the men refused to obey it and those who did went forward with great reluctance. The one brigade that got within easy range of the Confederates was cut to ribbons; after that, the men withdrew without orders and Warren canceled the attack."

I asked Matthew to describe the enemy's position. "It was not especially high ground," he said, "but the Confederates had made the best possible use of it. Much of the area in front of the hill was already open; where it was not, they had cleared enough of it to give them a clear range of fire. By the morning of the 12th they were well dug in, with brush and felled trees piled up in front of their trenches and *abatis*—logs with pointed ends—staked out all along the line. At one point, there were even three tiers of trenches, so that overrunning one or even two of them would still leave us fatally exposed. One of the officers present described the Confederate works overall as 'frowning.' They were certainly enough to inspire a sense of futility in anyone attempting to carry them. And to make matters worse, the Confederates had positioned their artillery behind the crest of the hill, where the advancing infantry could not readily attack it."

At this point Matthew paused, as if not certain whether he should continue. Though I had some trepidation, I was already more easy in my mind than when we had begun our conversation and wished to know the rest. "So," I said at length, "another attack was ordered?"

"Yes. Grant was determined to try every point of the line, certain that there had to be a weak point somewhere. Warren resisted, of course, even more vigorously than before, but under threats from Grant's adjutant and assurances that Meade would take responsibility for the consequences, he eventually relented. The attack got under way shortly before ten o'clock.

"It went poorly from the start. Griffin's Division advanced first—ahead of the others—and was immediately repulsed with heavy losses. That and the delay in our own division's advance left Cutler's Division exposed on both flanks. The first units got as far as a ravine, where they paused to await the others. Owing to their exposure, however, they came under an enfilading fire that took a heavy toll on them. The division ultimately made several determined attacks, but without result. Cutler then requested permission to withdraw, which was granted.

"Meanwhile our own division had started forward. For a while we had the cover of a wood, but as we came into view the Confederates opened up with a murderous fire. The men instinctively took cover as the officers pondered the best line of advance. Colonel Reed was hit in the chest as he was raising himself to study the terrain with his binoculars." Colonel Thornton had given me a few of the details in his letter to me afterwards. It was John's custom to position himself at the head of the regiment during the initial phase of an assault so as to give the men encouragement. When the enemy were actually engaged, however, he would drop back to get a clearer view of developments. On most occasions, he was armed only with a pistol, which he seldom used; his brain and a good pair of field glasses were his principal instruments of war.

"I was not near him at the time," Matthew went on quietly, "but was told that he was killed instantly. One of the other company commanders saw to it that his remains were carried back to our lines as soon as possible." He paused for a second, then added that an assault was subsequently made but to no avail. "The commanders on the field did not press it very hard. By then there was a general consensus to avoid unnecessary sacrifice."

We were silent for several moments as I turned the matter over in my mind. Then I asked the obvious question, whether it had not been pointless to order that assault upon Laurel Hill. Matthew replied, calmly but with apparent discomfort, that in battle it is not always possible to know the wisdom of an action ahead of time, that one simply does what seems best at the moment. "But surely," I said with some impatience, "Warren was right in thinking that the assault would be suicidal—there was ample evidence of that already." In response, Matthew simply took my hand and said quietly that he was sorry; his face had a look of unspeakable sadness. Instantly I felt the sting of remorse at having challenged him, this dear friend who was in such a difficult position. I was about to apologize when he put his finger to my lips and said no, that it was all right and that he understood. Wiping away the tears that had come into my eyes, I asked him to continue.

"Well," he said hesitantly, as if having lost his place, "Griffin's and Cutler's Divisions were shifted to the salient, leaving our division and a few smaller units to hold the army's right. Fortunately, there was no more fighting on our front. The battle for the salient, however, lasted another seventeen hours; it ended only when the Confederates withdrew to another line of works that they had been feverishly working on all that time. There was no fighting on the 13th, the exhausted armies simply staring at each other across a field littered with the carnage of the previous day. Several days of skirmishing then led to another major assault on the 18th, which also failed. A day or two later Grant resolved to abandon that position altogether and press on southward."

I then asked what we might say the outcome of the battle at Spotsylvania had been. "Tactically speaking," he said, "it was a draw: Though the Confederates checked our advance, they did not force us to retreat. In a larger sense, however, I believe that it held important lessons for both sides. To Grant, it brought home the virtue of patience: it was a war that would have to be won by attrition, not by a single decisive blow. Only once after that did he order a direct frontal assault on a well-entrenched enemy. That was at Cold Harbor, where breaking through the Confederate line would immediately put Richmond in our hands. As you know, that attack too was disastrous. To Lee, on the other hand, it must have signaled eventual defeat. After three years of outmaneuvering one Federal commander after another, he finally had an opponent who would give him no quarter, who would keep chipping away at his army until it could no longer resist. As early as June of that year his only real hope lay in the defeat of Lincoln at the polls in November. With that hope gone, it was only a matter of time."

That concluded Matthew's account. I thanked him profusely, saying that I was sorry I had become cross at one point. He said merely that he understood. We talked of a few other matters, then he rose to go. With his customary understanding, he undoubtedly knew that I wished to be alone with my thoughts just then.

Tuesday, February 11th

For the last three days, my mind has been generating images of the fighting at Spotsylvania. As befits his nature, Matthew's account of the battle was largely analytical, focusing on strategy and the movements of the various units. Then too, he may have wished to spare me the pain of certain details or to avoid reliving them himself. My nature, however, seems to require precise tableaux. And so I have had before me images as vivid as if I had actually witnessed those incidents. The regiment at the moment it commenced its assault, the anguished forms advancing slowly through the woods, rifles held nervously at the ready. The first contact with the enemy: the orange flashes puncturing the grayness, the dull thuds of minié balls penetrating human flesh, the sudden screams of agony. And especially the field afterwards, the guns now silent and the mutilated bodies being gently washed clean by a cool spring rain.

Productive as my mind has been in this regard, it continues to spare me images of John's death, however. When I think of him during the war, I envision him at the head of the regiment, conferring with his company commanders, or drafting a report at his field table. But always calm and self-possessed, giving thoughtful attention to the matter at hand—in a word, much as he was throughout our life together.

In this I have been helped by the fact that his death occurred at a distance, that I did not learn of it for some days (and then through a heartfelt but somewhat formal note of condolence from Colonel Thornton), and that I was not present at the burial. In that sense, there was an air of unreality about it all. But most of all it has been the mind's own instinct for self-preservation that has gotten me through. Without that, one could not bear such a loss.

Monday, February 17th

I spent a good part of the weekend going through John's letters again. There are quite a number of them; he wrote almost every week when the army was not on active campaign, and even then tried to send me a few lines as time permitted.

For the most part they deal with ordinary concerns—day-to-day life in the army, the affairs of the regiment, and so forth. They do, however, contain informative accounts of the campaigns in which he participated as well as some vivid battle scenes (some of which I permitted to be published in the *Clarion*). A few even have a philosophical tone, with musings about the larger meaning of the war and the prospects for reconciliation afterwards.

In rereading these letters I was struck by two things. The first is their excellent literary quality. John, of course, was a master of English prose whose natural gifts were bolstered by years of preparing meticulous legal briefs. Indeed, Judge Halston once remarked that it would be a pleasure to read anything that he wrote, even a laundry list.

The second thing that struck me about these letters is their warm, affectionate tone, which I must not have been so aware of earlier. Addressing me as "My dear Ellen" or "Dearest Ellen" or occasionally "Beloved wife," they invariably close with reminders that I am constantly in my husband's thoughts and that it is his deepest longing to be with me once again—that only his duty to the nation separates us.

Had I been a young wife, I would undoubtedly have read these letters over and over, cherishing every line. And though I did take great delight in them, I generally read them only once or twice before carefully filing them away, secure in our love and confident (I know not why) that my husband would return in due time. Even since his death, I have gotten them out only a few times.

The last letter, of course, is the most poignant. It was written on the 3rd of May, the day before the Army of the Potomac began its advance. The regiment had received its orders and John wasn't sure when he would be able to write again. There was, however, "a general feeling throughout the army that this would be the decisive campaign, that with it we would either drive the Rebels to the wall or finally have to own defeat." To be sure, with Grant at the helm, there was great optimism; but there was also a sense that "the war had entered a new phase and that from now on every gain would be purchased at considerable cost." By the benevolence of Providence, I received this letter before Colonel Thornton's, and before I was even aware of the great slaughter at Spotsylvania. Otherwise it would have seemed too cruel in its prescience.

I have other mementoes of my husband—his uniforms, his sword and pistol, his field glasses and personal effects. They have been carefully put away in a trunk that is kept in his closet. But it is his books and papers (even those from his law practice) that I treasure most, for it is in them that one can most readily see the sort of man that he was. And needless to say, it is these letters that are now spread out on the table before me that hold pride of place in my emotions.

Thursday, February 20th

This afternoon I sent Matthew my grandfather's copy of Prescott's *Conquest of Mexico* as a token of my appreciation for his telling me about Spotsylvania. Considering how greatly my grandfather prized his collection of American authors, it is a rather extravagant gift. And yet I am deeply grateful to this friend and know that with his fondness for history he will appreciate having the volume and will treat it with the greatest care.

Tuesday, February 25th

Word has just come that the President has been impeached. There are few details as yet, only that Representative Stevens informed the Senate of the House's action this afternoon and that it apparently stems from Johnson's attempt to dismiss Secretary of War Stanton, who has been actively colluding with the Radicals. The vote was a decided 126 to 47. Such a development would be shocking in any case, but it is all the more so in this instance because things have seemed fairly quiet on the political front of late.

Friday, February 28th

The situation in the capital has apparently turned very serious. Secretary Stanton has refused to accept his dismissal and has barricaded himself in his office; to prevent his forcible removal, General Grant has stationed a battalion of soldiers all around the building; and General Thomas, Stanton's would-be successor, has been arrested on charges of violating the Tenure of Office Act. Incredible as it may seem, there is actually talk of the possibility of a *coup d'état* by the President—with anxious inquiries as to what troops are at his disposal—as if he were bent on following the path of Cromwell or Napoleon III.

Judge Halston doubts that the government is actually in peril but says that in this state of heightened emotions "great harm may be done." He has pointed out two telling irregularities in the whole proceeding. First, it was the Joint Committee on Reconstruction that recommended impeachment, not the House Judiciary Committee, which would ordinarily have jurisdiction over the matter. And second, though the President stands accused of "high crimes and misdemeanors," there are no specific charges against him. "Apparently that pack of scoundrels hasn't gotten around to inventing them yet," the Judge says.

Saturday, March 7th

The political situation is markedly calmer than it was a week ago. No one now seriously expects a coup, and troubling as the proceeding against the President is it is being carried out in an orderly manner and with seeming deference to the law.

To prosecute its case, the House of Representatives has selected a "board of managers," all of whose seven members are prominent Radicals. Heading it, of course, is Thaddeus Stevens, who has spearheaded the opposition to the President all along. His principal lieutenants are Benjamin Butler and John Bingham (the one representative from Ohio to play a significant role in the proceeding), though George Boutwell and John Logan may assist at the trial as well.

The President has retained five attorneys to handle his defense. The most prominent are Henry Stanbery, who until recently served as Attorney General in Johnson's cabinet, and William Evarts, whom Judge Halston regards as one of the most distinguished lawyers in the nation. Though no friend of the President—just four months ago, Evarts made an impassioned speech against him—he knows his duty as an advocate and is expected to mount a vigorous and capable defense.

The board of managers has also drawn up eleven articles

of impeachment against the President. The first nine relate to his alleged violation of the Tenure of Office Act in attempting to replace Secretary Stanton, with one alluding to a "conspiracy" between the President and General Thomas and another to the illegality of appointing the latter even if he had the right to remove Stanton. That last article was apparently included to appeal to Senators who question the constitutionality of the Tenure of Office Act; to my mind, however, it relies on an interpretation of the act that defies all common sense.

The tenth article accuses the President of making "certain intemperate, inflammatory, and scandalous harangues" during the 1866 campaign that were aimed at turning the public against Congress. In this, the article alleges, the President had failed to preserve the dignity of his office. This article brought immediate scorn from the Judge, who said that if such delicacy is now the standard, "O Lord, who shall live?" The final article, said to have been crafted by Stevens to snag a few loose votes by an appeal to the Senators' vanity, charges the President with saying that the 39th Congress was not legally constituted because it excludes representatives from most of the Southern states, "thereby denying ... that the legislation of said Congress was valid or obligatory upon him."

Of course, there are unstated allegations as well, such as his apparent drunkenness at his inauguration as vice president, his support for the Ku Klux Klan, even his involvement in the assassination of President Lincoln. But the managers have evidently thought better of trying to make a legal case for such questionable assertions.

The Senators convened two days ago and were sworn in as jurors by Chief Justice Chase, who will preside over the trial. It is set to open on the 13th, just six days from now.

Monday, March 16th

The President's trial formally opened on Friday, but was immediately recessed for ten days to allow his attorneys additional time to prepare their case. They had originally requested forty days ("as long as it took God to destroy the world," Representative Butler said), but that was considered too long a delay since, as Senator Sumner reminded his colleagues, it would be necessary to suspend all other business until the trial was concluded.

It is also said that efforts are being made behind the scenes to avoid a trial by getting the President to agree to fill his entire cabinet with Radicals. But he clearly has too much regard for the prerogatives of his office ever to accept such terms. Even at this distance, the proposition seems utterly fatuous.

Friday, March 20th

The postponement of the trial has given us a welcome respite from that sad affair. However briefly, our talk has turned to more pleasant things, in keeping with the milder weather that we have been experiencing of late. This is no doubt just the calm before the storm, but we would do well to make the most of it.

I spent the afternoon comfortably ensconced with a book in one of the unused bedchambers upstairs along the southwest-facing side of the house. In terms of light and warmth, it is the best spot at that hour and season. Other parts of the house, of course, are favored at other times. The parlor and my own bedchamber are best in the morning, along with the little porch off the dining room when the weather is nice. The library is best in the afternoon and evening, particularly in cold weather; it seems to capture the warmth of the afternoon much as a greenhouse would, and after sunset one can draw the drapes to hold it in for a time. The piazza, naturally, is delightful in the late spring and early summer and other times when the weather is mild. Thus I find myself a sort of nomad within my own dwelling, seeking out the best spots for reading, sewing, writing letters, or simply enjoying the moment. These migrations are perfectly agreeable, however, and do much to keep things fresh.

Saturday, March 28th

The trial began in earnest this week, with opening statements by both sides and other preliminary matters. Evarts announced that the President would rely on two arguments in his defense: that the Tenure of Office Act was unconstitutional, such that he would be violating his oath of office in adhering to that act; and that whatever remarks the President had made during the 1866 campaign were protected by the right of free speech.

Representative Butler spoke for the board of managers—with more passion than reason if one is to judge by his printed remarks. He said that for the first time in history a nation had brought its highest official before the bar of justice. And it was well that it could do so, for this "elect of an assassin" was guilty even by a narrow reading of the case. Butler went further, however, asserting that the Senators were not bound by a strict interpretation of the law. On the contrary, they were entitled to consider the fact that although 300,000 Union soldiers had given their lives to suppress the rebellion, the President had eagerly restored its leaders to power. And they should ask themselves whether it would ever be possible to prevent "the usurpation of executive power" if the President were to be acquitted.

The first phase of the trial is to consist of the board's presentation of its case in detail. They have begun by reading into the record certain relevant documents, including the presidential oath of office and a certification of its administration to Andrew Johnson, Lincoln's appointment of Stanton as Secretary of War, Johnson's note dismissing him, certain of Johnson's speeches, and the testimony that Stanton gave to the impeachment committee. I suppose that this is a necessary formality, but to my mind it is a weak note on which to begin.

Monday, March 30th

A number of us lingered on the steps after church yesterday to discuss the trial. Admittedly, we have talked of little else for the last five weeks, but this occasion was exceptional in that it was the first time that Judge Halston has systematically expressed his opinion on the matter. According to Julia, he has been giving it as much attention as if it were a case being tried in his own courtroom. Night after night he has been up until the small hours of the morning reviewing the facts and pondering the state of the law with respect to impeachment. He has even instructed her not to touch his desk, which is now littered with legal treatises, decisions in cases that might serve as precedents, and numerous pages of his own notes.

As the Judge sees things, there is no merit whatsoever to the managers' case against the President. The charge of conspiracy with General Thomas is "patently absurd," those pertaining to violation of the Tenure of Office Act highly questionable. In all probability, that act would be found to be unconstitutional if challenged in court; certainly it seemed to go well beyond the Senate's duty to provide advice and consent in regard to presidential appointments. Even if the act is legitimate, the proper remedy for its violation would be to obtain a court order requiring the President to reinstate Stanton, not his removal from office. As to the President's speeches, they had indeed been intemperate; he ought not, for instance, to have called for the hanging of Thaddeus Stevens. But the Constitution makes no requirement that speech be wise and prudent, and the President was entirely within his rights in speaking as he had. Making that a ground of impeachment was of a piece with the Sedition Act of 1798, by which the Federalists had attempted to silence their political opponents.

The impeachment proceeding, then, was a blatantly political act that could in no way be construed as a criminal prosecution. The only question in the Judge's mind was why the Radicals had resorted to impeachment when they were in fact having their way with the reconstruction of the Southern states and the President would be out of office in less than a year's time in any case. There he could only conjecture that Johnson had deeply offended the Radicals, not so much by his caustic remarks as by his fundamental intransigence on the question of retribution. In his refusal to punish the South and completely overturn its social institutions, they perceived an affront greater than that of secession itself.

At least, the Judge said, that was the case with those who could be said to be acting from pure motives—Stevens and Sumner and the others whose zeal for redress had simply outweighed their reason. With an utterly "vile" man like Benjamin Butler, however, who could say? … though with *his* war record, any aspirations toward higher office would be imbecilic in the extreme.

As it happens, I have a very distinct image of General Butler, more so than of most of the other commanders sketches of whom appeared frequently in *Harper's* and the other illustrated newspapers. A porcine man with a deformed eye, he looks at once sinister and slow of mind—traits that at least some of his actions would appear to bear out. He was, of course, thoroughly incompetent as a field commander, so incapable of overcoming even slight resistance by the enemy that Grant got him dismissed in spite of his political connections. But it is the depredations that he committed as military governor of New Orleans that he is best known by: the hanging of a man said to have desecrated a United States flag, the jailing of a woman of good family for laughing during the funeral procession of a Union officer, and the order giving his troops the right to treat any woman who was disrespectful to them as a common prostitute—to say nothing of the widespread allegations of accepting bribes, illegally confiscating property, and trading in contraband cotton. For these things he was given the name "Beast," which I understand was used as freely by his own men as by the Southerners. As disreputable as he is, however, the Judge cautioned against underestimating him, as he is both shrewd and determined "in a way only the truly malevolent can be."

Toward the end of the discussion someone inquired who would become President in the event Johnson were convicted. "Ah," the Judge said with no small amount of sarcasm, "on what great statesman does the Constitution confer the mantle of authority in this hour of crisis? Why, on our own Senator Wade!"

There was a gasp from somewhere in the crowd, along with numerous looks of disbelief. Wade, of course, is familiar not only as an ardent Radical but also as a dour, largely uncultivated man who can be brutal in his dealings with others. He is even said to have been gladdened that Providence removed President Lincoln so that a sterner man might take his place. The great irony, the Judge says, is that although Wade (as president pro tempore of the Senate) is in line to succeed Johnson, his term as a Senator ends next year and the Ohio legislature (now controlled by the Democrats) has not reelected him. If he were to assume the Presidency, it would be tantamount to foisting off our own "unwanted goods" on the nation at large.

Thursday, April 2nd

There was snow this afternoon, a heavy, wet snow of the sort that commonly occurs at the end of winter. It took us a bit by surprise all the same: though the temperature has remained below freezing, it had been clear for some time and we had grown accustomed to the calm, bright days. As always, Mrs. Marshall put her finger on it, saying that the sudden influx of moist air must be related to the change of season, a transition that has its own "birth pangs."

By nightfall a strong wind was scattering the clouds, leaving the newly fallen snow almost iridescent in the moonlight. Though I rarely go for walks after dark, I decided to go out and see "the north wind's masonry" first-hand. It proved to be a whimsical masonry, all clumps and indistinct lines that distorted the natural shapes of things, very much as if the earth had been covered with an old, worn quilt. And yet there was a softness and grace to the landscape that I found very soothing … to say nothing of the immense quiet that invariably follows a day of snow, as if all of Nature were poised at the exact moment between breathing in and breathing out.

I went on in a sort of reverie for some while, until I became aware of a tall figure ahead of me in the distance. Although I could not make out any of the person's features, something about his bearing and gait told me that it was Matthew Carey. He must have sensed my presence at the same moment, for he turned around and, after studying me for a few seconds, waved warmly. I caught up to him and we continued our walk together.

For the most part we talked of small matters. He told me that although he often took walks after dinner, he particularly wanted to tonight because this would probably be the last snow that we would have this season. Indeed, "it would not be surprising if in a couple of weeks we were enjoying warm days and daffodils." That is a distinct possibility, as it is already late in the season and the turning point can come with little warning. Matthew thanked me again for the volume of Prescott, saying how much he was enjoying it. He offered to return it when he was done but I said no, he had done me a great service for which nothing could adequately compensate him.

By then we had reached the cemetery at the far edge of town, a natural place for us to turn around. We lingered there for a while, however, contemplating the orderly rows of headstones partially submerged in the snow. It looked so utterly peaceful to me that I could not but imagine those lying there as being perfectly at rest. I said as much to Matthew but he only nodded slightly in response. It occurred to me then that after what he had seen in the war he could never again see only innocence and tranquility in a churchyard.

It felt much colder on the way home, as the wind had picked up and we were now facing into it. Matthew offered me his arm, which I gratefully accepted, keeping close to him both for the warmth and for the special joy that I felt in being with him tonight. He offered to accompany me all the way home but I said no, it wasn't far and he must be cold as well. We parted near the church. Before releasing my arm he pressed it gently with his other hand, urging me to be careful on the way home.

Wednesday, April 8th

Matthew appears to have been correct in his prediction about the change of seasons. Though the day began cold and blustery, by early afternoon the wind had shifted to the southwest and it was nearly 70 degrees, with steam rising off the remaining piles of snow. It is impossible to describe the rapture one feels at such a time, the delight in throwing one's coat open and basking in the warmth after so many days of cold. It is as if the world were born anew and promised joys never before even imagined. Indeed, it is a time not for words but for complete absorption in the experience.

There was another pleasant surprise awaiting me when I got home: an invitation from Matthew to accompany him to a recital at the Scioto Conservatory the third week of May. He proposed that we take the three-thirty train to Columbus and have an early dinner at the State House Hotel so as to be in good time. He even included the program: Mozart's Piano Concerto in G Major, Beethoven's String Quartet no. 16, Schumann's Fourth Symphony, and selections from *La Traviata*.

Music, of course, is one of Matthew's great passions. He rarely missed a concert when he lived in Philadelphia and still plays the violin with some facility. It is completely different with me, however: apart from a few piano lessons shortly before my parents' death I have had no real instruction in music. Nor does my natural ability appear to be very great. Although I can listen intently for a time, fully aware of the different "layers" of a composition and the instruments assigned to them, my attention tends to wander and I have difficulty perceiving the overall structure. I cannot, for instance, always recognize a melody that returns after a long absence, my mind is simply not trained in that way. This is not to say, of course, that I am not fond of music. Quite the contrary: I enjoy it immensely, and though there are lacunae in my perception, I am still capable of being profoundly moved by it.

So I shall be pleased to accept Matthew's invitation, and all the more so since it should be a lovely outing in other respects as well.

Monday, April 13th

The board of managers has concluded the presentation of its case against the President. It does not seem particularly strong, at least to one untutored in the law. To support the charge of conspiracy they summoned the commander of the military forces around Washington, a General Emory, who testified that the President had inquired about troop dispositions in the area. The General could not say why this inquiry was made, however, nor did any actions appear to flow from it. (It is entirely possible that the President was concerned about his own security.) To support the charge of defamation of Congress, the managers examined the stenographers who recorded the President's campaign speeches. The only additional light that they could shed on them is that they had smoothed some of the language, a practice that is apparently fairly common among journalists. The President's remarks were essentially as reported, and they would have to stand or fall on his right to make them.

There has been one important development, however, according to the Judge. Concerned that Chief Justice Chase has been too lenient in his rulings on matters of evidence, the Radicals obtained passage of a resolution that permits the Senate to set those rulings aside by a simple majority vote—in effect making the Senators both judge and jury. "You cannot imagine the significance of this," the Judge says.

Sunday, April 19th

The warmer weather has held. Although we have had a number of the cool, damp days so characteristic of early spring, the intense cold of the last few months seems to have flown. Then too, there have been days such as today that are so bright and mild that it is the purest pleasure simply to be out in them. I did just that this afternoon, spending several hours on the piazza reading. I say "reading," but in truth my attention wandered a good deal. All around me were the signs of the awakening earth: the thick, green blades of the hyacinths forcing their way out of the damp soil; the tiny, ruby-colored leaves forming on the ends of the maple branches; the frenetic to-ings and fro-ings of the songbirds. On such a day it is immediate sensation that one craves, not intellectual truths however sublime they may be.

Friday, April 24th

The presentation of evidence in the President's trial has concluded; all that remains now are the closing arguments and the vote by the Senators.

The President's attorneys presented two prominent witnesses, General Thomas and General Sherman (to whom the post of Secretary of War had initially been offered). The purpose of calling the former to the stand was apparently to show how hapless and insubstantial a person he is—in other words, that he is utterly incapable of participating in a coup d'état. In this they succeeded, amply aided by Representative Butler in his cross-examination. (According to the Judge, they set a trap for Butler, which he, in his passion to obtain a conviction, allowed to be sprung on him.) As to the reason for calling General Sherman, it would appear to be to remind the Senators that the President had wished to replace Stanton with a man of unquestioned stature and loyalty; his testimony per se added little to the case either way.

The President's attorneys had also intended to call Gideon Welles, the Secretary of the Navy, to testify as to the deliberations within the Cabinet regarding the dismissal of Stanton and related matters. By exposing the inner workings of the administration, they apparently hoped to show that there was nothing untoward in the President's actions. The Radicals managed to prevent this, however: though the Chief Justice ruled that the testimony was admissible, the question was put to a vote of the Senators (under the terms of the resolution passed previously) and the ruling overturned. Whatever the outcome of the trial, it is certainly tarnished by this maneuver.

Tuesday, May 5th

I spent the better part of last evening reading extended excerpts from the closing arguments in the President's trial. Their length notwithstanding, they shed little in the way of new light on the case.

The managers' remarks, it seems to me, amount to little more than name-calling. Certainly, the incessant repetition of "incendiary" and "traitor" and "usurper" constitute neither evidence nor rational argument. It would appear that the Radicals are so beside themselves over the President's actions that they are incapable of presenting their case in any dispassionate way.

The President's attorneys, by contrast, seem to have made the best possible case for him. They reminded the Senators that he was the only Southerner not to resign his seat in Congress when his state seceded; that as military governor of Tennessee he had been vigorous in directing the defense of the state; and that throughout the war he had denounced the Rebels as traitors who should be hanged. Indeed, when he was first elevated to the presidency the Radicals themselves expressed pleasure at having such a staunch Unionist in the office.

As to the charge of violating the Tenure of Office Act, there were three points to be made: The act itself was probably not constitutional; it had not in fact been violated, as Stanton was still in office; and even if the act were valid and the President could in some sense be said to have violated it, that was hardly grounds for impeachment as those who crafted that provision of the Constitution construed them. There had been no violence against the Republic nor any unambiguous contravention of its laws, merely the attempt to replace a member of the Cabinet.

In his defense of the President's caustic remarks about Congress, Evarts resorted to the simple but ingenious stratagem of quoting members' remarks about him and each other. The *coup de grace* was the repetition of Representative Bingham's response to Butler's charge of incompetence in prosecuting the Lincoln conspirators: "Such a charge, without one tittle of evidence, is only fit to come from a man who lives in a bottle and is fed with a spoon." Evarts facetiously added that he had no idea what that meant; but as nearly everyone in the country is aware, Butler is renowned for repeatedly getting his troops "bottled up" and he acquired the soubriquet "Spoons" for the supposed theft of silver and other valuables from Rebel homes in Louisiana. By all reports, there was an uproar of laughter in the chamber. In any case, it was clearly shown that it would be difficult to fall short of Congress's own standards for political speech.

The final argument made by the President's attorneys is far and away the most serious: that his removal from office would destroy the balance of power among the three branches of government. If one branch were to become dominant, Evarts said, the whole American political experiment would fail—and "if that fails, what can endure?"

Thus the closing arguments. Unfortunately, it is neither logic nor evidence that is likely to determine the outcome but rather the Senators' calculations of their own interest. As Evarts himself said (quoting Cardinal Wolsey), in political times it is all too easy to assemble a jury that will find that Abel killed Cain. And the indications are that public opinion is running strongly against the President. Even worse, perhaps, it is said that the uncommitted Senators are being offered considerable sums of money in exchange for their votes. Each side has supposedly assembled a large fund for this purpose; the contributions, however, seem to be motivated more by the desire to control patronage than by any loftier principle. Sadly, it is all too probable that the Republic will be betrayed for thirty pieces of silver.

Sunday, May 10th

The day being pretty, Matthew and I walked along the river for a while after church. Somewhat surprisingly, we talked mostly about the upcoming vote in the President's trial. Hitherto Matthew had always shown a reluctance to discuss the matter, as if it pained him too greatly. Yet it was he who brought it up, I imagine because with things coming to a head the anguish of remaining silent was even more unbearable.

Yes, he said, he found it "very grievous" that the country had to endure this after all that it had already gone through. The bitterness of the struggle between the President and his enemies was so reminiscent of the strife between North and South in the decade before the war that it seemed that four years of war had settled nothing. Without question, Johnson was a poor choice for the presidency at this critical time—neither his temperament nor his views of things suited him for the task of reconciliation. Yet there were no legitimate reasons to remove him, and to do so would all but destroy the checks and balances on which our form of government hinged. The best we could hope for, he said, was the acquittal of Johnson and the election of a true statesman in the autumn.

I asked whether General Grant, who is on the verge of receiving the Republican nomination, was that man. "No," he said quietly, "I do not believe that he is." It was not a question of his integrity or his willingness to see a difficult job through. His conduct during the war had demonstrated those virtues beyond any doubt. His apparent motive in seeking the presidency was also quite laudable: to prevent the outcome of the war from being effectively nullified by the terms of the peace. No, the difficulty lay in the fact that he was a true babe-in-arms with respect to politics. By no means would he be able to command Congress as he had the Union armies. In all probability, the politicians now supporting him would see him as beholden to *them* and try to use him as their tool. Failing that, they would simply ignore him. Already he had been compelled to, in essence, collude with the Radicals over the impeachment question—to the point of openly opposing his commander in chief. The best that we might expect from a Grant presidency was indecision and infighting, the worst ... it was better not to say.

Matthew then fell silent, apparently mulling all of this over in his mind. When I judged the time to be right, I enquired as to whom he would prefer to see as President. At that he brightened a little, as if the prospect of an alternative afforded him some relief. "The situation," he said, "calls for a master statesman ... or at least one with deep experience. Seward, perhaps, or Chase; maybe some others." The task was twofold: to craft a practical scheme for the reconciliation of North and South that did not abandon the North's moral victory over slavery and to gain the support of men more accustomed to serving their own interests than those of the nation. It was, of course, an immense task. He doubted whether even President Lincoln, with his great vision and ability to appeal to people's "better angels," would have been able to accomplish it. As it was, we could only look forward to a difficult and perhaps shameful period.

I have experienced many emotions since the impeachment crisis began—confusion and trepidation and especially anger. But until this afternoon I had not realized the profound sadness of it all. The integrity of a nation founded on the highest principles, the aspirations of good people everywhere, the enormous sacrifices of so many—all set at naught by vanity and ambition. It must not be. And for the first time, I burst into tears.

Saturday, May 16th

The impeachment crisis has passed; the denouement came this morning with the Senators' vote on the eleventh article (the one on which it was thought that the President was most vulnerable and thus the one taken up first).

Most of the village gathered at the train station to listen to the votes as they came in over the telegraph. There was, of course, a good deal of tension, with some rather heated exchanges of views. As far as I could tell, opinion was about evenly divided, so that whatever the outcome many were bound to be disappointed. Nor was the outcome at all clear from the outset. Enough Senators remained uncommitted to permit the verdict to go either way, a fact that had apparently occasioned intense lobbying behind the scenes. To secure conviction, the Radicals had gone so far as to try to accelerate the readmission of Arkansas to the Union, thereby gaining the votes of two Negro Senators. In the end, they had to content themselves with making passionate appeals to their colleagues—and whatever pressure they could bring to bear on them. For their part, the President's supporters have endeavored to convince wavering Senators that he would not run riot if acquitted. To that end, they have gotten him to nominate the well-respected General Schofield as Secretary of War and to offer personal assurances of his intention to abide by the Reconstruction Acts.

To keep track of the votes as they were reported, Judge Halston had prepared a tally sheet with the names of the Senators who were known to favor conviction in a column on the left, the names of those who were known to favor acquittal in a column on the right, and those of the uncommitted Senators in the center. With this arrangement, he could easily move a name from the center to one of the other two columns and so keep running totals. There were 54 names in all; 36 of the Senators would have to vote for conviction for that to be the verdict.

The crowd fell silent when a long message began to come in over the telegraph. After taking it down, the operator read it aloud: Chief Justice Chase had called the session to order, admonishing those in the galleries that any disturbances would be met with arrests. The Senators were to be polled in alphabetical order. Each would be asked the (to my mind, excessively lengthy and formal) question: "Mr. Senator _____, how say you? Is the respondent, Andrew Johnson, President of the United States, guilty or not guilty of a high misdemeanor, as charged in this article?" To avoid falling behind, the telegrapher would report only the last names and responses of the Senators, abbreviating the latter to the letters "G" for guilty and "N" for not guilty.

Several minutes passed before the telegraph key again sounded. Then the operator intoned the words "Senator Anthony," and a moment later, "guilty." There was an immediate reaction by the crowd, so loud that the operator had to plead for silence in order to hear. Although this proceeding had been anticipated for many weeks, it was still something of a shock when it actually commenced. The Judge remained perfectly impassive, however, merely nodding and putting the number 1 by that Senator's name, which was at the head of the left-hand column.

A minute or so later, the telegraph key sprang to life again:

"Senator Bayard ... not guilty." Bayard's vote was widely anticipated, as he is a Democrat from a border state. Senator Buckalew, a Democrat from Pennsylvania, soon followed suit. The next eight Senators all voted for conviction. When Senator Conkling's name was called I heard the Judge mutter something that sounded like "despicable bastard," but both the code of silence that had been imposed on us and the Judge's acid look discouraged any request for him to repeat it. Conkling, of course, is the leading exemplar of the new men in the Senate, men whose only guiding principle seems to be their ambition.

There followed a series of predictable votes, some going one way and some the other. By then we were able to recognize the code and tell the result before the operator announced it: two longs and a short signified guilty, a long and a short not guilty. When Senator Fessenden's name was called there was complete silence. The first of the uncommitted Senators to be polled, he was thought to be something of a bellwether whose vote would influence the others who were still on the fence. A brief time later, the telegraph key tapped twice—the Maine Senator had voted for acquittal. To judge by the looks on people's faces, this vote came as something of a surprise both to the President's supporters and to his opponents. Visibly relieved, the Judge drew an arrow from his name to the right-hand column and entered the appropriate number in the margin. Senators Fowler of Tennessee, Grimes of Iowa, and Henderson of Missouri, also previously uncommitted, soon followed Fessenden's lead. The Judge smiled broadly when, as he had hoped, Senator Reverdy Johnson cast his vote for acquittal. Although the Maryland Senator had previously indicated his support for the President, there were lingering doubts because, out of a spirit of compromise, he had been the only Democrat to vote for all of the Reconstruction measures.

The Judge then made a quick calculation. If the remaining votes went as expected, there would be thirty-five for conviction. The only name remaining in the center column was that of Senator Ross of Kansas. "It will all come down to Ross," the Judge whispered to me. As with the other uncommitted Senators, there had been a good deal about him in the newspapers. A modest man and a printer by trade, he had been appointed to the Senate only two years ago when his predecessor committed suicide, supposedly because of the criticism leveled at him for supporting the President. At first Ross had seemed a sure vote for conviction, but as the trial went on doubts were raised by his votes on certain procedural matters. Word had it that the Radicals had been pressuring him heavily.

When at length his name was called, there was a palpable tension in the room. Most of those present avoided looking directly at the telegraph operator, either staring at the floor or cocking their heads so as to hear better. Glancing up at the Judge, I noticed that his eyes were tightly closed, as if he were uttering one last prayer. Finally, after what seemed an eternity, the telegraph key sounded again. Two taps—not guilty. Able to contain itself no longer, the crowd erupted, some in elation and others in disgust. Soon, however, people began drifting away—for good or ill, it was now done with. The Judge and I remained until the last vote was cast, just to be certain of the outcome. It was precisely as one would have expected once Ross's vote was known: thirty-five for conviction, nineteen for acquittal. The President had been spared by a single vote.

After his initial elation, the Judge became unusually pensive, almost somber, and as I did not wish to intrude on his thoughts we walked much of the way home in silence. At length, however, he revealed his mind to me. "You know, Ellen, one has to feel a bit sorry for them, Sumner and the rest. They have devoted their entire lives to the rights of the Negro and with but modest success. Now, with their powers failing, the country is losing interest in that question altogether. It is the Conklings who will dominate affairs in a few years' time. To be sure, the Radicals have done a great deal of harm, and yet ..." He did not finish the thought, possibly because it was not fully formed in his mind but more likely because it was too painful for him. He, after all, was of much the same age as the leading Radicals and had shared many of their principles, if less passionately. As he was speaking, I recalled the newspaper accounts of Thaddeus Stevens at the trial. Too ill even to walk, he had had to be carried into the Senate chamber in a chair, where he had sat wrapped in blankets, his eyes closed much of the time, unable to deliver his speech for conviction himself. Obviously close to death, he had summoned his remaining strength for this one last effort. It was indeed a sad circumstance, one would prefer to see him defeated a whole man who might recover from the defeat. And yet, as the Judge had made clear throughout, it was far better that he not prevail.

We parted a few blocks from the square. I had intended to head right home but decided instead to go inform Matthew of the outcome of the vote, just in case he had not heard it.

Friday, May 22nd

My mind is awash in impressions from last evening's excursion: the vista from the train window of broad expanses of rich, dark soil, freshly furrowed and planted, set off against the pale green of distant woods; the noise and confusion of the station in Columbus, the smoke and steam from the engines so thoroughly suffused with the late afternoon sunlight as to be almost blinding; the quiet elegance of the dining room at the State House Hotel, its placidity unmarred by the fact that the legislature was still in session and a good deal of business was being transacted in the lobby and the adjoining bar-room; and, of course, the exquisite sounds of what Matthew termed incomparably fine performances.

In imagining this evening, I had instinctively placed us in a concert hall reminiscent of the ones I had known in Europe, that is, in a large, ornate cavern with tiers ascending to the ceiling and done largely in red velvet. It turned out, however, that the recital was held at the Columbus Lyceum, a plain lecture hall with an unfinished wood floor and straight-backed chairs; rather than looking down on the stage, we actually had to elevate our heads somewhat to see the performers. Although the Conservatory has a more elegant performance room, Matthew said that it can accommodate only a small number and the spring recital tends to draw audiences from across the state. "Then too," he added with a laugh, "as Americans we must guard against too much corrupting luxury."

Though the hall was unadorned, most of the audience was brilliantly attired like ourselves, the gentlemen in evening dress and the ladies in richly colored ball gowns. It was evident that people had taken a great deal of care with their appearance on this occasion (one senses that even in the capital there are few opportunities to indulge in such finery), and the pleasure it so obviously gave them proved contagious. I took a delight in it because it gave things a festive air and seemed to harmonize with nature's own dress at this season.

After studying the program again, I asked Matthew about the selection of the pieces. He replied that because the recital (which, it turns out, extends for four nights, this being the second night) is a sort of final examination for the students and the pieces are chosen as much for the demands that they place on the performers as for their appeal to audiences. Even so, most of the compositions presented are true masterpieces, and the performances they call forth tend to be extremely good. He had been drawn to this particular program, he said, because of the Beethoven string quartet, which was the last of the sixteen such quartets that the composer had written and, in fact, his last completed work.

"The late string quartets," he added, "are something of a cause célèbre in the world of music. They are all fairly difficult—by then Beethoven had entirely abandoned the delicacies of eighteenth-century chamber music and was using his string quartets to make bold statements." The one that we were to hear was the most traditional of the set but it too had distinctly foreign elements. In the second movement, for instance, there was a highly disjointed phrase suggestive of a man limping along a road as well as a passage in which the second violin, viola, and cello seemed to be cursing under their breath, as if resentful at being relegated to the accompaniment. And in the fourth movement, which is (for no obvious reason) titled "The Difficult Resolution," there are two three-note phrases that are said to mimic the utterances "Must it be?" and "It must be!" (The cadences of these expressions are apparently the same in German.) *What* must be, however, the composer does not say, and opinions have varied widely, some holding that the phrases refer to the attainment of a mystical state, others that they simply represent the demand for payment of a bill.

I was glad to have this advance intelligence from Matthew, for it enabled me to listen to the piece with more comprehension than I otherwise would have. With one exception, however,

I cannot say that I truly enjoyed it. That was the third movement (marked *lento assai, cantante, e tranquillo*), with its peaceful hymn-like melody and plaintive undertones. That portion of the piece truly transports one into another realm, taking us completely beyond ourselves and our mundane concerns. It is in such passages that one can perceive the transcendent qualities in music that led one of our writers to call it "the flower of language, thought colored and curved, ... its crystal fountains tinged with the sun's rays."

I also found the Mozart piano concerto very agreeable, particularly the first two movements. The first movement, in fact, seems to offer an interesting study in what might be called the psychological response to music. On the whole it is very lyrical, but it proffers such an intricate interplay of melodies that it tends to leave one a bit breathless. We find a refuge from this storm, however, in the clear, precise notes of the piano, which summon us soothingly and guide us along almost without effort. Indeed, the pianist played with such single-minded devotion that she must have known that she was our fixed point of reference. The second movement prompted no such lofty thoughts, but with its brooding, almost melancholy undertones readily gave me a sense of immense yearning. The final movement, a theme and variations, seemed much more conventional. Yet as Matthew pointed out, it too has its original elements, including a mock-heroic passage near the end that almost made him laugh out loud.

It was, however, the selections that formed the second half of the program that intrigued me the most, for they offered an interesting contrast in the portrayal of emotion. That of *La Traviata* is simple and direct; the opera wears its heart on its sleeve, as it were, and pulls forcefully at ours. That of the Schumann symphony, on the other hand, confronts us with nuances and ambiguities that we are largely left to interpret on our own; in that it seems the truer to life.

Not that I did not enjoy the Verdi—on the contrary, I found it perfectly delightful. The lovers' dawning recognition of their affection for one another ("Ah, fors è lui"—perhaps he is the one, after all this time) almost moved me to tears. And how well the composer has captured the all-transforming nature of love in the phrase ending in "il univers' intero." Thus it is with a sense of shock that one hears, just moments later, Violetta dismiss the idea of committed love so completely out of hand ("Follie! Follie!"). And thus it is that one can understand Alfredo's bitterness ("Ogni suo aver tal femmina"—*anyone* can have a woman like this … simply by paying for her!) after his father has persuaded her to leave him. There is immorality here to be sure, but it lies far more in the mores of society than in the actions of the courtesan.

Yet for all its claims to realism, there is a fundamental artificiality to *La Traviata*. I suppose that this is true of all opera—to be effective on the stage it must exaggerate both the circumstances and the feelings of the characters. As with so many other things, to profit from it one must take it on its own terms.

This I found very easy to do with the Schumann. I accepted its aesthetic so naturally that there was never any question of coming to terms with it—from the very first notes I was led along effortlessly, a quite willing follower. I believe that what most appealed to me in the piece was its balance, the expression of emotion through controlled, highly refined melodic lines. The symphony opens, for instance, with a forceful melody in which we immediately sense power and energy even though the phrase is very lyrical. Insistently it repeats itself, asserting its dominance. Though gentler passages follow, they always culminate in the original, driving melody. Always it is impelling the piece forward, even when it is absent it is lurking in the back of our minds, ready to spring. Whether it causes us anxiety or confirms us in our own strength, it takes firm hold of us until the very end of the symphony, and beyond.

The scherzo contains another instance of the same sort, though of an entirely different character. It consists of a long, descending line, dominated by the strings, that is played over and over, as if the composer had no thought of time or were so pleased by the line that he could not let go of it. What Schumann had in mind when he wrote it I cannot say, but in mine it conjured up the image of young girls chasing butterflies in a field on a warm Sunday afternoon. As they are still in their Sunday dresses they run rather cautiously, always arriving at the flower in question just a moment too late. They are undeterred by this, however, and summoning their strength scurry off in pursuit once more. This happens again and again, until they finally tire of the game—but what fun it has been.

When I mentioned this to Matthew afterwards, he said that that was interesting because one of Schumann's best-known compositions for piano is a piece called "Scenes from Childhood" (he had actually written a piece called *Papillons* as well, though there the butterflies are dancers at a ball and the music is more dramatic); so perhaps there was something to my instinct about that melodic line. He said that he would get the sheet music so that his sister could play it for me. I should like very much to hear it again, for I find both a grace and a richly human warmth in this composer.

It had turned rather cold by the time we left the hall. I slept most of the way home on the train, my head against Matthew's shoulder. When I awoke, just as we were entering Westerly, I found that, ever thoughtful, he had draped a blanket over me. As it was late, we did not linger over our good-byes. But in the calm matter-of-factness of our parting, each of us seemed to recognize that we had crossed a threshold.

Tuesday, May 26th

For several days now, when not fully engaged elsewhere, my mind has tended to fill with sensual images. They have come unbidden yet of such intensity as to leave me on edge, longing for a more complete resolution of the passions they arouse within me.

The first of these experiences occurred as I was leaving church on Sunday. I was just starting down the steps when my eyes were drawn to a girl of about fifteen standing by the gate with several of her friends and two young men. I have known her all her life, but since last autumn she has come into womanhood, her hips full and her ample bosom pressing tightly against the plain front of her dress. There was color in her cheeks as well, and the whole suggested nothing so much as an exotic fruit that had just ripened. The poses she was striking (for she was flirting with the young men) made it clear that she was intensely aware of her physical nature and not in the least hesitant about asserting it before the world. She will give herself willingly, I thought, and have numerous lovers. And whether it brings her happiness or not, she will always act with abandon and have no regrets. Try as I might to suppress it, the image of this girl remained with me for the rest of the day. At times I was even audacious enough to picture her in the act of love itself, her boldness and freedom in full play. Though this gave me a cold shiver, I could not (as it were) turn away.

Last night my thoughts turned to the sensual in art. The human body, of course, is frequently used to represent some ideal of beauty or virtue, and not many works of painting or sculpture are erotic in the purest sense of the term. The sheer loveliness of Praxiteles' *Hermes* or his followers' *Aphrodite of Cnidus* (in which the goddess is shown gracefully setting aside her garment and stepping into a pool) virtually rules out baser desires, and the same may be said for most of the great works of the Renaissance. Yet few if any of these artists could have been completely insensitive to their subjects, and here and there one can detect subtle erotic undertones.

Nowhere (to my mind) is the tension between the sublime and the sensual more pronounced than in Titian's *Sacred and Profane Love*, commissioned to decorate a bridal chamber in 1514. There is the obvious contrast between the sumptuously clad but chaste-looking young noblewoman on the left (presumably representing the face that the betrothed was to wear in public) and the nearly nude Venus on the right (representing the side of her that was reserved for her husband's private pleasure). Yet even within the second figure itself one senses considerable tension. To be sure, there is a distinct innocence to this figure, the painter having endowed her with a classical head and pose and given a serenely graceful flow to her body. Her thighs, too, are demurely kept together, with a wisp of white cloth delicately draped over her intimate parts. Yet the model is very young (I would put her age at seventeen) and in the first bloom of womanhood. Her limbs and torso are rich and smooth, and there is longing in her sideward glance and the almost imperceptible parting of her lips. However subtly, she is a portrait of desire; surely the painter was in love with her, or at least ached to possess her.

Our modern painters, of course, have shown less restraint—witness David's portraits of ladies in diaphanous gowns and Ingres' openly seductive *Odalisque*. It is, however, in the relative subtlety of the latter's famous *Baigneuse* that the erotic seems to become the most intense. We are shown the figure from behind as she is preparing for her bath; all that is really visible to us is her back and a bit of her neck, her delicate skin almost glowing in the soft light. Still, from the calm repose of the body and the assured angle of the head, we immediately sense that she is an experienced lover, a mature woman capable of giving the most sublime pleasure. Indeed, it is her unbroken serenity that arouses such uncontrollable passions in her paramours.

Not content with remembered images, this afternoon I got out some of the "life class" sketches that I made during my year in Italy. Signor' Antonelli was very insistent that we learn to draw the human form well, as this would not only lend realism to our work but also compel us to shed our inhibitions and attain to the boldness that true art demanded. To that end, he had us draw an astonishing number of models—including the aged and repulsive (people literally from the street) as well as the young and comely—in a variety of natural and artificial poses. I believe that the sketches I made during these sessions were generally competent, at times even inspired. But I never achieved the perfect composure and daring that Signor' Antonelli wanted, and to the end he was admonishing me not to be so *protestante*.

I came closest, however, with a young working man of about my own age who sat for us only a few times. One could not call him an Adonis—indeed, he had a rough, even criminal, aspect to him. Yet he was distinctly attractive with his well-proportioned limbs, smooth, almost hairless skin, and taut muscles. At times his disheveled hair and dark, intent eyes gave him the look of a satyr, a wild, virile look born of a passion for living. All this I have captured in my sketches, which even now seem so perfectly natural that my hand must have been working from instinct alone, all attention to technique erased by my absorption in this image. There is even something of his scent about them. He appeared to bathe infrequently and always came to the studio with the manly odor of work about him. I recall this as distinctly as if there were droplets of his sweat preserved on these sheets of paper.

In the first sketch that I made of him I "finessed" the sexual parts, adopting an angle from which they would not be clearly visible. Severely upbraided for this, however, I then drew them boldly and in detail off to the side, where they are far more prominent than they would be if I had been less self-conscious to begin with. The effect is a bit comic, I suppose, but I now see in these routine sketches a depth of feeling that has only rarely found full expression.

All of which is to say that I have fallen deeply in love with Matthew, and desire him intensely.

Tuesday, June 2nd

Shall I give myself to him then? This is the question that has occupied almost all of my waking thoughts these last few days, to the virtual exclusion of all else.

Society, of course, would unequivocally say no, and there is wisdom in that. Yet its objections seem to have little merit in this case: much as I cherish my husband's memory, his death has released me from my vows to him; there is no question of my being taken advantage of; and there is virtually no chance of my being gotten with child. Some, no doubt, would object on the ground of simple morality, but I can give no credence to so archaic a view. We live in our own times, after all—not those of the Old Testament—and must be guided by our own lights.

Then, too, one must seriously question a morality that denigrates so integral a part of our being. Are we not physical creatures who relate to the world largely through our senses—and through our experiences of pleasure and pain? Are not our sexual urges the source of the greatest intimacy we can know with another person as well as the continuance of the race itself? At times, I confess, I have awakened from an erotic dream to find that I am touching myself; no sense of shame has then kept me from indulging in those exquisite sensations. The revelation of this would no doubt be appalling to many, yet I cannot believe that I am alone in such pleasures. Indeed, I suspect that there is a good deal of hypocrisy about all such matters.

If there is anything that gives me pause about lying with Matthew, it is the desire to avoid our becoming the subject of malicious gossip. Apart from the possible injury to our reputations, I do not want our relations to be seen as simply another of those sordid affairs that one hears so much about. But I cannot control

117

public opinion, and I imagine that there is at least some tittle-tattle already. The best that I can do is to be discreet and to carry myself with no sense of shame.

I say all this as if it were only my own desires that mattered, as if Matthew would willingly become my lover if I gave my assent. In truth, I cannot tell where his feelings about this might lie. Although he has shown me great affection, his conduct towards me has always been entirely proper—and I can well imagine his not wanting to entangle himself in the complications of a love affair. So shall I resort to seduction? The very thought makes me smile: it is not in my nature, and it would not be fair to him in any case. No, our lying together must be a mutual desire and I would be reluctant even to hint at it without a definite sign from him. The respect that I owe to him counsels patience. In time we may be lovers; if not, it will be better so.

Sunday, June 7th

Matthew and I have lain together. In the end it came about quite naturally, without the least awkwardness or hesitation. It was early afternoon, and we had just finished having luncheon on the piazza. As often happens on Sundays in the summer, the world had grown very still—apart from the soft thrumming of an insect, the only sensations of which I was aware were the delicate fragrance of the roses and the bright circles of light radiated onto the tablecloth by a wine glass caught in a ray of sun. Matthew had been staring off into the distance for several minutes, silent but seeming a bit unsettled in his thoughts. When at length his eyes again met mine, the meaning was plain. Rising and extending my hand, I said simply, "Come upstairs with me."

I led him to the unused bedchamber opposite my own, which I knew would be particularly pretty in the afternoon light. To my great joy, we undressed in front of each other, Matthew even assisting me with the buttons to my dress and holding it up by the shoulders as I stepped out of it. It gave me an unquestionable shiver of delight to stand before him in only my chemise and petticoats, to be for once forthright and *im*modest in my love. Emboldened, I advanced and helped him to remove his coat, then loosened his cravat and began to undo the buttons to his shirt.

Having done watercolors of him, I knew the general proportions of his body as well as the tone of his skin. And from my life class studies, I had even been able to imagine him completely nude. But nothing could have prepared me for the actual sight of him a few feet from me, serenely beautiful in his nakedness, his eyes ardent and adoring. We stared at each other almost in astonishment for few moments, until I motioned toward the bed.

He took his pleasure calmly, with great control, and yet seemed utterly transported at the end, his eyes closed and his mouth slightly agape, a low sigh coming from far down in his throat. I was bolder in seeking my own pleasure, my movements growing more and more vigorous as the sensations in my loins, at first just pleasurable, became absolutely insistent. When at last it came it was with such force that I nearly cried out, clutching Matthew fiercely and raising myself to meet each wave of sensation as it coursed through me. I was enormously grateful for his weight and the firmness with which he pressed against me, for it seemed that without something solid to break against the waves would simply have overwhelmed me. When the last of them died away, I lay back almost exhausted, my skin warm and damp with perspiration, my mind in a sort of cloud. I felt perfectly at peace, however, and wanted nothing but for that moment to endure.

We talked quietly for a time, and then, overcome by lethargy, drifted into a deep sleep. I was awakened about an hour later by the chiming of the clock in the downstairs hall; it took me awhile to come to full consciousness, however, the exertion and the warmth of the afternoon having lulled me into a sort of drugged state. Matthew was still sound asleep, motionless except for his gentle breathing. Raising my head very carefully so as not to disturb him, I lay there looking at him, at his kindly, intelligent face, his solid torso, and his long, still youthful limbs, the muscles firm even in repose. I was aware, too, of my own body—one that was softer, fuller, more obviously curved—and thought that here were the two great principles of life: the male and the female, each the complement of the other and incomplete without it. Immediately I felt a twinge of desire and a longing to touch him. Turning on one side, I drew my forefinger gently along his upper arm several times, and once across his breast. At that he began to stir, so I withdrew my hand. He did not come completely awake, however, and I was able to indulge in this moment a little longer, touching him only with my eyes. When at length he awoke, he gave me a loving smile and drew me to him; we nestled together for some while, feeling a quiet but intense happiness.

We parted with a light embrace and a gentle kiss. I remained by the window as he descended the stairs, then followed his figure along the street until it was lost to view. I then dressed, came downstairs, and began to clear away the things from the table. Alicia will be here before long, and she will no doubt notice some household detail that I've overlooked in my preoccupation with the events of this afternoon—that is, if my radiance does not give me away completely.

Thursday, June 11th

I have spoken with Lucy about last Sunday; I wanted her counsel, and I suppose, too, that I simply wished to tell someone. Far from disapproving, she expressed great happiness for me and counseled only a bit of discretion. After all, she said, most people will naturally assume that my relations with Matthew are entirely platonic and those who suspect otherwise will not force the issue unless I am too open about it. My natural sense of decorum will undoubtedly serve me well in this regard.

Understandably enough, she asked whether we might marry at some point. To this I could only respond that I do not know. Given Matthew's age (he turned thirty-four just last month), he may well wish to begin a family before long, and for this he will naturally prefer a younger wife. Then too, I have never seen marriage as the goal of my relations with him. On the contrary, ours has simply been a close friendship, one soul bonding with another in such a way as to remain above the mundanities of day-to-day living. I suppose that it would be asking too much for us to go on like this forever—something is bound to put an end to it and, in all probability, relatively soon. It is ours for the present, however, and I must not spoil my current happiness with the thought that it is not secure for all time. Nothing ever is, as I have learned beyond a shadow of a doubt already. But for all our sorrows, there seems to be a Providence that ultimately means us well.

III. 1875

Thursday, March 18th

It seems remarkably calm this afternoon. The day is bright and clear with no wind, and although it is as yet rather chill one senses a certain softening in the earth, a relaxation of that grip with which winter has held us since early December. The sounds coming from the village are rather muted, as if all activity were suspended there; perhaps it is that day in early spring when we sense that we no longer have to struggle against the elements and can lie back on our oars a bit. Such a day is naturally conducive to contemplation, what Mr. Williams has called "the soul's private communion with the universe"—and so it is with me now.

My principal reflection is that the years have been quite kind to me: my life remains one of quiet purposefulness and, though outwardly uneventful, is as rich and satisfying as I could desire. At its center, of course, is my drawing and teaching. Yet even its more peripheral elements—my reading, walks, social engagements, and other pleasure pursuits—are important for the variety and balance that they give to it; otherwise I should probably be too lost in abstractions.

I have another great blessing as well: my relationship with Matthew. We have become what might be called "loving friends."

Though we are occasionally intimate, our bond is principally one of the mind and heart—an attraction of kindred souls who delight in one another's company. To the extent that it is love, it is the quiet, assured love of a long-married couple rather than the intense passion of youth.

Westerly seems to have accepted all this without complaint. We take care, of course, not to flout propriety too openly, and by now the sight of us together is so familiar that no one gives it a second thought. Then too, my age and the fact that I am widowed largely exempt me from the scrutiny to which younger, more physically attractive women would naturally be subject. Women in particular seem to be glad for me: at a time when so many others are enduring a lonely widowhood, I have been granted the happiness of another true life's companion.

I had long assumed that Matthew would eventually marry and our idyll thus come to an end, but it appears that this was not his wish. And as it happens, he has in a way become head of a household of his own. His father died several years ago, leaving him the principal source of support for his aging mother and an unmarried sister who suffers from neurasthenia. The situation of the latter is very sad; she has no real friends and, in fact, seldom leaves the house. She has proved to be quite adept at managing it, however, and the large Italianate structure just off the square is widely said to be a "trim ship." I have done what I can to befriend her, and I believe that she appreciates my attentions.

The felicity of my own situation, however, stands in marked contrast to that of the nation; indeed, in many respects it is the worst of times for us as a people. Since the autumn of 1873 we have been in the midst of an economic crisis, brought on, it is said, by the collapse of Jay Cooke & Company after its failure to place millions of dollars in bonds for the Northern Pacific Railroad. The railroad went into bankruptcy, to be followed by numerous others in subsequent months. As one of the Northern Pacific's principal shareholders, Cooke & Company were swept away as well, leading to a full-fledged panic among the financial houses. From there it was a downward spiral: the cessation in railroad construction led to less call for iron and that to less call for coal, the distress in those two industries ultimately having repercussions on many others. The hardship is now widespread, particularly for the workers. Even those who have managed to keep their places have had to accept large reductions in their wages, with the result that strikes and even violence are now quite common. Sadly, we may have crossed something of a threshold in this regard, for I cannot recall a time when the conflict between workers and owners was so bitter.

The root cause of all these troubles, I am told, is the unbridled speculation in railroads which has absorbed much of the nation's capital since the end of the war. Many thousands of miles of new track have been laid, often (as the Judge puts it) "with far less prudence than schoolboys exercise in trading marbles." The fact that the major financial houses provided the credit to support this speculation only created a house of cards that sooner or later had to collapse.

There is, however, another factor in all this: the corruption in high places that now seems almost universal. The most notorious instance of this, of course, is the Crédit Mobilier scandal of several years ago, in which an inner ring of Union Pacific stockholders systematically siphoned off that railroad's profits and (as a guarantee against interference by the authorities) awarded shares of the company's stock to influential members of Congress. But Cooke & Company, it seems, had done much the same, using bribery to obtain grants of Federal lands for the Northern Pacific. Even reputable members of Congress are known to be on retainer to the railroads, so there is little hope of that body's acting purely on principle where they are concerned.

Saddest of all, the plight of the Negroes has been almost entirely overshadowed by other events. Reconstruction, now in its death throes, has left them little better: Southern resistance has proved too great, Northern resolve too weak.

It began auspiciously enough. Even before the war's end the freedmen had begun to establish their own churches and schools and other institutions of a civic nature. Indeed, the eagerness with which they sought to acquire literacy and the ability to manage their own affairs was nothing short of remarkable. With the 1868 elections they acquired a small measure of representation in government, and in most cases used their authority wisely and fairly.

The new state constitutions that they helped to draft were models of enlightened governance, providing (for the first time) for public education and civic improvements that would benefit all of Southern society. It is difficult for one to imagine a more responsible citizenship.

But it was all too much for the Old Guard, which is in some degree understandable. In no time or place would the dominant class readily accept the loss of its privileges, and such a radical upheaval in social relations was bound to engender resentment and fear. Still, the wave of violence and intimidation that has followed has been surprising in its intensity. Across the South, the freedmen and their white supporters have been taken from their homes at night and beaten, maimed, or even murdered; their homes, schools, and churches have been burned to the ground, other property looted or destroyed. Officeholders have been particular targets, along with Negro militiamen, those who have been bold enough to exercise their right to vote, and all those whose work in any way serves to advance the Negro race. This with the blessing if not the actual participation of the planter aristocracy and other "respectable" elements of Southern society. I am told that newspaper editors have even praised the commission of these outrages, calling their perpetrators "patriotic" and urging an expansion of this reign of terror. Nor can the membership of the secret societies that are responsible for it be terribly secret in a community that accords them such honor.

The government, to be sure, has not stood idly by. Congress has passed several "enforcement acts" in support of the Fifteenth Amendment; hindering anyone in the exercise of his right to vote is now a felony under Federal law, and violations are to be adjudicated in the Federal courts. In extreme cases actions to intimidate or obstruct voters may be deemed a "rebellion" and lead to the suspension of the writ of *habeas corpus*. President Grant has at times used these powers aggressively, notably in suppressing the Ku Klux Klan in South Carolina. He has also ordered in Federal troops to quell two civil disturbances in Louisiana: the occupation of the State House in New Orleans by the White League last September and the Democrats' attempt to take control of the legislature this past January by forcing the legislators to allow five of its members to fill disputed seats.

All the same, one senses that it is ultimately a losing battle. In all but four of the former Confederate states the Conservatives have regained control, a situation they are pleased to call "redemption"; there are few Federal troops left in the South with which to prevent outrages; and the President himself is seeming increasingly reluctant to do battle with such determined opponents. The reality is that we in the North, whether from simple weariness or a fundamental ambivalence about the Negro, are abandoning the struggle. Having stood in the sunshine of liberty for a brief while, the freedmen are now being pulled back into the shadows of a near-slavery. To our everlasting shame—if we had the moral acuity to feel shame.

Sunday, March 21st

This morning after services there was a lengthy discussion of the currency question on the church steps. I listened intently, as I know that this is an issue of some importance, but not being versed in financial matters I could not completely follow the argument. I said as much to Matthew over luncheon. He responded by saying that that was perfectly understandable given the complexities of the issue and its somewhat abstract nature. Still, it would be useful for me to have a firmer grasp of it, as it was one of the leading questions of the day and would undoubtedly be with us for some time. He then offered to give me a short lecture, to which I readily agreed—there is no one who can bring greater clarity to a subject once he has mastered it.

"As you know," he began, "prior to the war all paper currency was 'backed' by gold, that is, freely convertible into a given amount of gold on demand. The intent, of course, was to make the country's money sound, so that a lack of confidence in it would never become a drag on commerce. The exigencies of financing the war, however, led the Treasury to suspend convertibility and issue a purely paper currency, the 'greenbacks.' The value of that currency in terms of gold fluctuated rather wildly, often following the fortunes of the Union armies. It hit a low of 35 cents in the summer of 1864, when it had become clear that the siege at Petersburg would drag on for some months and not, as hoped, put a quick end to the war. By the end of the war it had risen to 78 cents, but even now greenbacks trade at a significant discount to gold."

I vividly recall these fluctuations. One never knew from one month to the next what a greenback would be worth; the tendency was to part with them as soon as possible when their value was high and to hang onto them in anticipation of a rise when it was low.

"After the war, the Treasury began to slowly retire the greenbacks. This seemingly appropriate measure had the effect of slowing commerce, however. Money, as it happens, is a sort of axle grease, and if the total amount in circulation declines too precipitously business will suffer. Within a couple of years there were numerous complaints of hardship, so the policy of retiring the greenbacks was reversed and a re-issuance authorized.

"Now, too rapid an increase in the amount of money in circulation has an unfortunate consequence of its own: inflation, or a marked increase in prices generally. This is precisely what happened during the war years and it remains the principal concern in many quarters.

"So here we have one of the two main battle lines in regard to the currency question. On the one side are those who insist on withdrawing the greenbacks and returning to strict convertibility as soon as practicable, on the other side those who are wedded to the maintenance of 'soft money.' Needless to say, which position one takes tends to reflect his own financial interests: the farmers, small merchants, craftsmen, and so forth, who are heavily dependent on credit, almost universally favor soft money; the new industrialists tend to take the opposite view, in part from principle but in part because they know that a return to hard money will make things more difficult for their smaller competitors.

"The other main battle line has more of a moral character. As you will recall, as one means of financing the war the Treasury issued a large number of bonds and for the first time promoted them to ordinary citizens as well as the large investors. Many households that had never before owned so much as a share of stock purchased these bonds; indeed, Cooke & Company first rose to prominence peddling them to such households. The purchasers, of course, had to pay for them in gold, even though the bonds themselves frequently didn't stipulate the currency in which interest and principal were to be paid. As time went on, the smallholders became more and more convinced that the government was going to redeem the bonds in the devalued greenbacks. Many decided just to cut their losses, selling out to speculators at highly unfavorable prices. Subsequently, of course, Congress passed the Public Credit Act, which required repayment in gold and thus handed the speculators a large windfall. Naturally, the smallholders who had sold out felt cheated and the whole business became a highly charged political issue."

Matthew then enquired whether I recalled the "Ohio idea." The term was familiar, to be sure, but I could not say precisely what it signified. I said as much to him.

"It was the invention of George Pendleton, the prominent Peace Democrat from Cincinnati, who put it forth as part of his bid for his party's presidential nomination several years ago. It called for redeeming the bonds with new issues of greenbacks wherever the bonds themselves did not specify repayment in gold. To preclude an inflation of the currency, notes issued by banks (the principal means by which they extend loans) were to be eliminated. As Pendleton saw it, the scheme had the virtue of retiring the government's debt and advantaging the farmers while giving the speculators 'as good money as they had given.' It was quite popular throughout the Midwest, where there are many small producers and there is little love for either speculators or banks. Though Pendleton did not receive the nomination, the Ohio idea found its way into the party's platform. As a formal matter, it died when the party lost to Grant, but the sentiments behind it are still very much alive."

I then enquired about the role that Ohio's Senator Sherman had played in all this, as his name seems to have become inextricably linked with the currency question.

"He," Matthew replied with unusual conviction, "is the architect of the present solution, which to my mind is a true masterpiece of diplomacy as well as sound policy. It puts the country's finances on a solid footing while at least nodding in the direction of the soft-money interests.

"It has three elements. The first maintains the amount of

greenbacks at its current level—about $350 million—instead of retiring them outright. In time, of course, they will become an insignificant fraction of the currency, but for now they will provide a certain cushion for commerce. The second element authorizes the Treasury to replace the bonds issued during the war with longer-term ones at lower interest rates, both principal and interest being payable in gold. This has obvious benefits for the Treasury, while not unduly disadvantaging the current bondholders and putting an end to all of the uncertainty surrounding the situation. The third element, which was enacted just this past winter, restores convertibility to gold by the beginning of 1879. It is, of course, the keystone of the entire edifice, but the delay in its implementation allows for a gradual adjustment to the return of hard money."

At that point Matthew fell silent, pursing his lips as if to say "So there you have it." I, too, was silent for a time, mentally retracing the points that he had made. At length I remarked that there indeed seemed to be a certain artistry to the solution crafted by Senator Sherman, that his growing reputation for statecraft was well deserved. Still, I was puzzled by the fact that the currency question was apparently not settled—at least, that was what I had gathered from the discussion after church.

"No," Matthew said with a certain resignation, "it probably isn't. Now that the Democrats have regained control of the House of Representatives, there is certain to be an attempt to repeal convertibility. And whenever times are hard or some group perceives itself to be disadvantaged by the adherence to hard money, there will be agitation for abandoning it. Already there is talk of basing the currency on silver as well as gold. It is difficult to say what the final outcome of all this will be, but it's a fair bet that the question will be with us for quite a while."

Luncheon being over, we took our customary walk, this time eastwards along the river. Although it was pleasant (the afternoon had turned quite mild and the clouds had lifted a bit), my thoughts remained fixed on the things Matthew had talked about. My grasp of the currency question has certainly improved, even if I am not completely at home with it. What strikes me most of all, however, is that this is yet another impossibly thorny issue— complex enough by itself but rendered all the more difficult by the competing interests attending it—with which our poor country must grapple.

Wednesday, March 24th

The first warm day of the season, the thermometer outside the headmistress's office registering 68 degrees by mid-afternoon. There was heavy fog during the first part of the day, but by noon it had lifted and the soft warmth of early spring had settled over us. "Zephirus eek with his sweete breeth," in the words of the instructor in early English literature, and indeed, many a mind must have seen the munificence of the West Wind in this welcome event.

The result was a distinct restlessness in every quarter, an urge to be outside that overcame all one's sense of duty. The girls in my afternoon classes found it almost impossible to concentrate, their attention repeatedly drawn to the windows (as was mine, if the truth be told). Although it goes against her principles, Mrs. Marshall eventually gave in and awarded us an hour's holiday to refresh our spirits. The delight with which all of us abandoned our desks was truly palpable.

On returning home, I decided to change into my outdoor clothes and walk back through the orchard into the woods a ways. I was not gone long, as the day was already turning cool again—the first notes of spring are always fleeting and leave us, however subtly, with the anguish of a frustrated desire.

Tuesday, March 30th

For the last two days I have been pondering a question that Meredith Sims chanced to put to me after church last Sunday: whether I have noticed any changes in the character of my pupils over the thirty years that I have been teaching. My first instinct is to say "no," that they have always been marked by a certain restiveness, an enthusiasm bordering on giddiness that is probably natural to girls of that age. On further reflection, however, I must admit to a difference. There is not quite the same innocence, the same assured delight in things; rather, the girls I now have in my classes seem to be more on edge, more suspicious of authority, even a bit more defiant at times. One senses that, however subtly, they perceive the larger world as harsher and less reliable than did their counterparts of a generation ago. None of this should be surprising, however—one cannot expect the prevailing ethic to have left no mark on the young.

Saturday, April 3rd

There is a cold rain this afternoon, and occasional gusts of wind. It is quite dark in the house, as it always is when the clouds are low. One would not immediately suspect that spring is advancing rapidly; but spring wears many different gowns, one of which is this somber one.

Matthew and I are comfortably ensconced in the front parlor, he reading (some work of mediaeval history) and I penning these notes. Alicia left us with a good fire in the grate and we have brought in a couple of lamps from other rooms. However inhospitable the world outside our windows, it is bright and warm in here. And despite the absence of natural light it reminds me of one of Vermeer's interiors.

We spent much of the morning tidying up the grounds, raking up the downed branches and other debris of winter and beginning to open up the beds where the annuals will go. It was cold and raw, and we were thoroughly chilled when we came in for lunch, but the rain held off until we were done. When it came, we were only too glad to retreat to the parlor, our sense of comfort enhanced by our earlier labors in the cold and wet.

My attention wanders a good deal as I write this—to the storm outside, the things coming up this week, and particularly to Matthew. I love to watch him reading, his limpid eyes tracing the words across the page, his nods of satisfaction when an idea "registers." At times he will look up, gazing off into the distance; then, I know, there is something that he does not fully comprehend, that he is taking a moment to puzzle it out. At such times he will often pencil a note in the margin, either a point of clarification or a question to which he will return later. I have never known anyone to read with greater care or to go to such lengths to integrate what he reads in one book with what he finds in another. This, it seems to me, is the true spirit of scholarship, which is as natural in him as his good judgment in the world of affairs.

In a little while I should look to supper. Matthew will no doubt offer to assist me with it, but I will encourage him to go on reading; he can help with the cleaning-up, and then we will have the whole evening together.

Wednesday, April 7th

This afternoon I received my invitation to the annual meeting of the firm's shareholders, to be held in two weeks' time. These meetings are usually just a formality: the firm has a long history of sound management and there are seldom important questions to discuss. Still, as a major shareholder, I feel a certain duty to attend. It is also a way of honoring the memory of my grandfather, who was one of the firm's founders and a member of the board of directors until his death.

As it happens, this year I have a special reason to attend. Elisha Caldwell is retiring and Henry Thornton is to be installed as the new president; the current treasurer will take his place as vice president and Matthew is to become treasurer. There will be a celebratory dinner at the hotel after the meeting.

Thursday, April 15th

I am greatly troubled by an incident which occurred this afternoon. Shortly after I got home, a Negro man knocked on the kitchen door and asked if he might do some work in exchange for a bit of food. Out in the lane that runs between the backyard and the orchard was a wagon with a woman and two little girls—and, it would appear, all of their possessions. I replied that I had no work that needed doing but would be pleased to offer his family something if they would step into the kitchen. At first he was reluctant, saying they would just take the "victuals" with them. He relented, however, when I said that it would actually be simpler for me to serve them at table and that a little rest would undoubtedly do them good.

The meal that Alicia and I put together for them was rather make-shift: just some leftover ham and potatoes, canned green beans, and apple butter. Alicia had baked some bread that morning, however, so we were able to offer that along with fresh butter and milk for the girls. While they were eating I assembled a basket of foodstuffs that wouldn't spoil for them to take with them when they departed.

They were from the western part of Virginia. The husband had been free before the war and had owned a small blacksmith's shop. He had prospered because he was known to be diligent as well as skillful and was well liked and respected throughout his native county. Now, however, everything was overturned; with all the hatred and suspicion toward the freedmen he could no longer make a living at his trade. He was hoping that one of the iron foundries up near Cleveland would take him on—he ought to have some advantage over the immigrants by virtue of his experience and command of English.

They had actually set out last autumn. To avoid using up all of their savings they had stopped wherever they could find a few days' work to do. Generally they slept in barns but on occasion were compelled to make do in the open. It had been difficult crossing the mountains in the winter; even now, they sometimes felt that they would never get warm.

From the first I had been struck by the man's self-possession and well-spoken manner; now it was clear that these traits were coupled with intelligence and a resolute character. I remarked that with such attributes he would surely get on well in the North. He thanked me very politely and said that he hoped so, adding in a more subdued tone that there was one thing against him—though as they were going to an area of great Abolitionist sympathies he trusted that that would not matter. He then informed me, as a sort of afterthought, that he could read quite well and regularly read a newspaper and some books.

By this time the girls had finished eating and were growing rather restless. So that the parents could have their coffee without rushing, I suggested that they be allowed to play outdoors until the family was ready to leave. This was well received and they scampered off after being admonished to check the mules and not to climb any trees. I gather that their parents are fairly strict with them, but they seemed quite happy nonetheless.

Before we broke up I wrote out the name of a Quaker woman who lives along the road they were taking and who would be able to offer them accommodations for the night. I do not know whether they pursued this, however.

It is fairly commonplace, particularly in rural areas, for travelers to seek food and lodging at the houses they come to; few, if any, are ever turned away. And yet this simplest of things must be very difficult for travelers such as these. They must always be exceptionally deferential, perhaps even servile, and even then they cannot be at all certain how they will be received. Many a night they must go hungry or have to sleep on the ground for want of common courtesy. Nor can they have any real assurances as to what awaits them at the end of their journey. Ordinarily such determination in the face of hardship and uncertainty would earn our admiration. But for these people, at this time, it is simply not so.

It has been said that this is the Negro's time of wandering in the wilderness. What we fail to realize, however, is that it is a wilderness that we ourselves have created out of our ignorance and mistrust.

Thursday, April 22nd

To my surprise, the meeting of the shareholders yesterday was quite enjoyable, at times even uplifting. Indeed, in some respects it might be compared to a religious service.

We gathered in the customary place, the large vestibule on the second floor of the building in which the offices are located, at three in the afternoon. It is an attractive, well-lit room at any time and had been specially arranged for this occasion, with orderly rows of chairs facing a lectern and a long table draped in green felt. As always, the firm's employees had been given a half-holiday, so that the entire grounds were quiet.

The first order of business was the installation of the new officers, which was done by the chairman of the board. Each of them was introduced in turn, formally invested with his new responsibilities and congratulated by the chairman, and given vigorous applause. Although he seldom shows a great deal of emotion, on this occasion Matthew looked very happy, almost beaming. As well he should—he has worked quite hard these last nine years.

There followed the customary reports, beginning with that

of the chairman. Of most interest, of course, was the treasurer's report. In a satisfied but measured tone, Matthew announced that the financial condition of the firm was actually quite good, given the poor state of commerce in general. As always, the firm had benefited from its excellent reputation and the fact that it serves a rather small and specialized market. Orders had also been bolstered by the growing number of laboratories at both universities and industrial concerns. This, he said, could be expected to continue for the foreseeable future. Matthew then summarized the trends in the major items of receipts and expenses, noting their effects on net earnings. He concluded with some remarks on the level of the firm's cash reserves. In response to a question, he gave a brief account of the ways in which the idle balances were invested. Although the payment of dividends lies entirely outside his purview, it appears that the firm's financial position would permit the approval of at least modest ones, which would no doubt be welcome to many.

After Matthew's report, Henry Thornton advanced to the lectern to present his vision for the firm. It was, in a word, remarkable. We were living, he said, on the verge of a new age of science and industry, an age in which the ever-increasing sophistication of products and the processes by which they are made would offer almost boundless opportunities for a firm such as ours. For the immediate future, he intended to focus on certain applications in the chemical and metallurgical industries, but in time the range of the firm's activities would doubtless become a great deal wider. Prudence, indeed, dictated that every step be taken with care, but even so we would have to accustom ourselves to much broader horizons than ever before.

After the meeting we were invited to accompany Mr. Hoffmann into the showroom to see the new products that the firm would offer this year. My artist's eye has always delighted in the firm's "line" of precision instruments. Their intricate designs—the precise orderings of small, finely machined parts—has always made them seem more like works of art than workaday tools, and their gleaming brass surfaces offer a distinct pleasure to the senses. Among this year's offerings I was particularly taken with a small binocular microscope (intended, I think, mainly for use in the field); its graceful lines and the almost imperceptible "flow" of the twin barrels into one another reminded me of a classical sculpture of a rearing horse. This sculpture, however, has the additional virtue of enabling us to penetrate some of Nature's deepest secrets.

At dinner there were numerous encomiums to Elisha Caldwell, "whose steady hand had guided our ship to safe ports" time and again. Though the speakers were warm and sincere in their praise, I could not help but think that these tributes paled a bit when the firm's achievements under its outgoing president were set against Henry's grand vision. Mr. Caldwell's stewardship had been responsible in the highest degree, but it had not been bold; it was better suited to an earlier era, when expectations were not as great.

Still, this recounting of the firm's history had a certain poignancy for me, reminding me as it did of my grandfather. To a great extent, that history was also his own history and, at only a slight remove, mine as well.

As I was leaving, Lucy Thornton took me aside and invited me to come have a look at the new house that she and Henry have been building north of town. It is very grand and she was anxious for someone else to see it. We agreed that she will call for me at the Academy about two this coming Tuesday.

Tuesday, April 27th

This afternoon I accompanied Lucy to her new home, which they anticipate being able to move into in a few weeks' time. The past winter not having been too severe, the workmen have made good progress since Christmas and are now adding the finishing touches to the interior.

The house is situated on a long ridge about three-fourths of a mile north of the village. To the east is an old meadow, the openness of which affords a nice view of the valley below. The site of the house itself and the long driveway leading to it have had to be cut out of the woods, however, and there are still a great many stumps and much slash to be removed. Adding to the sense of isolation, the nearest habitation of any sort is perhaps a third of a mile away.

If one were expecting a rude cabin, however, he would soon be disabused of that notion: the structure is indeed on a grand scale. It is in the very latest style as well, all asymmetries and interrupted lines. To the right is a mediaeval turret, to the left a classical pediment, both extending up to the third story. The two small windows in the center of the second story look as if they might collapse under the weight of the steeply sloping roof right above them, into which a disproportionately large dormer has been set. The roofline is irregular, as are many of the exterior details. Some of the finials are Italianate, others Flemish; the "texture" is thoroughly uneven, stone and slate being juxtaposed with clapboard and wooden shingles of several different shapes; and neither the broad verandah along the front of the edifice nor the porte-cochère to one side of it seems well integrated with the rest. The whole says "whim," increasingly one of the hallmarks of our era.

However odd the exterior, the interior can only be described as sumptuous. The foyer is large, extending two full stories in height. It is entirely done in a dark walnut, the walls being lined with recessed panels of a traditional design. Large columns support a graceful staircase, which seems to sweep effortlessly to the floor above. The study, to the left as one enters the house, is similar in its décor, though with bookshelves lining two of the walls and little benches that have been built into the slightly bayed windows. To the right are the parlor, part of which lies within the turret, as well as Lucy's pride and joy, the dining room.

Particular care has gone into the design and decoration of the latter. On the outside wall is a large, south-facing window the upper portion of which forms an arch. On the opposite wall is the fireplace, which is faced in black marble and surmounted by an intricately carved mantel with Corinthian motifs. Above that, and extending all the way to the ceiling, is a sort of reredos portraying classical figures at a banquet; the delicate carving reminded me of the stitching in a French tapestry from the late Middle Ages. The lower portion of each wall is covered by wainscoting, which is plain but of a rich, highly polished wood. The upper portion is hung with a wallpaper of dark green and gold in a scalloped pattern which the Thorntons were at some pains to acquire. Lucy is eager to begin entertaining in this room and envisions many happy times there.

The family bedrooms on the second floor are generally light and airy, with ample sitting areas. Their arrangement is so convoluted, however, that one has the sensation of being in an old palace, uncertain as to which passageway leads to a particular chamber. Indeed, one might well imagine some sort of intrigue behind every door. The rooms on the third floor are small and unadorned, being reserved for servants.

In keeping with the grandeur of the house, each room is to be elaborately furnished. A number of new pieces have been ordered, all in the dark woods and rich fabrics that have become the fashion of the age. The carpets and draperies for the lower floor are being specially woven in Belgium. In time, Lucy hopes to acquire a suitable array of *objets d'art* with which to complete the adornment of each area of the house. No detail, it seems, is being overlooked.

On the way back Lucy finally posed the question that she had clearly been anxious to ask all along, namely, what I thought of it all. I naturally replied that the house was very impressive and that I wished her every joy of it. Privately, though, the whole business rather troubles me. As a matter of aesthetics, I much prefer the lighter, more delicate lines of my own house and its furnishings, which date, of course, from the early part of the century. To my mind they evoke a sense of grace and refinement that is altogether missing from the ponderous modern style. Then too, I am decidedly uncomfortable with so much luxury, which seems altogether alien to the American spirit and cannot but have a deleterious effect on the soul. Worst of all, however, is the sheer amount of *display,* the desire to lord it over one's humbler neighbors. Curiously, it was Henry who insisted on so much extravagance—left to her own devices, Lucy would have been content with a more modest dwelling. In truth, she herself may have some misgivings, as she allowed that it may all be "too much" for a community such as ours.

From my first glimpse of the house I had the feeling that I had seen something like it before, but I could not quite place it. Now it has come to me: the chateaux in the Loire Valley, beneath the elegance of which one can often detect the lineaments of the original fortress.

Tuesday, May 4th

The first truly heaven-sent day of the year, one as pretty as the proverbial morning in May. Although the days have been growing milder for some weeks, it is only now that spring seems to have come into its full glory, the coolness and dampness of April having given way to that warmth and freshness unique to this month of flowers. It is at once exhilarating and enrapturing: we have greater energy, but at the same time we are aware of an enormous calm in everything around us, a calm that conduces to repose and quiet contemplation rather than activity.

So it was with me. I had intended to spend the latter part of the afternoon in my classroom, marking the girls' latest round of essays. However, the intensity of the light coming through the windows (even covered, as they were, with the dust and grime of a long winter) proved too seductive and I soon found myself outside, strolling in a leisurely way about the grounds. There were, of course, a number of others there as well, either walking or lounging about the lawn in small groups. For that number of people, however, it was remarkably quiet. Such conversations as there were were in low tones, as if those engaged in them were mindful of not disturbing others. Like myself, most seemed content simply to revel in the day, to gaze transportedly off into the distance or savor the warmth of the breeze on our faces. In a sense, that is our proper work on a day such as this.

Saturday, May 8th

Matthew came by unexpectedly this afternoon, saying that I must take a short walk with him, that he had something to show me. Though I was busy with other things, there was such schoolboy enthusiasm about him that I could not say no.

We went west along the river, into an area that is mostly woods, and turned down a path leading to an old boathouse that was almost lost in the tangle. With a bit of difficulty Matthew got the doors open, then stood aside so that I could see his newest possession: a wooden canoe about eighteen feet long, which was resting upright on a pair of sawhorses. It had belonged to an old trapper but had not been used for many years. Matthew had engaged a cabinetmaker to sand it down and apply several new coats of varnish, work which was already far advanced. It is to be ready in about a week and Matthew envisions taking a trip in late summer.

"It's quite well built," he said as I leaned down to get a better look, and indeed, the craftsmanship did appear to be remarkable. Despite its age, the ribs, thwarts, and gunwales were all solidly in place and even the boards on the outside did not seem too badly distressed. Two different woods appeared to have been used, a softer, more flexible one (possibly ash) for the basic frame and a harder one for the exterior. The whole had real artistic qualities, and I imagine that it will be quite attractive when it is refinished. I am invited for the maiden voyage whenever that takes place.

Sunday, May 16th

This afternoon we took the canoe out on the river for the first time, giving it, in effect, its baptism. Matthew has taken to calling it his batteau after the sturdy craft used by the French voyageurs two centuries ago—though it is not expected to have to perform such arduous work.

The sensation of being on the water was quite remarkable and, for me, entirely new. I have, of course, crossed the Atlantic twice, but that was in much larger vessels—never before had I been right down in the water, separated from it by only a thin shell. And sitting in the bow as I was, with only the tip of the canoe visible to me, I frequently lost sight of the boat altogether and imagined myself hovering unsupported just above the water's surface.

Equally delightful was the sensation of buoyancy. As soon as Matthew had slid the prow free of the bank I had the feeling of being liberated from gravity, of being capable of moving effortlessly in any direction, as if granted a special privilege from Nature. You are constantly aware of this in a canoe: the continual rocking from side to side that results from the rhythmic strokes of the paddles is an effectual reminder as the boat dips first in one direction and then in the other, always righting itself before leaning away again.

I found a unique pleasure in paddling as well. The technique is to dip the blade into the water at a vertical angle, then to pull the shaft toward you with the lower arm. At first there is great resistance from the mass of water that has to be pushed out of the way; then, seemingly all of a sudden, the resistance gives way and the rest of the stroke is almost effortless. This has its parallel in the muscles: the beginning of the stroke requires considerable exertion, the end very little. This pattern of meeting resistance and then overcoming it, of tensing the muscles and then relaxing them, had a very soothing quality, the more so in being repeated over and over. Then, too, with each stroke I could see our progress through the water and confirm the power present in my own limbs.

We did not go any great distance, just a little way upriver and back. For now, Matthew just wanted to give me the feeling of being in the boat and some practice using the paddle. Later on we will practice turns and he will teach me to steer. He is very keen to have me accompany him on the trip that he has planned. It is tempting, certainly, but so unusual for a woman that I shall have to give it careful thought.

Friday, May 21st

Word has just come of a coal strike in the Hocking Valley; the editor of the *Clarion* posted the notice shortly after noon and within minutes a large crowd had gathered in front of the paper's offices. I myself made a detour there instead of going straight home.

There have, of course, been many strikes since the panic of the autumn before last, but this one is particularly close to home— some of the towns affected are no more than thirty-five miles from here. Naturally, there are concerns about violence, which has all too often accompanied strikes elsewhere. But there is also considerable incredulity that things could have come to such a pass in that particular area, where most of the miners have worked in the same mines for many years.

Discord has apparently been building for some time, however. The hours of work have been reduced since late 1873 and the miners paid mostly in ninety-day promissory notes and credit at company stores. While accepting these terms, most of the miners have nonetheless opted to organize under the auspices of the Miners' National Association. In response, the owners have formed a league of their own, each of them posting a $5,000 bond as surety against failing to act in concert with the others.

Matters came to a head two days ago when the owners announced large reductions in wages and demanded the dissolution of the union (its leaders had already been fired from their jobs). The miners did not challenge the wage reductions but insisted on the right to organize. To that end, they initiated a strike yesterday morning, which has been almost universally honored. Thereupon the owners promptly closed the mines and the battle lines were drawn.

The news brought diverse reactions. While most of the crowd had some sympathy for the miners, many held that they could not escape the "iron laws" of supply and demand, that the market would set their wages in any case. George Sims, who was standing close to me, proffered that, as a banker, he could well imagine that the owners were operating pretty close to the margin. Although the Hocking Valley is a major coal-producing region (accounting for more than a million tons a year in recent times), the large number of companies working those fields tended to depress profits even in the best of times. And given that the industry was naturally subject to large fluctuations, there were bound to be periods of instability and distress. While it was true that the owners might have acted with more decency, as a practical matter their hands were probably tied.

With that, the crowd began to break up; whatever more there was to say, people had to get back to their work. As for myself, I confess that my thoughts on this whole issue are as yet unformed. Clearly, it is one of the great questions of the age, but how it is to be resolved no one seems able to say.

Wednesday, May 26th

So far the miners' strike has been peaceful. Naturally, the men assemble almost daily to review developments and discuss the situation but there have been no moves against the owners or their property.

The owners, of course, fearing trouble and perhaps trying to intimidate the miners as well, have called upon Governor Allen to send the militia, but at least for now it does not appear likely that he will. Sent to investigate reports of violence, the state's Inspector of Mines found them to be groundless. And next week a group of prominent citizens from the affected towns is to meet with the Governor in order "to give him the facts."

There has been one comic moment as well: in New Straitsville, one of the mine owners brought in armed men from Columbus "to protect his investment." After a loud public protest in which men, women, and even children paraded through the streets, town officials had the owner's men arrested for disturbing the peace (the actual arrests were made by striking miners deputized as special police). They left town immediately after posting bond and no one seriously expects them to return for trial.

So, though the situation remains serious, there is reason to hope that it will not end in bloodshed.

Thursday, June 3rd

It has turned quite sultry, and I fear that our lovely spring weather is now gone for good. Indeed, it is much like being in a greenhouse these days, the air so warm and heavy that it seems to weigh down the limbs and the slightest movement appears to take unusually great effort. True, such weather is not uncommon in this region during the summer, but I am particularly sensitive to it. It saps my energy and darkens my spirits, preying on my slight natural tendency to melancholy so greatly that I become very lethargic and despondent.

It is unfortunate that the season has turned so early this year, as there is still much to do to bring the academic year to a close. Indeed, it is one of the busiest times for me, what with final marks and awards to decide upon and ceremonies to attend. All this when my reserves of energy are largely depleted and I am really looking forward to the respite that summer provides. The end is less than a fortnight away, however, and I shall endure.

Thursday, June 10th

The sultry weather has abated somewhat in the last few days and hopefully will hold off until after the graduation exercises on Tuesday. Classes have now ended and the final tasks of the year are well in hand; there remain only the ceremonies themselves, which are always enjoyable. Along with some of the other teachers, I have been invited to have coffee with the board of directors that afternoon. Although there will no doubt be some shop talk, it is primarily a social occasion and should be quite pleasant.

If peace reigns within the Academy, however, it is far otherwise beyond its walls. There the talk is all of the strike in the Hocking Valley, on which opinion is now bitterly divided. The urban newspapers have been virtually unanimous in condemning the strikers, one calling them "a degraded class with the idea that the world owes them a living" and that is simply too shiftless to fend for itself. Commerce, it is widely believed, is subject to certain inevitable fluctuations against which one must make provision. As the *Chicago Times* has expressed it,

> The man who lays not up for the morrow, perishes on the morrow. It is the inexorable law of God ... The fittest alone survive, and those are the fittest, as the result always proves, who provide for their own survival.

There is also a deep antipathy to unions as something that is alien to "the American order." Memories of the Paris Commune are fresh, and no doubt there are fears that American *communards* will take matters into their own hands. The editors have seemed hesitant to draw the comparison, as if the possibility were simply too horrible to contemplate, but it is certainly weighing on many minds.

Within the Hocking Valley itself, however, there has been general sympathy for the miners. The editors of the newspapers there have been at pains to point out that the strikers are native born, that many served in the Union armies, and that a number of them hold positions of respect and responsibility within their communities. A goodly number have worked in the mines their entire lives and might be said to have a "moral claim" to their places there. In no sense are the strikers the "lawless Vandals" portrayed by the urban newspapers.

One of the more thoughtful editors, tracing the current troubles to the vast changes that have taken place in our economic life over the last fifteen or so years, has noted that we are all more vulnerable now to the "harsh, impersonal forces" of the marketplace and that "there is no going back, even if we would." But even so, it is well within our power to confront the new realities in the spirit of Christian charity rather than "the law of the jungle."

Ten years ago, at the conclusion of the war, we had the pious hope that peace would finally prevail in every dimension of society. That is evidently not to be. The old divisions have been superseded by new ones, which, though perhaps not as sharp, are certain to take many years to work themselves out. We had thought our work to be over, but it is not—and perhaps never can be.

Wednesday, June 16th

A cool, clear morning, with little droplets of dew glistening on the grass. There is a decided freshness in the air, as if the earth itself, exhausted by its long labors, had slept late and awakened unusually refreshed. It is the perfect commencement to the school vacation.

For the moment I have the delicious sensation of having no particular responsibilities—of being free to garden, read, and take long walks just as the mood strikes me. This will pass, of course, as I do in fact have some duties to attend to: drawing lessons to give, lectures to prepare, and committee meetings to attend. I should also try to take at least a short trip to Cincinnati to see some paintings and talk with the younger artists at work there. So before long I will have fashioned a new structure for my days. And it is well that I do so, for the soul seems to require order as well as liberty (indeed, complete liberty would probably be altogether unnerving). My summer's regimen, however, will be more relaxed and leisurely; I shall go at my own pace and change course as inclination and circumstance lead me to. Still, it is salutary, as now, to occasionally have the sense of an infinite horizon.

I have also agreed—in principle—to accompany Matthew on his canoe trip at the end of the summer. He proposes to head downriver for four days or so and then return. Unless there is an unusual amount of rain, the current should be light. The country through which we shall pass is said to be very pretty, there not being much settlement there. There will be little in the way of accommodations, however: we shall have to camp out and prepare virtually all of our meals ourselves. Matthew has already taken to referring to us as *voyageurs*.

It would have been difficult to say no in any case, as I would have the pleasure of being alone with him for an entire week in addition to the delight of being out in Nature. I have another reason for accepting, however: the desire to actually experience "roughing it." As much time as I have spent in wood and field, I have passed every night of my life under a roof, usually with servants of some sort to attend to me. I have never known the demands placed on generation after generation of pioneer women—to say nothing of those who accompanied their husbands to the war.

My task now is to increase the strength in my arms and build up my tolerance for spending long periods in the relative confinement of the bow of a canoe.

Thursday, June 24th

This afternoon we witnessed a very sad spectacle: a train with perhaps 200 Negroes bound for the coal towns in the Hocking Valley, to take the places of the striking miners. They had been recruited from as far away as Richmond and Memphis, offered high wages, and told little or nothing about the situation into which they were going.

The cars passed through town quite slowly so as not to risk injury to the numerous bystanders. It had apparently been decided that it was simply too dangerous to stop and allow the passengers to refresh themselves. Although there were a few catcalls, for the most part we greeted them with silent looks of disbelief and dismay. In the eyes staring back at us one could read mainly bewilderment, and perhaps a measure of fear. All too soon they would understand the sorry game in which they were pawns.

Word has also come that units of militia are being assembled at Athens and Chillicothe. It is hard to see how violence can be avoided now.

Tuesday, June 29th

The state of things in the Hocking Valley is not as bad as might have been expected, but there is still great cause for concern. Some 500 Negroes have been brought in and assembled at what is being called a "military camp." They have apparently been armed with muskets from a state arsenal and placed under the command of the county sheriff and his deputies, with instructions to defend themselves as well as the mine owners' property. A guard is being maintained around the camp, and no one is allowed into it without permission.

The miners, needless to say, have reacted angrily. For several days now, upwards of 1,000 men and their families have surrounded the camp, pleading with the Negroes not to involve themselves in a dispute that does not concern them. Mothers have even held up their children, pointing the Negroes out to them as the ones "who came to rob them of their bread."

Mercifully, all of the assaults have been verbal so far. The strikers have even had some success in persuading the Negroes to leave. About a hundred of them have walked out of the camp, many saying that they had been recruited under false pretenses and that they had no desire "to interfere with white folks' work." The strikers housed them overnight in the union halls and raised some $500 to pay their fare home. Still, enough of them remain to enable the owners to reopen the mines, which they are now doing.

Tuesday, July 6th

Our Fourth of July festivities (which were held yesterday because the 4th fell on a Sunday) were good but somewhat marred by the tensions occasioned by the situation in the Hocking Valley. It was, of course, the twelfth anniversary of Gettysburg, and speaker after speaker asked us to recall where the regiment had been at that fateful time—and the difference that it had made. The tributes were eloquent and heartfelt, and many were deeply moved by them.

The martial references, however, had the consequence of reminding us that not two days' march from here veterans are on the verge of moving against other veterans, and there is deep resentment over this. By all accounts the Hocking Valley men fought valiantly during the war and are "damn sure as good men as the ones bein' sent to put 'em down," as one bystander put it to me. Then too, the arming of so many Negroes in such a volatile situation is generally thought to be sheer lunacy.

After the formal ceremonies were over, Matthew and I opted for a quiet dinner on the piazza instead of staying with the crowd on the square. We had had enough of the tensions for one day, and it has gotten very warm again.

Friday, July 23rd

My first entry in more than a fortnight. It has been a period of oppressive heat and, in my case, a feeling almost of despair. I can tolerate a few days of such weather but any long stretch of it saps both my energy and my spirits. Indeed, a sort of panic often sets in, and I question how I can endure another minute of it.

It is generally clear at dawn, with enough freshness in the air to raise hopes that the spell is over. That illusion is gone by mid-morning, however, and by noon the temperature is well into the nineties. Then one feels the weight of the heat pressing down on him, and if there is any appreciable amount of moisture in the air begins to believe that his skin will lift off in raw, thick mats. By late afternoon very little is stirring in the village and an eerie quiet prevails. One then gazes out at the now-sear landscape, made all the more alien by the intense light at that time of day, and utters a silent prayer that the hours will pass quickly and that it will soon be night again. The coming of darkness brings little relief, however: the temperature drops only a little and, if anything, the air seems heavier.

By way of accommodation, Alicia and I have made a number of adjustments to our daily routine. We have taken to sleeping on the porch at the back of the house, on pallets over which we have arranged some mosquito netting. It is generally past midnight before it is cool enough to lie down, and even then our sleep is very broken. We awaken several times during the night, always bathed in sweat, and it takes us a while to recompose ourselves and return to our slumber.

We do only a little cooking, and that the first thing in the morning. In truth, neither of us has felt much like eating and we've taken to getting by on salt pork, bread, and fruit, all of which we consume cold. It has been difficult for me to give up my tea, especially since it would help me to overcome my sense of enervation, but the few cups that I have had have left me feeling quite flushed.

We spend much of the day in the cellar. It is damp and gloomy down there, of course (the floor is dirt and the entire space is musty smelling), but it the only reasonably cool spot in the house. The few times that I have ventured up to the second floor it has been unbearable, and even the first floor is uncomfortable after an hour or so.

I generally try to do a little work in the morning but by afternoon am so overcome by the heat and fatigue that I am able to sleep for a few hours. Upon awakening, I sponge myself off with the water in the rain barrel and change my clothes. It is not a proper bath (indeed, I have not had one in some days), but it does leave me feeling refreshed for an hour or so.

In the evening we poke our heads out, usually just ensconcing ourselves in chairs on the north side of the house until bedtime; occasionally, however, we will walk a little way down the road to converse with neighbors, which is a comfort. Sharing the burden, if only verbally, seems to lighten it a bit. Needless to say, the social life of the village has largely come to a standstill. Matthew has been good about coming by, but I'm afraid that I haven't been particularly good company. Nor would it have been possible to maintain anything like our normal relations in any case. He has been spending most of his evenings on the river, where there is often a bit of a breeze. But then, he is less sensitive to the heat to begin with and seldom lets it deter him from anything. If it keeps up, I am not sanguine about our trip next month.

Owing to the isolation that Alicia and I have imposed on ourselves, I have largely lost track of the world beyond our door. I have heard of several deaths apparently caused by the heat, including that of an elderly man living on the upper floor of a boarding-house. Despite all of the measures that have been taken to accommodate the extreme weather (the firm, for instance, has gone to half-days), there are those whose livelihoods or other circumstances will not allow them to lie low, and for them I have only the greatest sympathy. I imagine, too, that the heat is making things much worse in the Hocking Valley, causing tempers to rise with the temperature.

Saturday, July 31st

For the first time, there has been a physical confrontation in conjunction with the miners' strike. It was little more than a scuffle among a few men and hopefully will not alter the peaceful tenor that has prevailed up 'til now.

The facts, as far as I have been able to glean them, are as follows: the confrontation occurred last Monday just as the morning shift was beginning. Two of the strikers, their nerves apparently worn raw by the heat and the constant tensions of the situation, became abusive of one of the Negroes who was about to go down into a mine, shouting insults and even threats at him. A proud man, he went over to them, glaring at them angrily and brandishing his pick as if to strike them. What happened next is not entirely clear, but apparently someone struck the Negro from behind, knocking him to the ground. The two strikers then fell on him, seizing the pick and pummeling him with their fists. They fled when informed that the sheriff was coming to arrest them. When they could not be found after several hours, a small unit of cavalry was dispatched from Athens to track them down.

The fugitives took a northerly course, at first staying within the heavily wooded areas along the ridge lines. At length, however—local sympathy for the strikers being quite strong—they were drawn into the old Underground Railroad network that was formed to assist runaway slaves. Thereupon a series of "station masters" conducted them from one safe haven to another. Within a few days they should be far enough away that they will no longer have to worry about being pursued.

Though I cannot condone their actions, their frustration is entirely understandable—indeed, they are probably on the verge of utter desperation. Most of the mines are working again, the strike notwithstanding. To all intents and purposes it appears to have been broken.

Tuesday, August 3rd

Our spell of intensely warm weather seems to be over. The temperatures are now more seasonal, and though not entirely comfortable have largely permitted life to return to its usual courses. Thus there is nothing to prevent Matthew and me from making our excursion on the river, which is now set to commence on Saturday, the 21st.

He has assumed responsibility for most of the preparations, procuring a tent, blankets, cooking utensils, and the other pieces of equipment that we will need as well as giving thought to our meals. Our diet, naturally, will be rather plain. Although we may be able to purchase eggs and a few other perishables from farms along the way, for the most part we will be limited to what we can carry and procure from Nature. In the case of the former that means dried and salted meats, flour and cornmeal, potatoes, and some canned goods; in the case of the latter, late-summer fruits and nuts and (Matthew hopes) a goodly number of fish.

As far as the preparations are concerned, my only real task is to get together my clothes and other personal effects. I have settled on some old linen dresses, which should be fairly cool and which should dry easily; a straw hat that I wear when working in the garden; my walking shoes; and a light cloak, in case it turns cool in the evening or after a rain shower.

To my surprise, Matthew doesn't intend to take any books— just some old issues of *Harper's* and the *Atlantic* that he needs to catch up on. There is too great a chance of a book's being damaged, and in his view reading is an activity for the quiet of the library, not the rough-and-tumble of the out of doors. In this I shall not follow his example, however, as there will undoubtedly be times when the tranquility of the hour or the sublimities of Nature will make a book of verse or essays welcome. I shall wrap them carefully in oilcloth and they will not be my best books in any case. I shall also take a small notebook in which to record my impressions for later entry into this journal.

Friends have enquired whether I feel any trepidation about this trip. The answer is no, though as with any new experience, there is a certain anxiety about the way in which it will all unfold and exactly what I shall encounter. I have every reason to expect it to be pleasant, however, whatever adjustments it may call for.

Wednesday, August 11th

I turn fifty years of age today. By way of celebration, the Halstons are giving a small dinner party for me tonight. Matthew has already presented me with a special gift: a small figurine of a wood nymph in the Florentine style, done in the most resplendent white marble. By rights it should be on public display in the hall or parlor, but I have chosen to keep it on the mantel in my bedchamber, where it will share my private moments and where I shall see it the first thing in the morning.

Naturally, I have many thoughts on this day. Although I can easily trace in my mind the entire sequence of events that brought me here, it does not seem possible that half a century has gone by so quickly; to all appearances, it is no more than a dozen or so years, a virtual blink of the eye. And yet, the world of my youth—the 1830s and 1840s—now seems very, very distant. No one born in the last twenty years would even recognize it, so great have the changes been.

All of which makes me wonder what lies ahead, and how many more years there will be. I cannot, of course, know the answer to either of these questions, and it is probably just as well. But I must be mindful that my horizon is no longer unlimited and make the most of each day. Whatever pleasures or instruction it offers I must take hold of with a grateful heart.

Monday, August 16th

Two days of heavy rain. The river will be up some, but Matthew does not believe that this will impair our excursion—though the current may be a little stronger on the outbound segment, the higher water level should generally make things easier for us.

Wednesday, September 1st

I have spent the last two afternoons working up my notes from our eight days on the river. Herewith an account of that event, as it unfolded day by day:

SATURDAY

We "cast off" a little before ten in the morning from a level, sandy area just downstream from the village. Matthew had gotten there ahead of me, sending a man and wagon for me and my things. By the time I arrived he had most of our gear securely stowed beneath an oil-cloth in the center of the craft. It took only a few minutes to get my own things aboard, and then we were off.

The morning was cool and fresh and the water sparkled delightfully in the brilliant sunshine—a thousand pinpricks of light shifting kaleidoscopically in an irregular but steady rhythm. And once again I felt the exhilaration of gliding along almost effortlessly as well as the pleasure of exerting the strength in my arms.

The landscape through which we were passing was a familiar one—the broad valley that stretches for some ten miles east of the village. I have seen it hundreds of times on my walks, and it looks only marginally different from the middle of the river than it does from the road. It is a largely pastoral landscape, tidy farms with their fields of late-summer crops now beginning to ripen. It has something of a timeless quality, and indeed, it has changed little since I was a girl.

It was very quiet at that hour. Though Nature begins each day with a flurry of activity, by late morning it has all died down and a perfect stillness reigns. Apart from the sounds from some distant farms and the passing of the one train that runs on Saturdays, all we could hear was the wind and the lapping of the water against our bow.

We stopped briefly for luncheon a little after noontime. It became our practice to do most of our day's traveling during the cooler hours of the morning and to have our camp set up by mid-afternoon. That way we would have a chance to relax and explore our surroundings before dinner and would be well ahead of any late-afternoon thunderstorms that might occur.

By the time we stopped for the day we had entered distinctly different terrain; in place of the familiar valley with its broad vistas were the steep banks and thick woods of a wilder landscape. It gave me a certain unease, particularly as night came on, as there was no way of telling what might be lurking just out of view. Probably nothing, I told myself, but in such close and unfamiliar surroundings one cannot help wondering. I said nothing about this to Matthew, however, quietly resolving just to set aside my anxieties and get on with the tasks at hand.

There is much to do in setting up a camp: erecting the tent, making up one's bed (which means gathering leaves and other soft materials over which to lay the oil-cloth and blankets as well as rigging up some mosquito netting), clearing a fire circle and locating some large stones on which to rest the pots and pans, and gathering enough firewood for the evening and the following morning. In a few days we grew quite proficient at this, however, learning how to parcel out the tasks so as to get them done in the shortest time.

That night we had a simple dinner and went to bed early. I was certainly tired and I believe that Matthew was as well. Before retiring, however, we walked down to the edge of the river to observe the stars and listen to the water slowly flowing by in the darkness. It was a truly sublime moment, of the sort that one often finds in confronting Nature face to face.

The final tasks were to turn the canoe over in case there was rain during the night and to hang our foodstuffs from a high limb, where they would be safe from any marauding animals.

SUNDAY

It was after eight when I awoke. I did not sleep particularly well that first night: I could not get comfortable, and the unfamiliar sounds of the forest kept me awake for some hours. It is remarkable how the slightest noise—the creaking of a branch or the scuffling of some small creature in the leaf litter—is magnified when one is lying on the ground and everything is shrouded in darkness. The brain seems to perceive the least stirring as a possible threat, and we are ever on the alert. When at length I drifted off, it was into a drugged sleep from which I did not emerge until well past my normal waking hour.

Matthew, by contrast, had been up since first light. He had gotten a fire going and brewed some coffee and was in the process of baking biscuits in a Dutch oven. It was with the warm sense of being cared for that I went over to him, bleary eyed and a bit unsteady on my feet, and slipped into his arms. Knowing that I had had a difficult night, he urged me just to sit by the fire and have some coffee while he finished preparing breakfast. I was only too grateful to do so, hunched over my cup and finding a familiar comfort in the warm steam curling upwards from it. In a little while I managed to shake off my stupor and gain a sense of the day, which promised to be quite pretty.

We were under way by half past nine. The day had the feel of a Sunday, quiet and leisurely with the soothing tones of church bells in the far distance. This stretch of the river, however, was more irregular than that through which we had passed the previous day, with more bends as well as sand bars and snags. As the one in the bow, it was my task to "read" the river—that is, to keep a sharp eye out for any obstacles which we would have to skirt.

It was a task that came quite naturally to me. With my artistic training, I have an enhanced visual sense and take a real delight in the myriad colors and textures of the scene before me. In this case, however, there was the added dimension of not being a stationary observer but of actually passing through the scenes that I was witnessing. There were, of course, subtle changes in both the color and the shape of objects as I got closer to them, a phenomenon that came to fascinate me as the day wore on. But I believe that I was most struck by the sheer facticity of things, which was enhanced by perceiving them, as it were, in three dimensions.

That afternoon I made the first of the many sketches that I was to do over the course of the week. Some of these were of Nature, of course—the different landscapes we encountered as well as interesting rock formations and aquatic plants swaying gently just below the surface of the water. The great majority, however, were of camp life, "domestic" scenes from a very bare-bones existence. In these I have caught Matthew in many different moods: the vigor with which he would cut wood or heave our canoe up onto the shore, the intense concentration in his eyes when trying to get a fire going, the calm reflectiveness of reading, even the placidity of sleep. I have also placed myself in some scenes, having done enough self-portraits to be able to draw myself with ease and without the aid of a mirror. All of these sketches, of course, were done with charcoal and are fairly simple; over the winter I will redo the best of them in water colors or oil.

As we had the previous evening, we retired rather early. This time, however, having gotten my "sea legs," I slept soundly until nearly dawn.

MONDAY

We were off early this morning, as befits a working day—though how I was to know that it was a weekday when I was so removed from my customary tasks, I cannot say. Perhaps there is a sort of timepiece that resides within us, one formed by our following the same pattern week after week our entire lives. In any case, I felt a certain call to duty and took up my position in the bow with more resolve than on the previous two mornings.

The country through which we were now passing was much the same as that of the previous day, heavily wooded with but few signs of human habitation. To all appearances it has changed little since before white settlement, and I would not have been surprised to come upon a Shawnee hunting party around any bend. It is remarkable that for all our efforts to the contrary, so much of the wild world remains. Nature, it seems, is not to be cast off easily.

This thought was to find confirmation in a particularly delightful way a little further downstream. At that point the wooded embankment gave way to a low marsh, the river, now wider and shallower, dividing itself into several small channels that slowly threaded their way through the grasses. Looking down into the clear water, I could see that it was alive with all manner of little creatures: fish, of course, but also frogs, insects, and even mussels in clumps on the bottom. I was especially taken with the sight of the blades of grass emerging from the water, imagining that these plants, though secure in their watery element, were striving to attain the purer one of the air. There is a grandeur in Nature, for all that we hear of its being "red in tooth and claw." Indeed, the scene before me was so fresh and peaceful that the morning could easily have been the first one of Creation.

Being out of one's customary routine is conducive to reflection, and I had another intriguing thought as we were setting up camp. For three days our lives had been centered on meeting the most basic needs of our race—for water, nourishment, light and warmth, and shelter. And though we had tried to maintain our customary standards with respect to order and cleanliness, we were finding that impossible. Little by little, by the force of necessity, we were slipping into more primitive ways. In this condition, lacking so many of the usual amenities of life, I suddenly realized why the human race had been at such pains to create them—the feather beds and fine clothes, the pens and books, the telegraph and railroad, and all the other items of comfort and convenience. Without them life would be immeasurably poorer. All the same there is much that one can do without, and it is good to forgo life's luxuries from time to time so as not to become too greatly attached to them. It may even be that there are some that one can dispense with altogether.

I spent most of the afternoon reading, followed by a short walk along the river bank. Matthew went downstream a ways to try some fishing and returned with several small pan-fish to round out our dinner. As we set about making it, talking quietly in the stillness of late afternoon, I had an almost infinite sense of peace and well-being. The day had been full but unhurried, and at least for now there was nothing more I could want.

That evening we had the first of several remarkable conversations that, for me at least, were one of the true high points of our week on the river.

It was growing dark and we had built up the fire. We said very little at first, each being occupied with his own thoughts. For my part, I was mesmerized by the spectacle of the fire—the iridescent play of the flames amidst the tangle of twigs and branches; the upward leaps of the sparks into the gathering darkness; the slow transformation of the wood into glowing coals, as perfectly sectioned as if by some unseen craftsman. I was wondering how I might get all of this on canvas—not just the various images but the sentiments they aroused as well—when I heard Matthew sigh softly.

He had, it turns out, been thinking about the miners' strike, the implications of which now seemed much greater than they had previously. To his mind, it (and the hundreds of others like it that had taken place over the past two years) represented nothing less than a sea change in our economic life—indeed, in the very character of the nation itself.

"Before the war, enterprises tended to be rather small and to serve predominately local markets. In consequence, there was a natural comity between the owners and their workers. One's relations often extended beyond the shop floor to the church, the public square, and many other places; the lives of owner and worker were bound together in a hundred ways.

"It is altogether different now. The railroad has made it possible to serve distant markets, and the war has given rise to firms of a size never before conceivable. The dominant fact of our economic life now is anonymity. Owners and their employees are unlikely to have any relations other than economic ones, a situation that will naturally lead them to see their interests as opposing. That, I think, is the reason that the 'good' people of Cleveland and Chicago have so little sympathy for those hurt by the panic."

He paused for a moment, then added, "I believe that there is another factor at work as well, at least from the workers' perspective. Until recently, factory work and the like tended to be a temporary expedient: young women might do such work until they married, young men until they had acquired enough capital to purchase a farm or set up in business for themselves. Whatever period of servitude they had to endure, there was always the assurance of being one's own master in due course. That, too, is now largely overturned; particularly with the influx of so many immigrants, there has arisen a sort of permanent proletariat. And the prospect of spending all of one's life in a large, dingy workshop is bound to engender a certain amount of desperation. Where it will all lead is anyone's guess, but it does not seem that it can end altogether happily."

I inquired whether he thought that the greater anonymity of the present day was responsible for the increase in dishonesty and corruption. He pondered this for a while, then replied that although it had undoubtedly played a role the mere opportunity itself was probably a more potent factor; after all, vast fortunes were now more within reach than at any other time and some would stop at nothing to acquire them. But even that might not be a sufficient explanation—in morals, too, there seemed to have been a sea change, the old restraints had been knocked away and any qualms about this dismissed with the most casual contempt. The answer to my question no doubt lay in the workings of the human heart, but exactly what those were he could not say.

I had some difficulty getting to sleep that night. I found our conversation profoundly disturbing, even though little of what Matthew had to say was entirely new. Similar thoughts had been forming in my own mind but they had acquired an almost terrible force from being articulated so clearly.

TUESDAY

Fourth day on the river. By now it all seemed very natural: the narrow ribbon of water winding its way through the dense woods, the long hours of silently observing the passing scene, the rusticities of camp life. Indeed, it would require a bit of conscious effort to recall that this was simply an interlude in my customary comfortable and well-ordered life.

Not long after we got under way we passed a small creek entering on our left. Although we had encountered a number of them since we began our journey, it was only now that I gave any thought to the vast network of waterways in which we were enmeshed. As with the branches of a tree, the smaller tributaries flowed into larger ones and those into still larger ones until one reached the main "stem." The watershed thus formed could be truly enormous, comprising the better part of a continent. The twig bobbing gently in the water alongside me could in principle be carried into the Muskingum River and thence into the Ohio and Mississippi Rivers, ending its journey in the ocean off the coast of Louisiana. By then it would have traveled many hundreds of miles, the distance greatly amplified by the continual winding of those rivers.

Toward noon we came to a small village along the south bank and decided to put in for fresh supplies. We got some curious looks, probably because the inhabitants couldn't imagine anyone—let alone a woman of any means—spending a week on the river purely for pleasure. It was certainly not our appearance, for most of the villagers were as unkempt and begrimed as ourselves. Nonetheless, they were quite cordial and soon put aside any misgivings that they might have had, apparently figuring (in the manner of country people everywhere) that we knew our business better than they did. By way of returning the favor, we followed their suggestion that we have lunch at the village tavern (an old stagecoach stop, apparently, a bit run-down but still charming in its way). It was not a great deal better than camp fare but was served with sincerity and warmth. In parting, we promised to stop again on our way back.

We stopped for the night about four miles further downstream, at what was apparently the site of an old homestead. There was no sign of a dwelling but we found the remnants of a rail fence and a small apple orchard, the gnarled trees now maturing diminutive fruits. Overall, the setting had a certain domestic feel that I found quite comforting.

That afternoon we made love in the soft grass beneath one of the apple trees. I was not the least self-conscious: the pleasure of baring my entire body to the vast vault of heaven, of feeling the warmth of the sun on it as well as the refreshing coolness of an occasional breeze, was so great that I did not care who might be watching. I took my pleasure with unusual vigor, as if something primal had been released in me.

Afterwards, while Matthew napped, I bathed in a small pool along the near side of the river. The overhanging branches afforded me almost total privacy, and I abandoned myself to the luxury of being enveloped in that soft, cool liquid. I swam alternately on my stomach and my back, rotating my body either forwards or backwards to reverse course, each time delighting in the feel of the current I thus set into motion. My greatest pleasure, however, lay in the buoyancy given to my breasts. Relieved of their ordinary weight, they seemed to float on the surface of the water, as full and firm as those of a young woman in her first bloom. Indeed, I had the distinct sensation of being a sylph or one of those delicate virgins employed in ancient rites.

I spent perhaps an hour in the pool, and another sunning myself on a large rock. By the end I was almost in a trance, all passion spent and possessed of the most complete sense of tranquility.

Our campfire was quiet that night. We exchanged a few thoughts but for the most part each of us nurtured his own in silence.

WEDNESDAY

About an hour into our voyage this morning we reached the small falls that we had agreed would be our turning-around point. It would have been easy to portage around it and continue downriver—in fact, there was a well-worn path for just that purpose—but as it would take us at least as long to get home as it had to get here, we really had to head back.

We did, however, put ashore to get a closer look at the falls. They were not particularly impressive, just a jumble of large boulders with a drop of about four feet. Still, it was remarkable how they transformed the smooth flow of the river into a tempestuous white froth, the once-steady current splintering into a hundred fragments tossed from one rock to another until they worked their way past the obstruction. I took particular delight in a little whirlpool that had formed beside a small boulder, finding a real grace and beauty in the slow but constant twirling of the dark water.

As soon as we were back in the canoe and headed upriver I was aware of the current. What had favored us in our outward voyage would now oppose us. All the same, the added resistance was not tha great and I quickly became accustomed to it.

Indeed, my thoughts were still on the falls—and on an idea about aesthetic perception prompted by my encounter with them: to be fully aware of something—to grasp it in all its many facets—we must cease to be aware of ourselves, must in a sense become one with the object. But to actually perceive it and derive pleasure in doing so we must reinsert ourselves into the scene, being conscious of our having such a perception. The aesthetic experience thus seems to have two contradictory elements, a disparity that requires some sort of resolution. Perhaps we achieve this by separating the elements in time, hewing first to the one and then to the other; or perhaps we never give ourselves over to either complete-ly, preserving a rough balance between them.

It is probably the same with other aspects of our lives as well. To do a task well, we must be fully immersed in it; but to find real joy in it we must be able to step back and recognize its place in the full scheme of things. Immediacy and distance—those would seem to be the joint principles of a genuine experience. I shall have to give this more thought when I return home; it is too large a question to decide on a relaxed, summer excursion.

As it happened, our campfire that evening was devoted to an even weightier matter. Matthew had been quiet, twirling the stalk of a maple leaf over and over with his fingers and obviously deep in thought. When I judged the moment opportune, I asked him what was on his mind.

He replied that he had been thinking about the scientific dis-coveries that had been made in recent years—Darwin's, of course, and the growing number of fossils that supported it, but also the progress of the geologists in reading the ages of the earth from the different rock formations. "The remarkable thing," he said, "is that it's all perfectly logical. Nature always obeys certain practical laws, and one can easily see how things change in response to new circumstances; even inanimate objects like rocks undergo a sort of 'evolution.' Compelling as Paley's argument is, it is almost certainly wrong."

William Paley, of course, was the English theologian famous for his analogy of the watch: if one found a finely made watch in a field, he would naturally infer the existence of a watchmaker who had crafted it. "But it appears to be different with Nature. There is much that we do not yet know, but what we do suggests that the natural world consists of vast, never-ending fluxions of matter and energy that drive everything from the stars to this leaf in my hand. In a word, the watch can essentially craft itself."

I enquired whether that meant there were no Divine Be-ing. He hesitated a moment, then replied that "as a matter of pure logic, we cannot know. It is simply not the sort of proposi-tion that we can put to the test—the agnostics are certainly right about that. Yet the number of phenomena attributed to super-natural causes has declined considerably over the centuries and undoubtedly will continue doing so. If there is to be a religion, it must be a more sophisticated one, one that is not at variance with reason and the things we can see so plainly for ourselves."

This, of course, is the direction in which the Unitarian Church has been tending for some years; in some quarters, it is even on the verge of forging a purely secular religion in which the divine is simply a vision of our higher selves. Though I have followed the debate with interest, I have always hesitated to adopt the new ideas wholesale. Perhaps they have seemed too radical a departure from my beliefs heretofore, perhaps I have simply not had the courage to venture onto such seemingly uncharted waters. I asked Matthew, if his view were correct, what remained of the transcendent and what it all implied for morality.

He did not reply immediately, apparently giving careful thought as to how to frame his answer. Finally he said that those were probably the central issues of the whole controversy, the cruxes on which the new ideas would succeed or fail.

"I believe that there are several forms of transcendence. Thought, certainly, particularly our ability to conceive of things in abstract terms and arrive at the larger truths underlying them. The sublimer emotions, such as love and compassion (here he turned to me with a tender smile). And most fundamental of all, our inward sense of ourselves. Mind you, none of these necessarily points to a supernatural power—they may all turn out to be consistent with the secular view. But clearly, a purely secular world would not be as cold and indifferent as some might imagine.

"And as to morality, it is a poor morality, it seems to me, that is based solely on the fear of divine retribution. Nor does such a morality always lead to good conduct. How many of our politicians and men of commerce are pillars of their churches and yet treat their fellow men and women with utter indifference?"

He paused a moment and then added, "The basis of a true morality, I believe, is fellow-feeling, the recognition that others are fundamentally the same as ourselves and thus have rights that we are bound to respect. Absent that, there is no end to the evil one can do. We could not have treated the Negro as badly as we have if we had seen him as our equal, it would have preyed on our conscience far too much."

He fell silent, but I could see from his expression that he had more to say. At length he found the words that he wanted. "Most of our religious ideas derive from other peoples and other times, some of them quite ancient. Perhaps such ideas spoke to their experience, but there is no reason for us to remain in thrall to them if they do not speak to ours. Ideas, too, evolve—however reluctant we may be to admit it." By way of summary, he added that whether there were a Divine Being or not the lineaments of our faith would be much the same, entailing respect for our own powers and recognition of the need to use them wisely and with due regard for our fellows.

At that point he got up and stirred the fire, staring into it as if some mystery were to be revealed there. At length, growing a bit wistful, he made his last point, a sort of coda to the whole conversation. "Unfortunately, all of this is very abstract. At best, it provides an intellectual comfort, not the sort for which people yearn so greatly." I asked him what he thought people wanted. "The best conception that I can come up with is 'wholeness'—the assurance that, at its heart, there is a moral order to the universe and that our lives have purpose and meaning. An assurance that the secular view cannot give so easily."

I lay awake for quite a while after we turned in, pondering all of this. There is much to Matthew's position, and it may someday prevail. But change is always a bit frightening, we resist moving in totally new directions until they have gained enough familiarity that the change in course seems inevitable. I recall the shock and disbelief with which Mr. Darwin's ideas were first greeted. This was entirely natural, for they ran completely counter to our intuition as well as the received wisdom. Now, however, they are gaining acceptance: we have had time to grow accustomed to them, to appreciate the logic and physical evidence behind them, and to realize that they do not overturn our world as much as we had thought they would. So it has been with many new conceptions, and so, perhaps, it will be with religion.

THURSDAY

Warmer and more humid today, as if Nature felt the need to admonish us not to take the fine weather of the last few days entirely for granted. By mid-morning the air was very heavy and we were bathed in sweat, the task of simply keeping the canoe moving forward having become real toil. That alone might have led us to make camp early, but the gathering of storm clouds shortly after noon settled the question for good.

By the time the storm struck, we had camp set up and our gear stored away as well as we could manage and had taken refuge beneath a rock ledge a good ways up the bank. It rained furiously for perhaps half an hour, with much lightning and high winds. We could see very little of it, however—the great mass of water cascading over the ledge formed a thick, silver curtain which our sight could not penetrate. Nor did the storm entirely abate after the initial downpour; it continued to drizzle off and on throughout the night, ending for good only after first light.

Despite our precautions, most of our things were wet. The wind had uprooted one of the tent pegs, and the stream of water flowing beneath the overturned canoe effectively rendered it useless as a shelter. We managed to get a fire going and to prepare a modest supper, but it was a pretty miserable night. Both my clothing and the bedding were damp, and it turned cooler during the night.

FRIDAY

We awoke to much lower temperatures and a light mist. Indeed, the morning had the distinct feeling of autumn, which was only enhanced by the sight of the purplish-red leaves of the dogwoods, always the first to turn.

We got a late start this morning, having to allow time for things to dry before we stowed them away. The rain, of course, had increased the current considerably and our going was slow. It was past five before we had come far enough to stop for the night.

By this point, I confess, I was eager to be home. It was less a matter of the hardships we were suffering than the fact that I was already in an autumnal frame of mind, my thoughts having turned to the Academy and the lyceum and the other things of that season. However pleasant summer may be, it always has an air of unreality. And since its end was inevitable, I wanted it to come quickly.

SATURDAY

A hard day of paddling brought us back to the sandy beach from which we had embarked eight days earlier (though it seemed a great deal longer than that). Matthew's man was waiting for us; he would cart me and my things home while Matthew sorted out the rest of the gear.

We bid each other adieu with a slight embrace and the sort of kisses on the cheek that a brother and sister might exchange. It would probably be several days before we saw one another again. I felt a pang of sorrow at our parting, as it is only rarely that I can enjoy his company so freely. I comforted myself, however, with the thought that the time until our next meeting would pass quickly—that, and the anticipation of a warm bath.

Wednesday, September 8th

It has been only ten days since we returned, yet our excursion on the river already seems fairly remote. By now I am deeply immersed in my autumn schedule—teaching, committee work, social visits, and so forth. I do think about our excursion a good deal, however, relishing its calm, unhurried pace and the feeling of being closer to essential things. Memories of it often come into my head when I am fully engaged in something else and least expect them.

It is well that I have this sort of refuge, for events on the national stage have turned ugly again. In the past week, ruffians have broken up two Republican rallies in Mississippi—not merely scattering the crowds but actually hunting down and killing the office seekers and other prominent persons. It is all aimed at the "redemption" of that state in the fall elections, which is now expected in virtually all quarters. The President, by all reports, is unwilling to take action against these outrages for fear of alienating moderate voters in the Northern states, so the Negroes and their few white supporters are left completely at the mercy of their enemies.

Next year is the centenary of our independence as a nation and a great celebration is to be held in Philadelphia. I suppose that that is as it should be, but clearly we are not altogether worthy of it.

IV. 1885

Thursday, January 22nd

An indifferent afternoon. It is warm for January though still too chilly for real comfort, particularly with the wind. There are high, thin clouds that allow us occasional glimpses of blue sky, but the light they admit is pale and attenuated, so that the scene outside my window seems indistinct, its colors (muted enough this time of year) as faded as those of old fabric. It is no season for grand enterprises, our spirits remain subdued and hesitant.

My thoughts, too, are of an equivocal nature this afternoon. As I often have in recent years, I have been pondering the enormous transformation that has taken place over the last two decades. It is an altered country that confronts us now, one in which life is a good deal more complex and, for many, unquestionably harsher. The exuberance and confidence of our early years have given way to struggle and insecurity, a certain amount of joy has gone out of living.

Nowhere is this transformation more evident than in the great issues of the day. One hears nothing of Reconstruction now, and very little of the Negro. The issue that dominated our national life for so long has, as it were, utterly evaporated. It seems that the South has gone into a sort of eclipse, an era of stagnation and nostalgia for the past it has lost. But whatever the state of affairs there, they are almost entirely out of our sight.

The issues of the present day mostly have to do with business, that is, the increasing concentration of economic power in the hands of a few and its effects on smaller competitors, workers, and the public at large. The emergence of large firms that was made possible by the war has led to attempts to monopolize entire industries. In some cases this has been achieved by willing collusion, notably through placing control of the competing firms in the hands of a single "trust." In others it has been achieved by disadvantaging competitors—through such measures as (temporarily) selling below cost or obtaining more favorable terms from suppliers, distributors, and so forth—and so driving them to the wall.

Matthew takes a more sanguine view of these developments than I do (indeed, it is one of the few things we have ever quarreled about). He points out, for instance, that in some industries, such as the railroads, firms have to be large owing to the heavy capital requirements involved—otherwise it would be difficult for the industry to exist at all. This is especially apt to be the case with the firms that are attempting to exploit new discoveries, such as electricity. Moreover, consolidation can confer distinct benefits. Until recently, for instance, we have had to purchase virtually all of our beef from the sole butcher in town, who enjoyed a local monopoly; supply was limited to what was available in the immediate area and price kept relatively high by that factor, the lack of competition, and the inefficiencies of producing on so small a scale. Now, with the advent of stockyards and refrigerator cars, we can obtain any cut we may wish at virtually any time of the year. Swift & Co. may have gotten rich in the process, but they have also done us a real service.

Matthew also believes that it is quite difficult for any one firm to dominate its industry for long. Large firms, particularly those in the newer industries, tend to have large "sunk" costs that they must cover, come what may. Past that point, to the extent that they increase their share of the market their profits rise rapidly. This, of course, is one of the principal reasons such firms desire to dampen competition—but it also indicates the intensely competitive nature of the situation. And in fact, most efforts to dominate an industry eventually come to grief because the colluding firms cheat on their agreements or their success in consolidating attracts new competitors. The latter have even resorted to a sort of blackmail; any number of refineries, for instance, have been started with the sole purpose of forcing Standard Oil to buy them out.

To be sure, Matthew has been very critical of some of the tactics employed by the new industrialists and is generally appalled by the extent of their venality. And he may well be right in his assessment of the new state of affairs in business. Still, I believe that there is much to be said against the current situation and that a level-headed person might well view it with alarm. For one thing, it would seem that there is a good deal more instability in our economic life now, that these battles among the industrialists can have serious repercussions on the well-being of the nation as a whole. For another, it seems more difficult for ordinary people to get a good living now. The man who a generation ago would have started a small foundry—and enjoyed not only a decent income but also the satisfaction of being master of his own destiny—is now forced to toil in one of the large mills, a virtual automaton working for a relative pittance. Certainly there is little contentment among such workers: the rising tide of violence against the large firms testifies eloquently to that. For my part, I cannot but see a certain coarsening of society in all this. No longer are we "equal on Sunday in the pew, on Monday in the mall," as the late Mr. Emerson has put it; we meet each other not on terms of mutual respect but of suspicion and resentment.

The revolution in industry has naturally left its mark in other areas as well. One of the most conspicuous is Wall Street, which has become little more than a den of thieves. One has only to think of the bitter struggle for control of the Erie Railroad some years ago, Mr. Vanderbilt's attempt to monopolize the lines serving the city of New York by acquiring a majority of the Erie's shares. Although the attempt failed, it left most of the contenders wealthier and put the Erie in the hands of two of the most unscrupulous men of the age, Messrs. Gould and Fisk. They used the railroad as an instrument with which to defraud British investors, curbing their greed only when faced with the possibility of a shareholder revolt. They followed up that "success" with an attempt to corner the gold market the next year.

Of course, the corruption on Wall Street pales by comparison with that in our government. There the change has been profound beyond belief. Tumultuous as our politics were before the war, they had a certain nobility of purpose: men of unquestioned integrity were struggling with issues of the greatest importance. There are few giants now, it is mostly small men who are driven by personal ambition and the opportunity for self-aggrandizement; the great questions of the day largely go begging.

One can see the change even in the way Congress works. Men such as Henry Clay and Daniel Webster acted primarily as individuals, attempting to carry the day through appeals to their colleagues' reason and sense of justice. With their successors it is entirely a matter of party loyalty, of holding onto power by means of strict discipline. Individual members take their cues from the party bosses and vote en bloc; there is no question of independent stands, let alone freedom of conscience.

The reward for all this, of course, is riches—which are provided in abundance by the trusts and other interests that the members serve; rare is the member who is not in someone's pocket and who does not leave office a far wealthier man. There is a cartoon that sums up the state of affairs quite nicely: the scene is the Senate chamber; seated at the senators' desks are small, timid figures, many of whom are glancing nervously about the room; seated in the galleries are much larger, supremely confident figures with grossly distended stomachs bearing the names of the various trusts. The caption calls it "the government of the monopolists, by the monopolists, for the monopolists." An exaggeration, to be sure, but one that contains no small amount of truth.

Corruption is nothing new, of course, either in business or government. But it seems altogether more pervasive now, it occurs on a much vaster scale. As one editorial writer has put it, deception and larceny have "gone wholesale." Our times have come to be called the Gilded Age, which seems an apt description. Gilded, not golden; however resplendent it may be on the surface, it is base metal underneath.

The natural question is what can be done about all this, and there I am afraid that I am not at all optimistic. True, there is some agitation for reform and a few successes to record: a professional civil service has replaced the old spoils system, and the trusts may well be outlawed before long. But our heart is not truly in it; there is no great sense of outrage, no absolute insistence that the indecency and corruption be brought to an end. Each of us, of course, is preoccupied with his own affairs, and many no doubt feel that the problem is too great to be solved. But most, I think, have simply come to accept the current state of affairs as inevitable.

This attitude is mirrored in the theory that society, like Mr. Darwin's tortoises, is subject to certain natural laws that we dare not attempt to contravene and that only the "fittest" deserve to survive. To my mind, this theory is utterly heinous and a complete contradiction of our humane tradition, but it is gaining currency in important circles. It is in this spirit, I think, that our courts have struck down laws intended to benefit workers by limiting their hours or mandating safer working conditions; it is not that such laws deprive workers of their "liberty of contract" under the Constitution (a right that Judge Halston insists has been cut from whole cloth) but that they interfere with the natural workings of the marketplace. Never mind that there is a decided imbalance of power between the contracting parties.

I confess that I would not know how to go about addressing all of the problems of the age even if it were in my power to do so. They are complex and to some extent a reflection of the natural evolution of things. But surely we are not helpless in the face of them, surely people of good will could devise a better way. For my part, I shall continue to do what I can, even if it is only to raise my voice occasionally. But I am growing old, and my energies are not what they were. Years of contending with difficult issues have taken their toll, and my spirit tends to recoil at the prospect of a new struggle. Instinctively I turn inward in search of some measure of repose.

Monday, January 26th

Yesterday after church there was an interesting discussion of the moral state of the country. I am not certain how we got into it—

perhaps someone made a casual remark about this as we were fil-ing out of the sanctuary—but it is certainly a subject that has been on all of our minds these last few years.

Mr. Williams proffered the view that in any age most people simply "follow the crowd," conducting themselves in accordance with the prevailing ethic. If there is a general tendency to rectitude, they will act rightly; but if dishonesty is widespread, they will feel no real compunction about being dishonest. Indeed, in all probability they will not even perceive anything wrong with their actions. In our day, corruption has reached a sort of critical point; like an avalanche, it has gained sufficient momentum as to carry virtually everything else with it. How it has gotten to this point—what has caused the mass of snow high up the slope to slip—he could not say, however.

Here Judge Halston had an important insight to offer. Each generation, he said, tends to have its own ethic, which derives as much from its particular experience as from what it has been taught by its elders. A new generation is rising, and it has a dis-tinctly different view of things. In particular, many of those in it seem to have an almost overwhelming compulsion to distin-guish themselves, to gain a measure of renown that will separate them from the mass. The acquisition of wealth is important not so much because it allows them to enjoy great luxury but because it places them among the elect. In a sense, wealth is simply a means of keeping score. To be sure, each of us derives a certain satisfac-tion from exercising his powers to the full and from leaving some-thing of his own stamp on things—that may be in our nature. But in recent times the desire to do this has gone well beyond the customary bounds, pushing aside whatever restraints there may have been in the past. Clearly, this is one of the forces that have perturbed the snow mass.

The Judge added that to make this theory complete he would have to explain the origin of this inordinate desire for distinction. Here he was at something of a loss; all he could say is that the times seemed to offer unprecedented opportunities for ambitious men, that present circumstances had given them "a vastly larger stage upon which to strut." None of us could take this argument any further, however, and the Judge's suggestion was seen as a distinct advance.

I chose that moment to raise an issue that has been much on my mind of late, namely, the idea that society is governed by certain natural laws and that inequality is the order of Nature. At this, a wave of agitation immediately swept through the crowd, and from somewhere in the back I caught the phrase "that damned fool Spencer again." It was Mr. Williams who ventured a response.

He was, he said, fairly familiar with Darwin's writings, having given them a good deal of attention owing to the controversy surrounding them. He had read much less of Herbert Spencer, the putative father of "social Darwinism," but nonetheless felt that he had an adequate grasp of the main ideas. It was his view that the popular conceptions pertaining to society and the natural order could not be laid entirely at either man's door.

Although the notion of struggle figures prominently in Darwin's work, the focus is on the derivation of new species from existing ones through the "natural selection" of traits that are valuable under given circumstances—it is not on the elimination of the unfit per se. Nor is Darwin in any sense a social philosopher. His subject is natural history pure and simple, and his writings might be said to be models of scientific scholarship. He adduces detailed evidence in support of his conclusions and avoids speculation except where it is necessary to round out his picture of things. Personally, by all reports, he is quiet and unassuming, devoted to his family and kindly disposed to mankind.

Spencer is in many ways Darwin's opposite. He has no family and few friends, living primarily for his work and not being overly mindful of others' sensibilities. He has taken all of reality for his subject and has a penchant for abstractions and overly broad generalizations. As a result, his thought often seems muddled and contradictory as well as indifferent to human concerns. Nonetheless, it would not be entirely fair to put him down as simply a misanthrope. Though society necessarily entails "the survival of the fittest"—the phrase is his, by the way, and not Darwin's—the ultimate end is a perfect society. For in his view evolution always results in progress. Spencer appears to favor laissez-faire because it has given rise to prosperous, peaceful nations such as Britain; the strict regulation of affairs, by contrast, tends to give rise to more militant nations, such as Germany.

Mr. Williams added that although one might well take issue with particular aspects of Spencer's theories ("he leaves himself open to attack at any number of points"), his failings appeared to be more intellectual than moral. One could not be as charitable with many of his followers, however. *They* had drawn on his ideas to justify not only the new state of affairs in business but also the denial of charity at home and the subjugation of "lesser" peoples around the globe. In essence, the notion that life is inherently competitive and that some are doomed to fail has absolved them from all responsibilities to others—a convenient view for those struggling to get to the top.

Mr. Williams concluded by expressing grave concerns about the uses to which the new scientific knowledge was being put. No matter how great our understanding of the physical world, he said, it would never obviate the need for moral judgments. Nature is no model for human society, for Nature is entirely amoral. We do not fault the hawk for pursuing the rabbit, or even attribute any moral capacity to the hawk at all. The same may be said for the competition between members of the same plant or animal species; we see no injustice in one maple seedling's shading out others by virtue of taking root earlier or growing more rapidly. It is simply the order of things. Humans, by contrast, are moral beings: we recognize certain distinct responsibilities to our fellows and place restraints on ourselves accordingly. The nature of these responsibilities has varied widely, particularly as to how far they extend beyond one's own community, but no society has been devoid of mores—quite the contrary. *That* is the point that is lost on too many of Spencer's adherents.

At that point Mr. Williams remarked that as we had managed to get a second sermon out of him this week there would be no need to hold services next Sunday. With that we let him go to his dinner, but not without someone's remarking that it had been a very fine sermon in any case.

Tuesday, February 3rd

I had a rare treat today: a letter from my cousin Elizabeth. She has never been a particularly good correspondent and is even less inclined to write now that she suffers from arthritis; but this was a fairly lengthy letter, full of family news.

She and George are well, apart from the "thousand natural shocks" of getting older. In recent years she has managed to persuade her husband to leave more of the business to the junior partners, both to relieve some of the stress on him and to give them more time to travel. They have spent the last two summers on the coast of Maine, "in a charming little town with magnificent views of the sea." This coming summer they intend to spend six weeks in England.

Her boys are both well launched. George, Jr., is with a prominent investment firm in Boston and fully immersed in the social whirl. He married several years ago and now has two daughters, both "adorable" but a bit prone to mischief. Henry, "always the more thoughtful of the two," is a professor of geology at a college in Pennsylvania. He spends his summers doing field work in the West, and his rooms are chock-a-block with dusty fossils and rock specimens. He seems to be a confirmed bachelor. His principal recreation ("this will interest you, Ellen") is drawing, most often with charcoal. He has put this to good use in his work, sketching rock formations and other objects of geologic interest; he has also done some nice landscapes and "picturesque" scenes from life in the field. She will try to get him to send me some of his drawings.

She closed with the hope that we will be able to see one another before long—I am always welcome in Lenox, and as her husband is eager to see something of the West they may stop for a visit on the way. Perhaps we can even arrange a sort of gathering at Christmastime, when both boys can be there.

I took an unusual degree of pleasure in this letter, not only because it is always delightful to hear from my cousin but also because her news offered a nice counterpoint to my weighty thoughts of late. In the midst of all our troubles, it is good to be reminded that life still holds such simple joys.

Thursday, February 12th

I spent the afternoon working on my Greek. In the five or so years since I took this up, it has become one of my greatest pleasures. It gives me a rare sense of calm, and I grow restless and even irritated when I am away from it for very long.

I wish I could say that it was the magnificence of Greek thought that first drew me to this study, but in truth it was something almost completely trivial. Mr. Williams was preaching on the opening verses of John's gospel ("In the beginning was the Word. . . ."), focusing on the rich array of meanings of the word logos. I liked the sound of that word, the two broad vowels (pronounced "aw") that gave it such grandeur and weight. When I mentioned this to him, he responded by reciting the full first sentence in Greek, with its wonderful sonorities: *lógos ... pros ton the·ón ... the·ós ... lógos* ("and the Word was with God, and the Word was God"). It has all the qualities of a chant, the repetition of that one sound being almost hypnotic. It clearly struck a chord.

Later that week Mr. Williams sent round the Greek grammar he had used in school in case I might wish to investigate the language a little further. As it happens, I had largely decided to make a formal study of it by that point. For some time I had been casting about for a new intellectual endeavor, and a knowledge of Greek is the province of every truly educated person in our culture. Having that knowledge, it seemed, would open whole new realms of thought to me as well as affording me readier access to some of our finest minds. Within a few weeks of first perusing the grammar, I had acquired my own copy and set about the task of mastering it with a will.

I had initially thought that the alphabet would be a significant hurdle, but as it turned out two hours' work was all that it took for me to become familiar with the letters, the accent marks, the rough and smooth breathings (the former sounded as an "h" before the vowel in question), and certain other fundamentals. The grammar took time, of course. Greek is somewhat more elaborate than Latin, its more familiar counterpart. Though it has only four cases (there being no ablative), there is an additional number (the dual, used with items that naturally occur in pairs, such as eyes), an additional voice (the middle, which serves as a reflexive), and an additional mood (the optative, which is used in place of the subjunctive in wishes and certain conditional clauses). Fortunately, though, the language also has a definite article, which is a distinct help to one whose own language relies on it.

From the beginning I took a particular delight in discovering the origins of many of our English words. I confess, though, that I have more often used my knowledge of English to derive the meanings of Greek words than the other way around. From our word "pharmacy," for instance, I could easily guess that *pharmakon* means "drug," and similarly with many other words.

Having mastered the basic elements, my only remaining tasks were to acquire a broader vocabulary and gain some experience in teasing out the meaning of actual constructions. That would require wide reading. My first foray into real literature was the New Testament, which had the great virtue of familiarity, so that I could read lengthy passages without having to look up a lot of words. The only drawback was that the words of the King James' translators were always ringing in my ears; it was virtually impossible to construe the original in any other way. But that did not lessen its value as an exercise, and it gave me some fresh insights into this tome that I have known since my earliest years.

When I had finished cutting my teeth on the New Testament, Mr. Williams suggested that I delve into an extensive anthology of Greek literature that is widely used in colleges. He offered to lend me a copy, but I insisted on having one of my own—I am in the habit of making extensive notes in the margins when I am reading, and more importantly, it would make me more serious about the whole undertaking.

The anthology consists of two large volumes covering poetry, drama, rhetoric, history, and philosophy along with a smattering of other genres. It has copious notes, some of which would only be of interest to scholars but many of which have proven invaluable in sorting out difficult passages. There are short essays on each of the authors as well, giving the essentials of their lives and times and noting where they fall in the literary tradition. One or the other volume has resided on my desk the past four years. I have spent countless hours with them, and I expect to turn over the final page sometime this spring.

It has been virtually a second education for me, so many rich experiences has it offered. There has been no author whom I have not read with pleasure or felt not to have been worth my while. Many have seemed to be a sort of bachelor uncle, a kind companion guiding me through a particular aspect of human life or thought. Then, too, there is a unique satisfaction in engaging not only the ideas of Homer or Plato or Plutarch *but their actual words*. Short of knowing these writers personally, one can come no closer to them.

Notwithstanding the catholicity of my tastes, I have my favorites. The lyric poets, for one, who have had the misfortune of being overshadowed by those writing on more serious themes. Yet how perfect are lines such as these by Sappho:

> To me he seems the equal of the gods,
> That man who sits close to you
> And listens to your sweet speech.

To be sure, they are simple and utterly restrained, with few of the flourishes that we have come to associate with poetry. But can one doubt the intensity of the speaker's love or the pangs of jealousy he (or, indeed, she) feels? As matter-of-fact as this statement seems, it reveals worlds.

In a similar vein are these lines from a pastoral poem whose title might be translated as "The First Fruits":

> There were wild pears at our feet,
> Apples rolled profusely at our side;
> The plum trees, weighted down with fruit,
> Even spread their slender branches on the ground.

Again, there are no flights of fancy, only a relatively matter-of-fact description of the scene. Yet one has an overwhelming sense of abundance, of the profusion of Nature's bounty. Though the poet must have had an entirely different setting in mind, I cannot read these lines without picturing myself strolling through one of our local orchards on a warm autumn afternoon, the air perfectly still, the sunlight gently filtering through leaves that are starting to take on hues of red and gold—a moment such as I love best. Such is the power of the poet's craft.

Of the major writers I am most drawn to Euripides. Although the other dramatists are unquestionably great, they seem much further from us. Their works are more formal, more purely literary; the authors fit comfortably into Athenian society, mildly admonishing their fellow citizens for their shortcomings, perhaps, but never actually throwing down the gauntlet before them. Euripides, by contrast, is the fiercest of critics. Indeed, he is sometimes said to be the Voltaire of ancient times: the implacable opponent of superstition and tyranny, a man deeply affected by human suffering. Many of his dramas are but thinly veiled representations of the state of affairs at the time.

In keeping with the general character of Greek literature, there is a certain restraint in his verses. His images tend to be rather simple, little more than a reporting of the facts. Yet what power there is in them! I shall never forget my reaction to the following lines from *The Trojan Women*, which Hecuba, once the proud queen of Troy, utters when the shattered body of her young grandson, Astyanax, is brought to her:

> Poor one, how pitifully your ancestral walls,
> The work of Apollo,
> Have cut from your head the curls
> That your mother cultivated with kisses.
> Now gore seeps from behind the crushed bone. . . .
> Sweet hands, so like your father's,
> Now hanging limply from the wrists.

The Greeks, of course, had ordered Astyanax to be hurled from the walls of Troy lest he someday avenge the destruction of the city. This at the urging of Odysseus, the great hero "so fearful of a little child." Though understated, Hecuba's contempt for her captors is complete.

Not long after she gives voice to a much more far-reaching contempt:

> The gods were simply determined to cause me suffering,
> Hating Troy more than any other city—
> It was in vain that we sacrificed our oxen ...

(then, addressing those who had brought Astyanax' corpse)

Go, take this lifeless body to its sorry grave.
It has all the garlands that it will need in the underworld.
I doubt it much matters to the dead
Whether anyone gives them elaborate funeral gifts—
That is only an empty show for the living.

Disdain for time-honored religious observances, even disdain for the gods themselves. In her outrage at the injustice and suffering visited on her, the very foundations of society seem to have been shaken.

It would not be fair to give Euripides the last word, however: he wrote at a time when Greece was descending into the chaos of the Peloponnesian War, and in terms of his own temperament is probably not representative of Greek culture at its best. For the Greek ideal, which permeates all of the country's noblest achievements, is a sense of balance. *Mē·dén á·gan:* nothing in excess. We see this very clearly in the graceful proportions of her architecture and sculpture, but it is also implicit in her giving primacy to reason in all things, in her embrace of democracy, and in her emphasis on moderation in the pursuit of pleasure. Not for her the ignorance, oppression, and gross excesses of other ancient cultures. At least, not to nearly the same extent and not without protest.

I believe that in Greece at her height we have—for perhaps the first time in human history—an advanced society in which the individual counts, authority does not derive entirely from tradition or force, and beauty is pursued for its own sake. A society that answers to our higher selves, and one in which happiness is not only esteemed but to some degree possible. That is her legacy to us, through all the turmoil from ancient times to our own.

As luck would have it, I shall have the opportunity to explore another aspect of Greek culture at the next session of our lyceum. Arthur Knowles, an old classmate of Mr. Williams who is now a professor of moral philosophy at Western Reserve University, is to speak on Epicurus.

Friday, February 20th

The lecture last evening was quite good. Given his field of study, I had expected Dr. Knowles to be rather severe, but in fact he was quite affable and even entertaining. A serious scholar, to be sure, but by no means an old pedant.

He began by thanking us for coming, saying that it was gratifying to see so much interest in philosophy. He would endeavor to make it worth our while, presenting the Epicurean view in such a way that we would be able to grasp it readily and see its relevance to our own concerns. It was one of his firmest convictions that knowledge should not be confined to the academy, that it had an important place in ordinary life. Although few if any of us would leave the hall confirmed Epicureans, he hoped that we would all gain new perspectives on the important questions—therein lay the real value of studying the old philosophers.

At that point, with a certain mischievous glint in his eye, he asked what came to mind when we encountered the term "Epicurean"… perhaps the image of a portly, good-natured gentleman who, having had a good dinner, is comfortably ensconced in his library with a snifter of brandy and a cigar? This drew a laugh, of course, but much of the laughter was rather sheepish, as many had no doubt envisioned just such a scene. "That, however," he went on, "would be to confuse an Epicurean with an *epicure*." As we would see, Epicurus counseled living a life of great moderation, even asceticism. In this, he was entirely in keeping with the finest elements of Greek thought and culture.

He began the lecture proper by giving us some historical context. Epicurus came to manhood during Aristotle's last years, the late 320s BC. Aristotle, of course, was the unsurpassed master of systematic philosophy. He had produced a comprehensive "system" addressing all of the great questions in philosophy (and many others) in a logical, fully integrated way. His approach was highly analytical, so closely reasoned that reading him can be rather difficult … as anyone who had tried to do this could attest. His system, moreover, had a very abstract character, often seeming to make little distinction between human concerns and inert matter. Aristotle, for instance, had equated God with "pure actuality," which has a certain analytical appeal but little relevance to everyday life.

Not surprisingly, then, philosophy underwent a profound change after Aristotle. It became more personal, focusing on offering comfort to people as well as guidance in the conduct of their lives. Epicurus himself best explained this shift when he said, "Vain are the words of the philosopher that provide no relief from suffering." The shift took several forms, including Stoicism and Skepticism along with Epicureanism. It is also possible to see the emergence of Christianity from this perspective. A common thread—the betterment of individual lives—runs through them all.

We could sum up the goal of the Epicurean philosophy in a single word: *ataraxia*, the complete absence of discomfort in body and mind. The true Epicurean would feel no pain or anxiety, would be perfectly at ease with all things. The well-being of the body would be achieved by living modestly, that of the mind by ridding oneself of common misconceptions about the true nature of reality. The Epicurean life, therefore, would entail a large measure of quiet contemplation, of withdrawal from the affairs of the world. Epicurus himself spent his days in precisely this way, conversing with close friends within the walled garden of his house at Athens. The image of being "far from the madding crowd" occurs quite memorably in a long poem that one of his followers wrote about the Epicurean philosophy:

> Nothing is sweeter than having a peaceful sanctuary,
> Well protected by the teachings of those with real
>   understanding,
> From which to look down on others as they wander
>   aimlessly,
> Missing the correct path in life,
> Endlessly matching wits with each other, striving for
>   distinction,
> And straining every nerve to gain the advantage and
>   acquire great wealth.

Epicurus says further that pleasure is to be our guide in pursuing tranquility, that we should adhere to those things that are pleasant and shun those that are not. It was an unfortunate choice of words, for it has given rise to the charge of hedonism. The fact is that the term "pleasure" is intended to be taken in a negative sense, that is, as the absence of troubling elements. Hedonism would have just the opposite effect. Overindulgence in the pleasures of the flesh, for instance, would not only be injurious to the body, it would also engender insatiable desires that would preclude all hope of tranquility of mind. For we easily become complete slaves to such desires.

Epicurus also maintains that the focus on *ataraxia* will lead to moral conduct, as the person who is at peace with himself will cause no trouble for others. Having a true understanding of the sources of happiness will militate against greed, for instance, and that will prevent a whole host of evils.

One of Epicurus' principal concerns was to dispel unwarranted fears, particularly those of the gods, of death, and of fate. To do this, he drew on his particular conception of the nature of reality. In Epicurus' view, everything in the universe consists of matter and void. Matter, in turn, is made up of millions of tiny atoms of various sorts, as Democritus had hypothesized; particular combinations of these atoms give rise to particular objects.

Epicurus went to some length to prove that reality is entirely material. We might think of our minds as belonging to another realm because it is with them that we conceive things and concepts per se are not material. But, to act on any of our conceptions, we must exert ourselves physically. If one decides to go for a walk, for instance, he must impart a physical impulse to his legs; as this comes from the mind, the mind must be something physical. Similarly with a sense such as sight: We are able to perceive objects visually because atoms "emanate" from their surfaces and penetrate our eyes, thereby giving us images of those objects. Our thoughts, in turn, derive entirely from our sense perceptions (a remarkable anticipation of the view that would come to dominate philosophy in the latter part of the seventeenth century). The soul, too, is a physical entity, made up entirely of atoms of a particular type.

Given this view of things, one would expect Epicurus to deny the existence of gods altogether. He may well have done so in his private thoughts, but it was far too radical a position to take publicly. Instead, he consigned them to the heavens, where they live lives of perfect tranquility and play no active role in worldly affairs. Certainly they cannot be bothered with all the day-to-day details of existence, such as how warm it will be and whether or not it will rain. And since human life is mainly toil and strife, they will assuredly steer clear of that, too.

In Epicurus' view, then, we need not fear the gods because they have utterly no interest in our affairs. The fear of death can easily be dispelled as well: when we die, our atoms disperse and we simply cease to be—nothing remains to experience either pleasure or pain. Although the act of dying might be difficult, death itself is literally nothing. Epicurus' solution to the problem of fate is of a more technical nature. Since atoms are constantly in motion, and since there is a certain randomness as to how far and in what direction they travel, nothing is completely predetermined. We may not be able to set our course with full confidence, but there is no particular fate in store for us.

Thus the main points of the Epicurean philosophy. Dr. Knowles then offered a brief critique of it, saying that he would try to address some of the objections that had no doubt occurred to us as he went along.

Epicurus' "science" is the most problematical element of his philosophy. It is entirely too loose and suffers greatly from lacking the concept of energy (it is, after all, reflected light that enables us to see and not the emanation of particles). Curiously, though, in a very general way Epicurus anticipated the view of matter to which modern chemists have come, namely, that objects consist of a limited number of elements in many different combinations. It may also turn out that phenomena such as thought and sense perception are fundamentally material in nature—that is, that they arise from processes rooted in physical laws alone. There is much yet to be learned about such phenomena, of course, but we cannot rule out purely natural explanations.

Epicurus is on surer ground in his prescriptions for living well. To be sure, one may question whether complete withdrawal from the world of affairs is honorable or even possible. But his counsel of moderation and reason would find favor with philosophers in all ages—indeed, with any thoughtful person. And we in our time can surely see the value of tranquility and ridding ourselves of the irrational fears that beset people in other eras. With the understanding that humanity has gained since the dawn of the scientific revolution has come not only a certain mastery over

Nature but also a more confident and benign view of the universe.

Epicurus has cast no long shadow in the history of philosophy; no later philosopher has consciously taken him as a point of departure. Yet he advanced views that were far ahead of their time; the naturalism and humanism that he espoused did not reemerge in even a rudimentary form until the Renaissance and did not come to full flower until the Age of Enlightenment in the eighteenth century. In that sense, he is thoroughly modern.

There was a good deal of discussion afterwards, and many favorable comments. Matthew in particular was very taken by the lecture. I have not yet had time to digest it fully, but will certainly put Epicurus on my reading list.

Matthew and I have been invited to join Dr. Knowles and the Williamses for dinner next Tuesday, as he expressed an interest in meeting me after hearing that I was one of "the foremost classical scholars in the village." As always, Mr. Williams gives me too much credit, but I am very much looking forward to the evening.

Wednesday, February 25th

Last evening at the Williamses was most interesting. Naturally, "Hellenics" rather dominated the conversation, but no one seemed to mind.

Though still very affable, Dr. Knowles seemed more serious than he had at the lecture. As soon as we had exchanged greetings and gotten settled in the drawing room, he turned to me and inquired about my Greek studies. I briefly recounted the way in which I had gone about them and the authors I had read, adding that I had found it very stimulating to engage such minds at so small a remove. At that he smiled broadly, saying that it certainly sounded as though I had done my work thoroughly. "Of course," he added with a trace of resignation in his voice, "it is fortunate that you did not pursue your studies at a college, for they would not have meant nearly so much to you."

This remark struck the rest of us as so odd that Mr. Williams asked him to explain it. He gave four reasons: first, my studies would have been a task, not a pleasure; second, the focus would have been on understanding the language rather than on coming to terms with the authors' ideas; third, I would not have had the vantage point of a lifetime of experience; and finally, I would not have felt so free to form my own judgments of things. On this last point he added that we tend to read the classics as we do Scripture, reverentially rather than critically. "We take it all as gospel," forgetting that classical literature is the product of many individual minds, each with its own perspective and its own limitations. In the same vein, we tend to impose a certain uniformity on the classical authors, imagining that they all reflect the same ideals. Even a moment's reflection would show that this isn't true, however: Homer and Euripides painted vastly different portraits of war, for instance, and the comic poet Aristophanes saw Socrates, now regarded as the first great figure in European philosophy, as hopelessly starry-eyed.

We commit another error as well, in Dr. Knowles' view: equating Greek culture with the achievements of its finest minds. Though we might view fifth-century Athens as a high point in the history of civilization, many ancient Athenians were profoundly disturbed by the challenges to traditional ways implicit in the works of her poets and philosophers—subtle thoughts and elegant verse would only lead to catastrophe if they made a mockery of the gods or undermined morality. In the end, Socrates was put to death over such issues, and Aristotle might have met the same fate if he had not fled Athens. Certain of Euripides' lines drew strong protests from his original audiences, and he too was ultimately forced into exile. "There seems to be something profoundly conservative in the human spirit, an ingrained fear of venturing too far from our earliest beliefs." At that point there was silence. None of us could add anything meaningful to Dr. Knowles' thesis, and we all—with deep regret—felt it to be true.

Over dinner the conversation shifted to other subjects, but toward the end it reverted to the previous one when Matthew inquired whether, given the great advances in our own times, Epicurus might not find more favor now. Dr. Knowles did not reply for a time, and when he did it was with a certain sadness. "No," he said, "I do not believe that he would. We, too, live in an Age of Faith; we have pulled back from the furthest advances of the last century, too daunted to go further or even to hold the ground that has been gained for us. Our high-water mark is now behind us—at least for the time being." There appeared to be some discomfort at this remark, as if he had gone too far in his condemnation of religion. To set things to rights, he then added that he found the religious instinct perfectly understandable, if by the religious instinct one meant the desire for a world that was ultimately intelligible and morally good at its core. The difficulty was that this desire, noble as it might be, had given rise to beliefs that were both extreme and utterly intransigent—to the point that they justified the most intense forms of violence, as the long struggle between Protestants and Catholics showed only too clearly. This seemed to smooth things over, even though there was no doubt that religion remained suspect in his mind.

It took me some time to get to sleep last night; I kept turning the discussion over in my mind, repeating to myself the things that Dr. Knowles had said. He is firm in his convictions, of course—firmer than I may ever be—but I too find it overwhelmingly sad that so many have retreated from the great questions, that for them the unexamined life is all too worth living.

Thursday, March 5th

Cynthia Edwards came by this afternoon with a petition on women's suffrage for me to sign. It is being circulated throughout the state with a view to presenting it to the legislature at the start of the next term.

I was pleased to add my name, of course, as it is a matter of simple justice. If there was ever a reason to deny women the franchise, there is no longer. In the last few decades we have engaged the issues of the day as seriously as men, and perhaps with greater objectivity; certainly, our views are less affected by personal interest and ambition. It is even thought that giving women the right to vote would do much to stem the tide of corruption in politics, not that the granting of fundamental rights should hinge on their practical effects.

All the same, one cannot be overly optimistic. Several petitions have been gotten up before this, and the legislature has simply shrugged them off. The time, apparently, is not right—more people will have to be won over before this fledgling of an idea can take flight. In time, however, it will acquire the force of inevitability, and then it will lift itself into the air as easily and naturally as if it had always been able to do so.

I confess that I myself have not felt the lack of the right to vote especially keenly. I have never enjoyed it, of course, and have often felt a certain relief at not having to deal with the sordidness of politics. Then, too, in most other aspects of my life, I have always had a voice, at times a commanding one. But in many ways I have led a privileged life; other women have no doubt suffered greatly from their forced silence.

Tuesday, March 17th

The spring is now well advanced; two weeks of unusually warm weather have softened the ground and coaxed a few buds into opening. On my walk this afternoon I happened upon a quince putting forth its first pink blossoms and cut off a stem to bring home with me. It now resides on my writing table in a little Oriental bud vase that John got for me years ago.

It makes quite a lovely sight, with the intense color of the petals set off against the more subdued blues and whites of the vase. But there are subtle harmonies as well. The iridescence of the petals is mirrored in the soft sheen of the glaze, and the finely etched design on the vase (also blossoms, but more abstract in appearance) echoes the delicacy of the living flower. There is a quiet grace to both parts of this composition, as if they were from the same hand.

I understand that European artists are beginning to introduce Japanese elements into their works. If so, it is no doubt because they want us to take a finer focus, to see life, as it were, in miniature and experience emotions too sublime to register on a larger scale.

Thursday, March 26th

The mild weather has continued, with the promise of many more such days to come. It has wrought a marked change in Matthew. Summer is his season, and though he accepts the darkness and cold of winter without complaint, his spirits are always lightest when the days are long and there are no impediments to an active life. On such days, he says, he can "stretch himself out" to the full.

Along that line, he has proposed an excursion to Grand Traverse Bay this summer. The area has recently become fashionable with the *haute bourgeoisie*, but is quite pretty and offers comfortable accommodations. There is even a sort of chautauqua for part of the summer, with lectures and concerts. He has warned me, though, that if he can arrange for a guide he would like to slip away to the "wilds" for a few days to do some fishing.

Though hesitant at first, I have now been won over. We do not usually venture so far from home, but the idea of being in a cool, northern place during the warmest part of the summer is very appealing, especially since there will be intellectual diversions as well. Nor do I mind being on my own for a few days—I am too old for roughing it any longer and quite capable of keeping myself occupied for so short a time.

Tuesday, March 31st

I have received a very odd letter, from a law firm in Cincinnati. It tenders an offer, on behalf of one of their clients, to purchase my shares in the firm for so much per share, adding that "given the condition of the firm, prompt acceptance of this offer is advised." The identity of the client is not revealed.

To my knowledge, this is the first time that an outsider has attempted to acquire an interest in the firm. Its shares are not publicly traded, and the few exchanges that have taken place have been among parties with close ties to the firm. Nor am I aware of any serious problems there; in a community as small as this they would certainly have come to light, however much the directors wished to suppress that fact. So I am completely mystified by this letter.

Friday, April 3rd

Other major shareholders have apparently received solicitations as well; indeed, there seems to be a concerted effort to wrest control of the firm from those who have held it since its founding. Naturally, this has led to a great deal of agitation, and Matthew has been at pains to reassure people that the state of affairs at the firm is sound. He has even gone so far as to suggest that the firm's books be audited by independent accountants.

Privately, however, he is very troubled by these developments. For one thing, it is not clear how anyone outside of the firm could know who the major shareholders are. For another, acquisition by a competitor would make little sense given that the market that the firm serves is small and very specialized and does not lend itself to mass production. "There is no industrial empire to be forged here; there is simply no opportunity for anyone to become a Carnegie or Vanderbilt."

Matthew has asked me to keep my ear to the ground but to say as little as possible about all this. He wishes to conduct an investigation of his own without the intruding eyes of others.

Thursday, April 9th

The possible sale of the firm is weighing heavily on us all. Even those without shares in it realize how greatly this could affect life in Westerly. All the same, many shareholders may be tempted to accept the offer, as the price named is some 18 to 20 percent above the per-share value of the firm's assets as Matthew reckons them. There is thus a tidy profit to be made by selling out.

As Matthew asked, I've been on the alert for any new information that may come to light. The only thing I've had to report, however, is a curious conversation that I had with Henry Thornton. I ran into him on the street two days ago and casually asked how he was bearing up under the strain of affairs at the firm. I would have expected him to be girded for battle, fiercely resistant to the idea of its being acquired by outsiders. Instead, he simply said, in a tone almost totally devoid of emotion, that a change in the ownership of the firm might be for the best. When I expressed astonishment at this, he replied that it was the way things were these days, that we were no doubt up against "superior forces" and it would be largely pointless to try to resist them. I did not argue the point further, but Henry's position seems so out of character for him that I can only wonder about it.

Monday, April 13th

The arrangements for our trip to Grand Traverse Bay are nearly complete. We are to leave on the 10th of July and return on the 3rd of August, thus giving us a full three weeks there. We have taken a room at a small hotel in Leelanau, a quiet village on a lake near the West Arm of the bay. It should afford us a measure of solitude while putting us within striking distance of most of the attractions. To my delight, I have learned that an eminent painter from Chicago has a summer home in the area and will be giving a couple of lectures at the chautauqua.

I am even somewhat looking forward to our time in transit. Travel by rail has become a good deal more comfortable than it was years ago (some cars, in fact, are as well appointed as the better hotels), and apart from the boredom is pretty agreeable. The first leg of our journey will take us to Detroit, where we will transfer to one of the new Pullman cars (a "sleeper," as they are called) for an overnight run up to Traverse City. It remains to be seen how much rest we will get, but I have been told that the motion of the train is very lulling. In any case, we shall be thoroughly au courant.

Saturday, April 18th

Matthew and I have had a very pleasant day, gardening in the morning and taking a long walk along the river in the afternoon. Virtually all of the plants are in leaf now, so that the landscape seems to consist not of distinct forms but of thousands upon thousands of small green specks in which one can only lose oneself, enraptured.

I hope that this outing has offered Matthew some respite from his worries about the firm. He can never entirely drive them from his mind, I realize, but there seemed to be moments when he was able to push them aside and just immerse himself in the delights of the advancing spring.

In all matters concerning the firm, emotions are running very high now. There is, of course, considerable tension between those who wish to sell their shares and those who do not. The most important source of discord, however, is the growing suspicion of collusion by someone within the firm itself. We have grown very guarded in our intercourse with one another, there is at least a glint of mistrust in every eye. Clearly, this state of affairs cannot continue very much longer—the cord will almost certainly snap somewhere.

At one point on our walk Matthew seemed to be on the verge of revealing some new fact to me, but then drew back. "No?" I said, by way of indicating that I would be pleased to have him share his thought or not, as he thought best. In return, he smiled tenderly as if to express his appreciation for my tact. "Not yet," he said, "but very soon."

Thursday, April 23rd

Matthew has informed me that he would like to hold a secret meeting with several of the firm's directors at my house this coming Monday at ten in the evening. He believes that he has untangled all of the threads concerning the attempt to acquire the firm and requires counsel as to what action to take now.

The time and place of the meeting, of course, have been chosen with a view to preserving its secrecy. In addition, Matthew has instructed the attendees to approach the house from the rear and enter by the side door, which is not visible from the street. They will meet in the library, where there are heavy drapes that I usually draw after dark. I have assured him that I will have everything in readiness, exactly as he has requested.

Monday, April 27th

It is late, but I want to record the details of the meeting before going to bed. I doubt that I would be able to fall asleep right away in any case.

Matthew arrived about nine-thirty, the others—Judge Halston, George Sims, and Elisha Caldwell, Jr., the firm's chief accountant and son of its previous president—shortly before ten. As luck would have it, a fairly dense fog had developed by late afternoon, obscuring the movements of anyone about on the streets.

I got everyone settled in the library and served coffee. I was about to go upstairs when Matthew asked me to stay, saying that my counsel would be valuable as well, to which the others readily agreed. I quietly pulled up a chair and joined them.

Matthew began by thanking us for coming and apologizing for the veil of secrecy that he had drawn over everything, the reason for which would soon become apparent. Since the beginning of this episode, he had been quietly endeavoring to run the various elements of it to ground. He had accumulated a fair body of evidence, and although much of it was circumstantial it all pointed to one person: the firm's president, Henry Thornton.

I gasped slightly at this news, so completely off guard had it caught me. The others looked quite grave but did not seem to be entirely surprised by it.

Matthew then laid out his case in detail. His suspicions of collusion from within the firm were aroused immediately by the fact that the would-be purchaser knew the identities of its principal shareholders as well as the value of its assets—facts that otherwise would have been very hard to come by. Henry had come into his sights owing to his tepid defense of the firm, a stance that seemed utterly out of character for him.

At that point, Matthew said, he initiated two lines of inquiry. First, he asked the Judge to sound out his acquaintances in Cincinnati legal circles as to whether anyone in the firm had had dealings with the law firm from which the solicitations had come. From this he learned that Henry had had two appointments with them, one shortly after Christmas and one in early February.

Second, he persuaded the clerk at the post office who sorts the mail to record the return addresses on all of the letters sent to the Thorntons. There were two of interest: one from the law firm, and one from a lens manufacturer in Connecticut that was one of our firm's main competitors. He did not know the contents of these letters, of course, but their very existence raised obvious questions.

The most telling piece of evidence, however, had appeared quite fortuitously. About two weeks ago, in his capacity as treasurer of the firm, he had received a statement of account from a bank in Cincinnati. Although the firm maintains accounts in several larger cities, it had never had one at this particular bank. Upon inquiry, he discovered that the account had been opened in early February by "your president, Mr. Thornton" in the amount of $10,000; there were two additional deposits the following month. Apparently the bank had sent the statement to Matthew under the assumption that the account was actually held by the firm.

Given all of the evidence, it seemed highly probable that Henry was in league with the manufacturer in Connecticut, that the law firm in Cincinnati had been engaged as a go-between, and that Henry had been paid a substantial sum of money either as an inducement or for any expenses that he might incur.

No one spoke for a few moments. Then Mr. Sims, sighing audibly, said that the facts which Matthew had presented were certainly disturbing but that there were two obvious difficulties with his conclusion: why, given that it was all such "small potatoes," anyone would go to such lengths to take over the firm; and how Henry, a man who had been such a pillar of the community for more than two decades, could bring himself to betray it.

With great deference, and choosing his words with care, Matthew acknowledged that these two points were weaknesses in his argument; he would, however, attempt to address them as best he could.

From a business standpoint, acquisition of the firm would make some sense, in that it would give the new owner greater control over the market. But on the whole this advantage seemed slight relative to the effort made to secure it. It would have made more sense simply to propose a merger of the two firms—though, admittedly, that would probably not have been agreed to. He was thus left with the feeling ("and it is no more than that") that the would-be purchaser had simply fallen victim to the madness of the times, that it wished to increase its standing however little it profited from it.

As to Henry's complicity in the affair, Matthew thought it quite probable that Henry had been offered a high position in the competing firm; at least, the inducements of which we were aware did not seem sufficient to procure such a shift in his loyalties. Matthew added that in recent years Henry had become rather enigmatic to him, that he had tended more and more to keep his own counsel; it was therefore doubtful whether any of us could truly say we knew Henry's thoughts at this point. None of this, of course, amounted to hard evidence, but it was at least a plausible explanation for what had occurred.

At that point I volunteered that I might be able to find out the contents of the two letters to which Matthew had alluded earlier, though I would have to take Lucy into my confidence to do this. That was thought to entail too much risk, however.

The Judge, who seemed to have been growing increasingly impatient with all the back and forth, now asked for the floor. In a firm and uncompromising tone, he said that we were giving Henry far too much credit in focusing on every trifling inadequacy of the evidence. To him, the case was clear: "Henry Thornton is a very ambitious man, and I think it is fair to say that he is largely without restraint when it comes to securing an advantage for himself. Our little stage has simply grown too small for him, and he proposes to climb over us to get onto a larger one."

The Judge's words were like a blow; recoiling from them we fell silent, no longer harboring any doubts as to their truth. We had been blinded by an unspoken desire to find Henry blameless; it was a natural enough desire, but one that would only bring us further trouble if we let it overcome our judgment.

"I suppose, then," Mr. Sims said at length, "that we shall have to take the matter to the entire board . . . and Henry will have to be given an opportunity to defend himself."

At those words, a shadow seemed to pass over Matthew. He acknowledged that that would be the logical course but said that there could well be a serious impediment to it. Several years ago, Henry had lent the firm a substantial sum of money in exchange for a note attesting to the firm's indebtedness. That note, however, was convertible into an equivalent number of shares of common stock, at his pleasure. If he were to exercise that option, and if he could find one or two allies among the major shareholders, he might control enough votes to block any action that the board might take.

Mr. Caldwell then asked if there were any legal recourse open to the board. The Judge replied that as far as he could see no laws had been broken. A civil action was always possible, of course, but it wasn't clear that even that would succeed, as the law tended to be fairly laissez-faire with respect to the internal affairs of commercial enterprises. Such an action would take time and be very divisive in any case.

In the Judge's view, the only option open to us was to confront Henry directly and force him to step down. He might refuse, but his gambit had failed and he was facing the condemnation of most if not all of those in the community—once his treachery had been exposed, he would have few friends.

In the end it was agreed that the Judge would confront Henry within a few days. In the meantime Matthew would speak privately with the other members of the board and try to elicit their support. The meeting broke up about midnight, the others slipping silently into the night at short intervals. Matthew was the last to depart. There was much that I wanted to say to him, but he was tired and anxious to get home. I let my embrace tell of my appreciation for the difficulties that he had been under and his courage in meeting them.

It will be a tense few days. I am especially anxious for Lucy, as this will be very hard for her. I realize that I cannot say anything to her, however.

Thursday, April 30th

It has ended tragically: Henry Thornton has taken his life. Julia Halston brought me the news; she was waiting at my door when I got home from the Academy.

The Judge met with Henry in his chambers yesterday in the late afternoon. Though momentarily taken aback by the confrontation, Henry offered no resistance, readily agreeing to resign his presidency and give up his financial interest in the firm. He did, however, request a few days' delay before it was made public so that the details could be completely worked out, to which the Judge consented. They parted amicably, at least as amicably as the circumstances would allow, the Judge feeling an enormous sense of relief that a potentially bitter struggle for the control of the firm had been avoided. Henry apparently left home before dawn this morning with his Army revolver. His body was discovered several hours later in a wood about two miles north of town, his skull horribly shattered by a bullet.

Lucy was now at the Williams', where she would spend the night. There is to be a preliminary inquiry tomorrow morning at which she will have to appear, but she would like to have me call on her in the afternoon. She will not be formally receiving visitors until tomorrow evening.

Before Julia left I wrote out a short note for her to take to Lucy. Then I went up to my bedchamber and wept uncontrollably. Never had I envisioned that things would take such an extreme turn. A line had been crossed, to be sure, and there was no returning to the way things were before: the Thorntons would have to sever their ties with Westerly and live out the rest of their days in shame. But I had pictured them settling into an obscure retirement, not ... *this*. For a time, I even reproached myself for my role in the matter, telling myself that I should never have been a party to it in any way. I soon righted myself, however. My relationship with Matthew had necessarily drawn me into it, and it was Henry who was undeniably in the wrong—the directors were entirely within their rights to call him out, however tragic the result.

Matthew came by about half past four. He seemed uncharacteristically upset, as if he too regretted the role he had played. "We could not have let it go on, we had to take action, ... and yet there are times when justice is too severe." I tried to reassure him that it was Henry who had elected to end his life, that justice itself did not demand so much. He pondered this for a few moments, then said with sad resignation that that might be true but with a man as proud as Henry there really couldn't have been any other outcome.

We talked for a while longer and seemed to find real comfort in sharing our anguish. He left a little before seven. Normally he would have remained all evening, but there was to be a special meeting of the board that he had been asked to attend.

Friday, May 1st

I spent most of the afternoon with Lucy. She seemed composed, but the strain of what she had been through clearly showed in her eyes, and there were times when she could not keep from tears.

We sat together on the small sofa in the family parlor, a

bright, cheerful room rendered all the more soothing by the gentle warmth of the afternoon sunlight. Our conversation followed no clear trajectory; Lucy moved from one topic to another as they occurred to her or as she had need to speak of them, often reverting to a previous one or anticipating one yet to be fully introduced. I said little, merely offering a word of comfort or encouragement from time to time. My task, I knew, was simply to listen.

As if by way of grounding herself, she first spoke of practical matters. There was to be a simple funeral service at six the following day, when most people would be at supper; only a few people would be permitted to attend—her sister's family from Dayton, her closest friends ("including you, dear Ellen"), and a few members of the regiment (her two children were too far away to arrive in time, and she had specifically requested that none of the officers or directors of the firm be present); there was to be no eulogy.

The house and most of its contents were to be sold. She would live with her sister until she could make permanent arrangements, though what those would be she could not yet say. Her attorney would arrange for the disposition of her investments in the firm; they should enable her to live quite comfortably come what may.

With that she fell silent for a time, perhaps pondering what she should say next, perhaps trying to master the pain that her thoughts were causing her. "I suppose that it was all inevitable," she said at length, "with his ambition. He had grown very dissatisfied with his station, with his 'quite ordinary' achievements; he had become almost desperate to be seen as one of the foremost men of business ... as a giant of the age. His reach had gone beyond all reason, it was folly through and through."

A pause, then: "One is tempted to attribute it all to the times, but it goes beyond that—it is our character that ..." She let the thought trail off, but its meaning was clear. I proffered that perhaps the times *had* played a role, in that in other times he might not have been so emboldened. She considered this, and it even appeared to give her some momentary comfort, but in the end she rejected it: "No, we are more than our times—we have to be."

Then, sharply: "He betrayed me as well." I had, of course,

heard rumors to that effect but had chosen not to give them any credit. I took her hand and said that I was sorry. She smiled weakly as if in appreciation of my gesture, then, looking away, said that it hardly mattered now. I said nothing, but instinctively felt that it did indeed matter and would as long as she lived.

We talked for some while, at times (by way of giving ourselves a bit of a respite) about insignificant goings-on about town, at others reverting to the serious issues at hand. Toward the end of our conversation, she sought my counsel on a matter that had evidently been troubling her: whether she should dress in mourning for the prescribed period. She thought the custom of widow's weeds a bit "barbaric," an excessive and even demeaning display of grief that, given the circumstances, could only cause her further pain; but she did not want to give offense or set tongues wagging. I suggested a sort of compromise, that she observe the custom until she left Westerly, then quietly forgo it; after all, few people in Dayton would be aware of her mourning period, and she would not be out in society in any case. This seemed a reasonable solution to her.

I took leave of her shortly afterwards, as she needed to get ready to receive her visitors. To my surprise, she suggested that I not return in the evening—that it would be a purely formal occasion, and I had already given her the best condolences that she could hope to receive. I thought it best to attend, however, and not flout custom. Indeed, though all of the condolences that she received that evening were heartfelt, there was a certain coldness and artificiality to their expression. I stayed only for the prescribed time and said the conventional things. I sobbed all the way home, however, my heart fairly breaking for her.

Sunday, May 3rd

Henry's obsequies last evening were simple but dignified. Mr. Williams, it seemed to me, struck just the right note, showing due respect for the deceased without extolling him in ways that would have rung hollow. As Lucy had requested, there was no eulogy, but Mr. Williams did find occasion to mention Henry's service during the war and his prominence in our community, indisputable facts that would place him in something of a positive light. The only truly sad note was that the minister's voice rather echoed in the largely empty sanctuary.

The ritual at the graveside is always the most poignant, particularly when the benediction is said and the first shovelfuls of earth are dropped onto the coffin. Lucy remained quite composed through it all, however. I would have expected her to be stoical in any case, but she actually seemed to be at peace, as if in the last two days she had come to terms with all the sorrows of her former life and found a quiet harbor for herself. This gladdened me more than I can say.

As I was leaving, I made a point of telling her that I would call on her soon. In response, she embraced me warmly, with a look of deep gratitude in her eyes. I walked home with a light heart, confident that all would be well. As it happened, it was a lovely evening, which I took as a sign that Nature itself was in sympathy with my longings.

Thursday, May 21st

The days seem to go by quickly now. There is much to do to bring the academic year to a close and, as always, it has become something of a race against time. Everything will get done, however, and the flurry of activity come to an end at a precise hour. In this we are like a canoeist negotiating a rapids: the current carries him faster and faster until, entering a patch of calm water, he comes to a virtual standstill in the blink of an eye. I have several projects planned for the summer but will be glad to have a couple of weeks of pure idleness before launching into them.

I have, of course, spent as much time as possible with Lucy, both by way of keeping her company and by way of helping her to prepare for her move. Although she does not really need to, she seems determined to part with everything that had been acquired specifically for the house, which comprises a large array of furnishings, carpets, draperies, paintings, *objets d'art*, bed and table linens, silver, china, and crystal, all of the highest quality and of considerable value. All this we have been sorting through, placing little tags on the larger items and collecting the others on tables in the parlor, dining room, and library. Much of the first floor now resembles a china shop—elegant, certainly, but with an air of wanton luxury.

We have been greatly assisted in our labors by Lucy's daughter, Camille, a pleasant woman now about forty with an absolute genius for organization. It is she who is compiling a list of all the items to be put on the block, each with a detailed description and notes as to its provenance and original cost. It should be of immense value to the auctioneer.

A caretaker has been found for the house, it being anticipated that such an elegant property will take time to sell. The person engaged is a young apprentice at the firm, the nephew of Mr. Hoffmann, the master lens grinder. For a monthly stipend, he is to live in the house and maintain the grounds; the current housekeeper is being retained to see to the interior. Though I am not at liberty to say this to Lucy, the Academy's board of trustees is considering purchasing the property as a residence for young teachers and a place in which to hold receptions and other formal events. I hope that this comes to pass, as it is difficult to imagine anyone else being interested in the house.

Lucy's financial affairs are falling into place as well. The firm has authorized an issue of bonds in order to repay the large loan from the Thorntons and entered into an agreement to repurchase all of Lucy's shares over the next fifteen years. Until these transactions are consummated, of course, she will continue to receive the interest and dividends due her.

The stage is thus set for Lucy to leave for Dayton about the middle of next month. She has shown a remarkable degree of equanimity through it all, calmly focused on the tasks at hand and betraying little of the emotion that she must be feeling. Only once has her mask slipped, and then only slightly. We had finished our work for the day and were having tea in the family parlor; Camille was busy upstairs. Gazing on the array of expensive things on the dining room table, she sighed audibly and then remarked, in a tone of deep regret, "This house … such vanity." With that she hung her head for a few moments and tears gathered at the corners of her eyes. She brushed them away, however, and summoning her resolve once again, said to me, "You must forgive me, Ellen" in a self-deprecating way, as if she had been guilty of some unwarranted outburst of emotion. I did not protest, merely saying that I understood. Despite her reticence, despite her determination to confront it all bravely, I believe that she finds a real comfort in my being with her at such times.

Thursday, June 4th

There has been one additional development in what the newspapers have taken to calling "the Thornton affair": several of the firm's directors have proposed that Matthew be made its new president. Though honored by this, he feels that it would be neither fair nor prudent for him to accept. In the first instance, there has long been a sort of *cursus honorum* at the firm, whereby one advances from treasurer to vice president to president, and there is no compelling reason to bypass the current vice president. In the second, he wants to allay any suspicion of ulterior motives in his accusations against Henry; cost what it may, his actions must be seen as honorable throughout.

This means, of course, that Matthew will soon become the firm's vice president—a happy event in any case.

Tuesday, June 16th

We saw Lucy off at the station this afternoon. On the surface, at least, there was a certain gaiety to the occasion, filled as it was with cheerful smiles and excited chatter. A casual observer might well have thought that we were merely saying goodbye to a friend who was to spend the summer in Europe. Our lightheartedness, however, was simply a shield against our sorrow at losing this friend. There was, of course, much talk of visits, but I doubt that many of these will actually come to pass. Once she is settled elsewhere, Lucy will probably have little desire to come back here, even for short periods—it will simply be too painful for her. And though I shall be faithful in my visits to her, I cannot imagine that there will be more than two or three of these a year. This, then, is the end of an era in our lives, whatever succeeds it will inevitably be different in many ways.

I try to console myself with the thought that everything of necessity changes, that even if there had been no "Thornton affair" the particular happiness that we had known would not have endured forever. Each year would bring new developments, we would grow increasingly infirm and less able to maintain our relations with each other; inevitably, our affections would be altered, if only in subtle ways. Still, in the normal course of events our losses would have accumulated gradually and we would have had time in which to grow accustomed to them; there would have been no one moment when everything was overturned so completely. It is this that causes us so much pain.

Sunday, July 12th

Two days of traveling have brought us to the north country, which is cool and lovely these midsummer days.

The journey itself was less arduous than I had anticipated. Our railway carriages were attractive and comfortable; indeed, the one for the first leg even hinted at the hand of an interior decorator: the walls were paneled in a light-stained wood finished with a soft varnish; the seats were richly upholstered; there were delicate lace curtains at the windows, no doubt a summer accent; and there were overhead lamps every few seats. There was even a stove in one corner, which, though not needed at this time of year, ensures that the carriage would be comfortable in winter as well. The only drawback was that the windows could only be opened a little way on account of the soot; fortunately, the day was not overly warm.

Matthew and I chatted for the first half-hour or so, as we passed through countryside intimately familiar to us. When we reached the flatter terrain of western Ohio, however, and the motion of the train became more regular, he settled into an eagerly awaited volume—the history of the regiment, published just two weeks previously. Soon he was oblivious to all else, his countenance reflecting the care and thoughtfulness that he always brings to his reading.

I, too, have a copy, but have thought it best not to delve into it until I have returned home. It is an impressive tome, however, both in its appearance and in its content. With respect to the former, it is printed on heavy stock and bound in a rich brown leather, with gold lettering on the spine; each chapter is headed by a small etching representing some aspect of military life—the colors, say, or crossed muskets; and there is a detailed map on onionskin that folds out from the center. Clearly, it is intended to be a keepsake as much as a historical record.

With respect to the latter, it reflects some ten years' research by several persons that has been worked into a coherent narrative by a former company commander who is now a professor of history at a college in Illinois. By all accounts, the author has a fine prose style, direct but refined, suitable both to the presentation of the facts and the elucidation of larger truths from them.

I myself played a small role in providing the materials on which this history is based. From the beginning, it was the author's intention not to rely on the official records alone but to supplement them with the accounts and recollections of the members of the regiment themselves. Thus began an extensive correspondence with surviving members and the relatives of deceased ones, asking them for information about numerous things and, whenever possible, the loan of journals and letters. I was reluctant to let John's letters out of my keeping, but I did go through them all and make copies of the portions that I deemed relevant; this amounted to some two hundred pages. I understand that others have been just as diligent in furnishing such items, giving the author a wealth of material with which to work. Although it is not the historians' usual practice to include so many personal observations—they naturally wish to maintain more distance from their subject—it seems altogether fitting for a history that is to be read principally by those who participated in it.

At midday we stopped for luncheon at a small hotel alongside the tracks in a town about half an hour north of Columbus. The hotel caters principally to railway passengers: at set times of the day it serves a limited number of dishes at long tables and without the usual formalities, the goal being to have everyone back on the train within forty-five minutes. Our meal—cold cuts and a potato salad—was good, if a bit plain.

I attempted to read once we were under way again, but soon grew drowsy and nodded off. When I awoke, the afternoon was well advanced and we were nearing the Michigan line. I could not immediately locate Matthew, as he had moved to the other side of the carriage in order to give me more room. He was staring out the window as if deep in thought, the regimental history closed on his right forefinger to mark his place. It took a few moments for him to notice me.

His thoughts, it turned out, were on the battle at Antietam some twenty-three years ago, of which he had just been reading. It was only the second battle that he had witnessed, and one of the most significant of the war. A Union defeat would have left the capital in peril and might have prompted foreign governments to formally recognize the Confederacy as well; it would certainly have precluded the issuance of the Emancipation Proclamation, which had the effect of turning a war for union into one against slavery as well. It was a hard-fought battle, and the losses were heavy on both sides.

For most of that summer the fighting had been concentrated in the environs of Richmond. Having stopped General McClellan's advance there, General Lee ordered his forces north in order to draw his opponent away from the Confederate capital altogether. In early September, Rebel forces crossed the Potomac River into Maryland. Confident that he could outmaneuver McClellan, Lee divided his command, diverting a substantial portion of it to the capture of Harper's Ferry a little to the west. As luck would have it, however, a copy of his orders fell into McClellan's hands; and as the Federals made haste to intercept the isolated Confederate units, Lee was forced to quickly gather what men he could into a defensive position. The ground he chose was not particularly advantageous in terms of height or cover, and the river was at his back, so that retreat would have been difficult. Thus the stage was set for a desperate battle on the 17th.

The Confederate line extended in a wide arc some three or four miles in length. Beginning at dawn, Union forces successively attacked the different segments of it, from north to south. For the most part these attacks were unsuccessful. Around midafternoon, however, the Ninth Corps managed to penetrate the southern end of the line and drive the Rebels back; it was on the verge of cutting off any possibility of a Confederate retreat when fresh enemy units from Harper's Ferry halted its advance. The entire battle thus ended in a stalemate. McClellan chose not to renew the battle the next day, and the Confederates subsequently withdrew unmolested.

The Fifth Corps, of which our regiment was part, was positioned at the center of the Union line. The entire corps was held in reserve, however, and took no part in the fighting. Matthew recalls that day as one of inaction coupled with great uncertainty—a combination that strained everyone's nerves immensely. From the noise and smoke they could discern the general course of the battle, but they were too far away to get more than fleeting glimpses of it; it was not until the next day that they received a full account.

The carnage wrought by the battle became widely known through photographs taken several days later that were exhibited in New York. It was this that first brought home the grim realities of the war to the Northern public. No longer could it be thought of as a romantic adventure or simply movements on a map—the horror and suffering were there for all to see.

Matthew, of course, saw it all firsthand: the wrecked and abandoned equipment littering the field; the houses, barns, and fences pockmarked by shot and shell; the bloated bodies grotesquely distorted in death. Some aspects of the battle even assumed the character of myth. One Union general said of the infamous Cornfield, where some of the heaviest fighting occurred, that "every stalk of corn … was cut as closely as with a knife, and the slain lay in rows precisely as they had stood in their ranks a few moments before." Another observer noted that the landscape itself seemed to have turned slightly red.

The great irony, to Matthew's mind, was that all of this took place in the most idyllic of settings. The countryside in that part of Maryland is gently rolling, with softly rounded mountains in the distance. The human presence is marked by neat farmsteads set within a mosaic of fields, pastures, and woodlots, quiet country lanes, and sturdy stone bridges with graceful arches. There is a special spiritual element as well, in the form of a small, plain chapel belonging to the Dunkers—a German Anabaptist sect known for its piety and pacifism. In short, it is a place of unusual beauty and tranquility, where one might expect to live a quiet life closely attuned to the unvarying rhythms of Nature.

The morning of the 17th was particularly pleasant. There had been rain during the night and the low-lying areas were shrouded in mist. There was even a hint of autumn in the air, a freshness that was welcome after the oppressive heat of summer. War, however, is no respecter of time or place, visiting death and destruction on even the loveliest ones.

Thus our thoughts as we neared Detroit, the end of the first leg of our journey, which we reached about five o'clock. As our connecting train would not leave until eight, we strolled around the nearby streets for a while and then had a leisurely dinner at the station restaurant. It had been some years since I was last here, and the place seemed very changed—larger, more bustling, and a good deal more polyglot. I could not place some of the languages that I heard spoken at all, and even had difficulty following conversations that I knew to be in Italian (true, I have not spoken that language regularly for forty years, though I have somewhat kept up with it through my reading; I suspect that the difficulty lay mainly in the fact that this was a southern dialect with which I am simply not familiar).

We boarded the Pullman shortly before it was due to depart. As advertised, it was very luxurious, a true palace on wheels. Though I am not one to shun comfort, this degree of luxury made me a bit uneasy; it seemed too much to lavish on a mere railway carriage, an excessive display of finery for such a utilitarian object. I was grateful when we got under way and I could distract myself with watching the countryside pass by in the fading light.

About ten o'clock a porter came through and lowered our two pallets from the wall, made up the beds, and drew the curtains. It was some while before I could get to sleep, however; the circumstances were so strange and the rumble of the train so much louder than it had seemed earlier. Then, too, I had the eerie sensation of being hurled through a dark tunnel into a strange, unearthly realm. I eventually dropped off, however, and slept soundly until after dawn. After washing and dressing, we had breakfast in the dining car. We arrived in Traverse City about half past ten.

The last leg of our journey was by stage up the "little finger" of Michigan, the long, narrow peninsula that separates Grand Traverse Bay from the vast expanse of Lake Michigan to the west. It was a pleasant drive through long stretches of woods relieved by occasional clearings that offered nice views of the bay and the picturesque if hard-working villages along the shore. As we drew near Leelanau, however, we began to encounter the well-appointed hotels that cater to summer visitors as well as the large, very fashionable "cottages" being built by the well-to-do, all quite new in appearance.

Our hotel, The Heights, proved to be an excellent choice. It is situated on a ridge above the bay, with superb views in all directions, and surrounded by wide lawns and old shade trees. The main building is three stories in height, with wide porches running the full length of the first two and a large, square cupola reminiscent of those in lighthouses. Covered walkways lead to two annexes offering more spacious accommodations for families and those staying for lengthy periods. The entryway consists of a large sitting room that extends the entire width of the building. To the right is the dining room, to the left a small library and the "gents' sitting room" (in which, we were told, several important business deals have been worked out).

Matthew and I have a spacious room on the second story, facing the bay. It is light and airy, the deep mahogany of the furniture balanced by the pastel greens and yellows of the wallpaper and woodwork as well as the light cream color of the lace curtains and chenille counterpane. There is a comfortable sitting area by the fireplace and (of particular interest to me) a small writing table beneath one of the windows.

Apart from attending services at the Congregationalist church this morning, we have lain low since our arrival, just resting from the journey here and acquainting ourselves with our new surroundings. The hotel is getting up an expedition to the dunes tomorrow, but for now I am content to sit beneath this spreading maple and study the comings and goings on the bay. I am particularly taken with the sailboats. From this distance their motion is all but imperceptible, and they remind me of so many white moths, their wings folded upwards, sipping from a shallow pool. They are the perfect image of a quiet Sunday afternoon—and the easy, boundless pleasures of summer.

Tuesday, July 14th

We set out for the dunes not long after breakfast yesterday morning in two large surreys, with a guide for whom the hotel had arranged. The hotel also provided us box lunches, as the excursion would take up the better part of the day.

The landscape changed markedly once we had gotten away from the settled area along the shore of the bay, the park-like setting giving way to dense forest pockmarked by numerous small lakes and streams, all very still and dark. My artist's eye took a particular delight in the whiteness of the birches, set off as they were against the deep green of the conifers. This splash of "color" had a whimsical quality as well, as if little fairies or sprites were peeking out from behind a large, heavy curtain. The woods at home lack this visual appeal and sense of charm; they are a plainer, more workaday affair.

As we approached the lake we began to see more signs of human activity. Here, Matthew pointed out, one could easily read the area's history in the landscape itself. The first settlement by members of our race had occurred some 30 years ago, quite recent by any standard. Their initial occupation was "wooding," that is, supplying cordwood to the numerous steamers plying the lake; this was clearly evident in the cutover areas near the shore and in other places with ready access to the docks, particularly those along the larger watercourses. Subsequent settlers had attempted to farm the cleared areas, but this had proved to be a hard go— hence the abandoned farmsteads and collapsing buildings that we had passed. The most recent endeavor was raising cherries and other fruits, to which the soil and climate seemed well adapted; and indeed, we had passed a number of recently planted orchards that in time should give the area a very pleasant, if completely domesticated, character.

I congratulated Matthew on his powers of deduction, impressed that he had been able to see so much in our surroundings. He confessed, however, that the manager of the hotel had given him the outline of this history, from which it had only been necessary to pick out pertinent pieces of evidence. Still, it shows how much we fail to see when we look at things casually. I have resolved to look deeper from now on, to see with the mind as well as the eye.

We stopped for luncheon a little way from the crest of the dunes, in a pleasant grove with views of the country we had traversed and, to the west, the distinct suggestion of a vast open area.

While we dined, our guide gave us a brief account of the nature and origin of the dunes. As we would see, they consisted of an immense ridge of sand that stretched for miles along the shore. At some points the dunes were little higher than the lake itself, forming pretty little beaches; at others, however, they rose to as much as 450 feet above the lake, giving the appearance of "sentinels standing guard along the coast." At no point were the dunes entirely stationary, though; they were constantly being reshaped by the action of wind and wave. Indeed, in some places one could see the "ghosts" of trees, lifeless skeletons half buried by the encroaching sand.

To the geologists, the dunes were the result of glacial tills being blown eastward by the prevailing westerly winds—a simple, natural process acting over aeons of time. To the Ottawa and Chippewa peoples who have inhabited the area from time immemorial, however, there was a more colorful explanation: Long ago, a forest fire along the western shore of the lake had forced a mother bear and her two cubs to swim for the Michigan shore, which was many miles distant. The mother reached the shore, exhausted; the two cubs, however, were not quite strong enough to swim the entire distance and drowned a little way offshore, within sight of her. In her anguish, she appealed to the Great Spirit, who transformed the cubs into the two large islands out in the lake, both of which have the Great Spirit's name—Manitou—in theirs. Overcome, the mother bear then collapsed where she was on the shore; in time she was covered entirely with sand. With a slight glint in his eye, the guide then remarked that it was not difficult to tell which of the two accounts our party preferred.

Luncheon over, we got back in the surreys and drove another quarter of a mile or so, alighting at a small, well-worn path. Here the terrain had the distinct feel of the shore of an ocean, the sandy path winding through low, spindly shrubs, then irregular clumps of beach grasses, then pure sand. Then, cresting the last rise, we were face to face with the vast blueness of the lake. It is a scene that must surely cause one's breath to catch, and all of us were silent for a time, overwhelmed by the immense panorama of water, sky, and shore. After a time, however, the different members of the party dispersed in different directions to carry out their own explorations. I did not go far, though, content just to feel the breeze on my face and take in the myriad details of the scene as if I were going to paint them; I was not even very diligent about that, however, soon abandoning myself to the sheer pleasure of being in this spot at this moment.

As we were strolling back to the road, one of the other women in the party remarked that seeing things from such a high vantage point made her feel altogether insignificant. My reaction, however, was just the opposite: I experienced a deep sense of satisfaction at having such a vast field of vision, of being able to take in the whole of a landscape ordinarily seen only in pieces. Psychologically, at least, for one brief moment I was master of all that I surveyed. I can recall only one other occasion like this, during my time in Europe. It was actually in a situation very like this one, on a ragged promontory high above the Mediterranean, with the ruins of several ancient civilizations visible in the distance. From that height, it was easy to envision those long-ago times as they must have been then, before the passage of some 2,000 years. It was as if I had transcended time as well as space.

The drive back seemed long, and we were all glad when we reached the hotel. I had a warm bath, then Matthew and I shared a simple supper in our room.

Thursday, July 16th

The days seem to be falling into an agreeable pattern. Matthew leaves about dawn to fish with a party led by an elderly Chippewa man. I linger in bed until the spirit moves me to get up, then have a leisurely breakfast in the shaded courtyard off the dining room. From then until midafternoon I attend lectures at the chautauqua, sketch or paint, take long walks along the shoreline, read, or write letters. When Matthew returns, we sit out under the maples and talk over the day until it is time to get ready for dinner.

Dinner is a rather formal affair, with numerous courses. One is expected to dress for it and to enter into the general conversation with the others at one's table, just as one would at a banquet. The chef works wonders with the many fresh foods available at this season. Fish figures prominently, of course, but we have also been treated to freshly shot quail and choice cuts of beef and other delicacies brought in from Chicago. The early-season fruits and vegetables from local orchards and gardens are a particular delight as well.

As there is still some daylight after dinner, we usually stroll about the grounds a bit before retiring, both to aid our digestion and to enjoy the last, colorful moments of the day. We go to bed somewhat earlier than at home, the fullness of the day making us more than ready for sleep.

So far I have completed only one painting—a small water-color of a white clematis trailing up a post along the walkway on the western side of our hotel. I was taken with this at my very first sight of it. The petals, of course, are large and "fleshy," but with such delicate folds in their centers that the entire blossom reminds one of a dinner napkin of the sort found in the finest restaurants. I am afraid that watercolors do not really do it justice (in particular, I was not completely able to capture the subtle sheen of the pet-als), but I am nonetheless very pleased with it, this private souvenir that now graces the mantle in our room.

Friday, July 17th

This morning I attended Mr. Cairns' lecture on "The Place of Tra-dition in Art," the one that I had been most anxious to hear since first seeing the program for the chautauqua. I was rewarded not only by a fine discourse on that subject but also by an invitation to visit him in his studio on Monday.

I confess that my first impression of Mr. Cairns was rather unfavorable, as his appearance is not at all what one would associ-ate with one of the country's foremost painters. To be sure, he was flawless in his dress and has keen, intelligent-looking eyes. But he is of no more than medium height and very solidly built; it is much easier to picture him behind the counter of a dry goods store than it is before an easel or a lectern at an art academy. My misconcep-tion was soon put to rest, however, for his very first words showed him to be a very thoughtful and highly sophisticated person. Curi-ously, though, his appearance reflects one important aspect of his character—that he has kept something of the common touch with respect to art and those for whom it is intended.

He began by briefly recounting his own tutelage in painting.

As a boy in Indiana he had been able to obtain reasonably competent instruction from local painters, but he realized that if he were ever to become a true master of his craft he would have to study in Europe. Hence his extended stay at the Royal Academy in Munich, one of the leading art schools in the world. He returned to America with the conviction that there should be institutions of that caliber on our shores as well, that his countrymen should not have to go abroad in order to become first-rate artists. It was his hope also that the establishment of academies and the staging of exhibitions would foster an interest in art on the part of the public at large. Americans, he said, were at their core a thoroughly practical people with little time for the purely aesthetic; the day was coming, however, when they would have an instinct for beauty as well, when they would produce works of art to crown their more utilitarian achievements. Thus it was that he had devoted so much of his career to teaching. His efforts, in fact, went beyond the training of professional artists to include offering summer schools for interested amateurs—which is, of course, what had brought him to Leelanau for the season.

He recurred to his own experience in introducing the topic of tradition. As a student at the Royal Academy he had been steeped in the old masters, and his early paintings were very much in that vein—old masters in modern dress, as it were. As time went on, however, he began to evolve his own style: his palette became lighter, his brushstrokes broader and more rapid, his images less literal and more suggestive. Few would immediately recognize the painter of today in his early works. Still, a trained eye would be able to detect the influence of the old masters in the way in which he composed his scenes and the solidity that he imparted to the principal subjects. This was particularly true of his portraits and still lifes—the two genres that account for the preponderance of his commissions—but it was evident even in his less traditional works. Paying homage to a tradition, then, did not mean slavish imitation of an older style but rather conscious adaptation of it: "something old, something new," we might say.

As natural as this conception of tradition seemed, however, he had had some difficulty in conveying it to his students. Each generation, it seems, is anxious to efface the preceding ones and rushes to the attack, utterly failing to acknowledge its debts to them. These debts extend beyond mere technique to style itself, which for the most part seems to evolve in a natural way. Even dramatic changes in direction reflect a sort of evolution. Would the pre-Raphaelites, for instance, have been so adamant about precise details if they hadn't been reacting to the perceived gauziness of Sir Joshua Reynolds and his contemporaries in the eighteenth century?

Ironically, some of his students commit the sin not of extreme rebellion but of too strict an adherence to the approach of some favored contemporary artists, such as the so-called Impressionists now active in France. Here his duty was to persuade them that their work will find more favor if it appears in its own guise rather than that of another, that they will achieve nothing if they come to be seen merely as imitators of Renoir.

The mature artist, then, must attend to his own vision while being conscious of his place in the whole "sweep" of artistic endeavor. After all, all artists are in a real sense allies—their mission is to reveal important truths to their fellow beings in ways that are especially compelling. While the ways that are most appropriate for this purpose will change from age to age, and even the truths themselves will evolve to some extent, the artistic mission itself remains essentially unchanged.

When the lecture was over a crowd gathered at the podium, ostensibly to ask him questions but more, I thought, simply to bask in his celebrity. Figuring that it must be an awful bother for him, I chose not to join them. As it happened, however, I was to have a private audience with him in the afternoon.

I had set up my easel on the hotel lawn and was working on a pastel of the bay when I spotted him coming along the shore road. He saw me at about the same time and, to my surprise, changed course and came up the hill toward me. Begging my pardon for the interruption, he said that he had noticed me at his lecture and that his remarks had seemed to particularly register with me; from this he had guessed that I had a more than amateur interest in art. When I told him my profession he grew very excited, peppering me with questions about my approach.

I replied that, of course, my situation was quite different

from his, in that I was not training professional artists; my pupils were girls who would draw or paint for their own pleasure and, incidentally, as a way of attaining a deeper appreciation of art itself. Many of my lessons were necessarily devoted to technique, but in my art history lectures I try to take a broader view, pointing out the dominant themes in the different painters' work and their varied conceptions of themselves as artists. I also stress that no work of art is produced entirely in a vacuum—it has its own particular context, which includes not only the prevailing style at that time and place but also the expectations of the one who commissioned it and, perhaps most importantly, the artist's own evolving vision. I remind my pupils that every work of art is individual, that it has its own unique origins and purposes and is never merely a token of some technique or school. I encourage them to study each painting as carefully as if they were doing it themselves.

I felt a bit self-conscious in saying all this, as I had the distinct sense that it was just what Mr. Cairns would wish to hear. Still, it was all true, and I saw no reason to conceal it. "Excellent, excellent!" he responded, beaming broadly, when I was done. "You are getting your students to look deeply and not just parrot the conventional judgments." More modestly, I then said that I really could not tell how successful I had been in this. Nonetheless, he replied, I was leading the students in the right direction, and that counted for a great deal.

At that point he asked if he might see the piece that I was working on. I was reluctant to show it to him—although I believe my technique to be highly developed, my style is painstakingly realistic; my canvases tend to be exact reproductions without the imaginative touches that make for true art. But he was standing beside me before I could object.

He studied the drawing for a moment, then pronounced it "remarkable for its precision"; it was beautifully detailed, with brushstrokes as fine as Dürer's, "a highly polished piece of work withal." His praise pleased me, of course, though I noted that it was confined to the technical aspects. But then, I have never thought of myself as having true artistic inspiration—that is given to only a very few in each generation.

We talked a while longer, then he said that he really must be going. He would, however, like me to visit him in his studio after his morning classes on Monday if I wished and the time was convenient. Naturally, I was delighted and would make the time.

This evening I have been pondering something that I often tell my pupils: that beauty per se is not the sole aim of art—if by beauty we mean mere perfection of form. Lovely as a work of art may be, we would tire of it relatively quickly if it did not engage us emotionally, if it did not speak some truth to us. We would not linger over the Mona Lisa, for instance, if it were not for her enigmatic half-smile—an expression into which we can read our own hidden desires and uncertainties.

Monday, July 20th

I called on Mr. Cairns about two o'clock this afternoon.

His residence, located on a small cove a short way up the shore road, is the very essence of a fashionable summer house—light and airy with large, open rooms and full-length windows. A broad gallery runs the entire width of the house along the front; this is done in the soft hues of summer and, of course, hung with numerous paintings by Mr. Cairns himself and other contemporary artists.

He met me at the front door and, after allowing me a few moments to study the paintings in the gallery, escorted me to his studio out back. This, it turned out, was a converted boathouse with only a few, high windows. Though he might have had them enlarged, he prefers to work in subdued light and it keeps him from being distracted by the superb view across the bay. There is another advantage as well, it seems to me: the restricted visibility enhances the sound of the waves lapping against the shore, which must be very soothing even if one is not fully conscious of it.

As one might expect, the studio was crowded with paintings at various stages of completion. A few of these, including an imposing portrait of a Chicago industrialist, were commissions slated for delivery in the fall. The great majority, however, were of a more personal nature—portraits of members of his family and local scenes. Although a number of these would be offered for sale at various exhibitions over the winter, I sensed that he produced them primarily for his own pleasure. Those of which he was particularly fond, of course, would never go on the block.

In perusing the collection, I was particularly taken with the portraits of women; indeed, Mr. Cairns seems to have a gift for conveying the intricacies of thought and feeling underlying the sitter's external appearance. One of the most remarkable was a portrait of a comely, well-dressed woman in perhaps her early twenties. She is seen largely in profile, highlighting her finely wrought nose and chin. Though mostly in shadow, her eyes nonetheless have an alert, intelligent, but kindly look. One senses that she has some education and, though well placed socially, is determined not to lead the life that is customary for one of her class. There is a quiet resolve in her countenance, and perhaps a strong desire to effect improvements in the world.

The most charming of the portraits were the ones of his ten-year-old daughter, Milagro. She is rather plain, with a long face and nose, and her dark eyes have something of a melancholy look about them. But she is clearly the favorite child and, I am assured, exuberant enough when not forced to sit long hours for her father. Still, there is an element of sadness about her, and one hopes that life will be gentle with her.

One of the portraits was so unusual that it almost gave me a start: that of an Ottawa girl of about thirteen or fourteen. One is immediately drawn to the difference in physiognomy, the high cheekbones and other features so characteristic of her race. But the portrait is not, as so often happens, a "type"; rather, it is one of an individual to whom the artist is clearly sympathetic. The alertness and sensitivity of her eyes bespeak understanding beyond her years, her erect posture and the firm set of her jaw genuine pride in her people. But there is resignation in her countenance as well, a note of alienation and subjection. The contrast with the first portrait could not be more marked.

Mr. Cairns' local scenes were enjoyable as well. Here he has captured not only the picturesque details of places around Leelanau but the subtle and shifting moods of a summer's day in this distant northern region. In his portrayals of children playing along the shore and well-dressed ladies having tea on the terrace of a hotel, one senses the pure joys of the season, be they ebullient or leisurely. Conventional as such scenes are, our souls respond to them; they offer us comfort and the reassurance that there is yet happiness in the world.

The two scenes that most struck me were of a more equivocal nature, however. The first shows a lone party of tourists ascending a dune from the lee side. The light is rather subdued, and there is a strong wind off the lake; the woods in the background are dark and indistinct, almost threatening in their utterly primaeval character. It is a landscape in which humans seemingly have no place—the party should have chosen a milder day, when there would be more people about.

The second scene is more subtle. It shows a delivery wagon on a country road just after a heavy rain; dark clouds continue to roll across the sky and the air is heavy with moisture. There are, of course, no tourists abroad, just the lone driver contending with the swollen ruts in the road. This is Leelanau in the autumn, when the visitors have gone and the permanent residents face loneliness and the unrelenting harshness of the elements. It is as if the brilliant summer season were but a momentary illusion.

We spent perhaps forty-five minutes in the studio, though it seemed much longer owing to my complete absorption in the paintings. As Mr. Cairns guided me out, I thanked him profusely for the opportunity to visit him in his inner sanctum, adding that it was unusual for an eminent artist to grant such a privilege. I had expected him to take the compliment in stride, and to a degree he did; but then he grew decidedly wistful, remarking that one must not become too fond of glory. Sensing, perhaps, that I would conclude that I had given offense, he went on to explain: eminent as he might be, there were already signs that his day was passing. Certainly the current generation of art students was turning to other models, and it was only a matter of time before he lost favor with the public. There was, in fact, a predictable course that his future reputation would follow. He would retain some popularity as long as his own generation was still on the scene, perhaps a little longer. At some point, however, he would go into almost complete eclipse. Four or five decades later (if he were fortunate), he would be rediscovered and collections of his works exhibited in museums, but by then he would be a "historical figure" rather than a living artist. One's moment in the sun was necessarily brief, one must be content to have had it.

Brightening a little, he remarked that all this raised the question as to what his contribution had been, what he had managed to accomplish with his art. Early in his career he had been criticized for not aiming high enough in his choice of subject, for focusing on relatively ordinary people in familiar settings. There were in his work "no mountains, no presidents," as one prominent critic had put it. In time, of course, he had seen himself vindicated by public acceptance. In recent years, however, he had come under attack by a new school of artists asserting that his canvases were entirely too pretty, that they failed to portray the often-grim reality of things ("as if slums and industrial grime were the only proper subject for painting!"). Taken together, these two criticisms had revealed to him what had unconsciously been his aim from the beginning: to elevate the quotidian, to discover the beauty hidden within it. "Our lives, as a rule, are not grand, but there is a loveliness that attends things of which art—more than any other instrument—can make us aware. We have but to learn to perceive things aright."

I was about to compliment him for this profound insight, but he forestalled me with the suggestion that we leave off such serious conversation and retire to the courtyard for coffee. There we were joined by Mrs. Cairns, a pleasant, attractive woman with distinct Mediterranean features. Milagro even put in a brief appearance, coming up to ask her mother whether she and a friend might play on the beach until dinner time. She is a lovely child, a bit shy perhaps, but with an ethereal quality that makes it obvious why she has so often appeared in her father's work.

I had much to think about on my way home, but my chief impression was of being hugely confirmed in my profession. Only in works of thought and imagination does life achieve anything like perfection, and it is in service to this cause that I have spent much of my life. Though I have not scaled the heights that Mr. Cairns and other well-known artists have, my work has meant a great deal to me, and perhaps through me others will derive a sense of elevation as well. In this mood I took a renewed delight in my surroundings, in the soft evening light and the slight breeze gently rustling the branches overhanging the road.

Tuesday, July 21st

This morning I attended a lecture on contemporary European politics that was given by a retired diplomat. It is not a subject to which I ordinarily pay much attention, but in view of its prominence in the newspapers of late I thought that I should try to become better acquainted with it. The lecture was almost painfully dry, but I found it valuable nonetheless.

There were two principal themes. The first was perhaps the most significant development of the last two decades: the unification of the various German states, with Prussia at the core. This, of course, was brought about by the consummate skill of Otto von Bismarck, who engineered a general war with France for just this purpose. With that, there were three powerful autocratic states in Europe—Germany, Russia, and Austria–Hungary—and two essentially democratic ones—Britain and France. None of these nations fully trusts the others; the foreign policy of each is aimed at maintaining a rough balance of power, so that no nation will benefit from aggression against another.

The second theme followed directly from the first, namely, the tense and unbelievably complex relationships among the major powers. Here, I confess, I found the vast array of details rather difficult to follow. The main thrust is clear enough, however: the principal powers of Europe are engaged in a highly intricate sequence of moves and countermoves, each carefully calculated to secure an advantage (or to deny one to an opponent) without tipping the scales so much that it all degenerates into open conflict. With luck, they will continue to be successful at this game; otherwise, it is difficult to see how a major conflagration can be avoided. Even though peace had largely reigned since the fall of Napoleon, this could by no means be taken for granted.

On my way back I stopped in a little tea room. I had just been served when a woman whom I had seen at the lecture approached and asked if she might join me. She had caught my eye, I believe, because the opulence of her dress stood in such sharp contrast both to the occasion and to her plain, rather plebeian features. Her name is Phillips, and she is "in society" in Chicago. I gather not the very highest rung of society, for her every effort seems directed toward gaining entrée to that august station. In any event, her husband is a senior officer at the Board of Trade and will no doubt be its president before long.

To make conversation, I asked her what she had thought of the lecture. She replied that she had found it all very dull, that the organizers really should have taken pains to obtain a more engaging speaker. But then, she added, what was the point of such a lecture anyway? Europe was so distant and less and less important all the time. She had been there, of course, and admired its refinements and culture. But it lacked the "sheer dynamism" of America (I presume that she picked up this phrase somewhere, for it did not seem at all natural to her), which would soon put our country well ahead of it.

Seemingly without taking a breath, she changed the subject to the cottage that she and her husband were having built a little south of town. It would be one of the grandest in the area, but unfortunately would not be finished until next season; for the time being they would have to make do with a hotel. Of course, *she* would have preferred a more fashionable resort than Leelanau; they had only come here because her husband was so fond of "traipsing about in the mud after fish."

In the course of our conversation she did ask me a bit about myself, but I chose to answer in the simplest possible terms so as not to give her an opening. At the first opportunity I excused myself with a vague remark about having to meet someone for luncheon.

Thursday, July 23rd

General Grant died this morning. I got the news from a shopkeeper who was draping his window in black as I was returning from a walk south of town.

Even from a distance, it was obvious that something serious had occurred. There were very few people in the streets, and those there were seemed to have pressing business that they were trying to conclude as soon as possible; there was no lingering in front of shop windows or for idle conversation. The usually gay mood of the town had given way to a very subdued, indeed somber one, as if indulging in even the simplest pleasure would be a sacrilege at such a time.

The country remains in deep mourning. The initial shock is over, however, and people are beginning to circulate a bit more and (in quiet, respectful tones) to articulate their grief. Tomorrow's church services should be a real comfort, in that they will give that grief formal, public expression.

A few more details have emerged. The general was suffering from a cancer of the throat and had spent his last weeks at the home of a friend in the Adirondacks finishing his memoirs, so as to give his family a source of income after his death. To remain lucid enough to work, he often refused the morphine that would have alleviated his pain. He completed his task barely a week ago. The details of his funeral have not yet been announced, though it will undoubtedly be very elaborate, perhaps surpassing even Lincoln's.

I spent the better part of the morning in reading a lengthy remembrance in the local newspaper. Naturally, it focused on the war years, giving only a cursory account of his troubled presidency and his unfortunate career on Wall Street. That is only fitting, I suppose—it would be unseemly to dwell on the negative aspects of his life at this time. It does, however, raise the question as to how, in the end, we are to judge this man.

With his character and motives there can, of course, be no quibble. We must forever be grateful for his fortitude in pressing the war home and finally bringing it to an end. Then, too, he appears to have sought the presidency less out of personal ambition than to prevent the fruits of his military efforts from being dissipated by Southern resistance and Northern apathy. In terms of his personal qualities, he clearly stood apart.

With respect to his actions, however, we must be more critical. He clearly was not entirely equal to the task of governing, allowing his administration to be consumed by corruption and partisan interest. And even his military decisions are open to question: his attempt to bludgeon the Confederates into submission at the beginning of the 1864 campaign cost a good many men their lives—to my mind, quite needlessly. I own, though, that I cannot be completely objective about this.

It is qualified praise that we must grant him then, in my judgment. I wonder, though, whether any of our contemporaries would truly have been equal to such enormous tasks. Rarely are we given a statesman of real vision and ability; in most cases we just stumble along without a clear direction, conducting our affairs more or less badly.

In the midst of these reflections I received a bit of comic relief, in the form of an invitation from Mrs. Phillips to dine with them at their hotel on Monday evening. She had shown some ingenuity in locating me, as I had not told her where I was staying. We shall have to go, of course—courtesy demands as much.

Tuesday, July 28th

As I had expected, our dinner with the Phillipses last evening was a rather lavish affair. They had even engaged a private room off the main dining room and arranged with the chef to prepare a special menu (including fillets of trout that Mr. Phillips had caught just that morning). And, of course, there was no question of our paying for anything.

I had thought that the death of Grant would dominate the evening's conversation, but in fact most of it was devoted to affairs *chez eux*. Mr. Phillips, it turned out, had not been in the war; he had sent a substitute and spent the war years amassing the nucleus of his fortune by purveying dried beef to the army. He had avidly followed the various campaigns in the newspapers, however.

The only other part of the conversation that I recall distinctly had to do with Matthew's position at the firm. As a man of business, Mr. Phillips was naturally impressed by his vice presidency. Though Matthew, ever modest, tried to put this in perspective by noting that it was a rather small, tightly knit firm, Mr. Phillips brushed this aside: That was no matter at all, and by and by Matthew would "do better"—a man of ability and ambition had only to apply himself. Matthew nodded politely, but seemed relieved when the conversation turned in another direction.

Back in the privacy of our room I asked Matthew what he made of the evening. He immediately laughed out loud, as if to give expression to the absurdity of it all. Having given it a few moments' thought, however, he added that the experience, while not enjoyable, was unquestionably salutary for us, for we led a rather sheltered life in Westerly and were apt to forget how brash the larger world had become.

He paused briefly, then said that he believed he had observed Mr. Phillips before, in the company of his fishing guide. On that occasion he had been the soul of calm and patience, perfectly at ease in his surroundings and gratefully accepting the guide's advice. All of which suggested that this was the true version of him and the aggressive man of business merely a role that he had forced himself to play; or, more likely, that both traits resided in the same person, predominating at different times or maintaining a balance by some other, less obvious means.

Imprecise as this analysis was, there seemed to be wisdom in it. I would not be surprised if the same had been true of Henry Thornton. In any case, we are spared the duty of reciprocating the Phillipses' hospitality, as they left for home today. I made a point of sending them a note of thanks early this morning, so as not to have to be in possession of their address in Chicago or to give them mine.

Saturday, August 1st

Our final week in Leelanau has been quiet. I have attended only one lecture and done no socializing. I have, as it were, drawn a heavy cloak about myself, the better to bask in the warmth of my own company.

Pleasant as it has been here, I am anxious to be home. I am always uncomfortable being away for too long, and there is a distinct unreality to life here much of the time. Instinctively, I find myself rehearsing my autumn lectures in my head.

Tuesday, August 11th

My sixtieth birthday. If there is a threshold to old age, it is surely this. Yet I do not feel particularly aged—my health remains good, and I am blessed with looking a good deal younger than my years. So I shall not give this milestone more significance than it deserves.

The years have taken a toll in one respect, however: my reserves of energy are markedly diminished. Not that I can no longer be active, merely that I cannot go on and on without giving it a second thought, as if harnessed to a steam engine running at full speed. I have to concentrate my efforts on the most important tasks and pace myself in performing them; otherwise I shall soon wear myself out. This is a small price to pay, however, for continuing to share in the rich rewards of living.

Thursday, August 27th

With the beginning of the school year rapidly approaching, our focus now is on having everything in readiness. There has been a general meeting of the faculty, as well as one of the curriculum committee, which I head. I have also been putting the finishing touches on two new lectures that will come up early in the term. It has not been all work, however: I have found time to sketch, and putter in the garden, and otherwise indulge in the pleasures of the last days of summer.

Monday, September 7th

The start of school, with its customary excitement, confusion, and nervous energy. There was a real poignancy to Mrs. Marshall's opening address, as it is to be her last: she will be retiring at the end of the school year. This intelligence, of course, meant little to the girls and even the younger members of the faculty; but to those, like myself, who have a long association with her, it marks the end of an era. However subtly, life at the Academy will be different from now on. We are being rudely thrust into the future, where our place is not altogether certain.

The search for a new headmistress will commence soon. Several members of the board wanted to offer the position to me, but I convinced them that it would be better to have someone younger. I have, however, informally agreed to remain at the Academy until Mrs. Marshall's successor is firmly established. This entails no hardship for me, as I had no intention of relinquishing my post just yet in any case.

Friday, September 18th

A leisurely afternoon on the piazza. My work for the week done, I am luxuriating in the warmth of early autumn, the first hints of color in the earliest-turning leaves.

My classes are going well. The girls' enthusiasm has proved contagious, and it is with a real sense of mission that I introduce them to the sublimities of art. It is all new to them, of course, so that each advance in technique or aesthetic furnishes them with fresh marvels.

I have also had a letter from Lucy, the first in some weeks. She has decided to remain in Dayton, taking a small house near her sister's with extensive grounds that will give her some seclusion as well as a picturesque landscape. By now the circumstances of her leaving Westerly have become generally known, but everyone has been very kind; no one holds this against her, and she has been afforded numerous opportunities to join in the life of her new community. Although her natural reticence and lingering sense of shame have held her back to a degree, she is beginning to surmount those obstacles through charity work—which, in addition to being needful, can only earn her the respect of all.

Naturally, she would like me to visit as soon as possible. Anxious as I am to see her, I have decided to wait until the Christmas vacation; that way I will be able to spend an entire week with her.

Thursday, September 24th

I have spent the last four evenings reading the history of the regiment. I put this off until now in order to give it my full attention, to read this volume with the care—even reverence—that it deserves. As it happened, the events it describes are such an integral part of my own life that my mind wandered very little in any case.

Much of the volume consists of military history in the strictest sense; that is, it recounts the myriad movements of the regiment in some detail, with occasional references to the larger context. Thus, there are many sentences of the sort, "The regiment with its division advanced four miles on the morning of the 20th, halting at such-and-such a crossroads until late afternoon, then resuming its march." The long litany of such matter-of-fact details is, however, relieved by personal observations culled from the members' letters and journals. From this we gain a sense of the war as it was actually lived—of the heat and dust, the fatigue, the confusion, and, at times, the utter terror.

Thus we have the following description of the terrible fighting at Cold Harbor:

> Orders had been given for a general assault along the whole lines at half past four. The gray light of dawn was struggling through the thick envelope of clouds, and a light pattering rain was falling. All was still as the grave, yet in a few minutes the storm of battle was to burst forth along a stretch of six miles. At half past four the signal was given. Suddenly, from behind the rude parapets, there was an upstarting, a noiseless springing to arms, the hushed command of officers forming the lines. Swiftly the lines move to the attack. One, two, three, a dozen, a hundred shots break the silence; a roll, deep, heavy, prolonged, like the rush of a mighty river. Above the awful roll is heard the cannon—boom, boom, boom, five, ten, twenty, one hundred discharges in a minute. How it deepens. It is terrific, yet grand and sublime. The great reaper of death is out there upon that field, stalking unseen between the trenches, walking in darkness, bordered with lightning, showering it with leaden rain, making it the valley of the shadow of death. The battle was "quick, sharp, and decisive." In twenty minutes, the fierce charge, the deafening volleys of musketry, the thunder of artillery, the wild yell, and the battle is over. Twenty minutes after the first gun was fired, ten thousand Union troops lay stretched upon the sod, calm and still in death, or writhing with wounds. Our lines were repulsed at nearly every point with awful slaughter.

The concluding chapter is in a largely reflective vein. It enumerates the enormous sacrifices of our community in seeing the war through—of those on the home front as well as those in the ranks, those who came through unscathed as well as those who paid the ultimate price—commending their courage and selfless devotion. The final paragraph attempts to draw the moral from the whole experience:

> As a Nation, may we never learn war any more. May future generations never again be called on to enact its bloody drama. The curse of human slavery—the cause and pretext of the war—has forever been abolished, and the Nation has been purified by the fiery ordeal. Thank God, every star in the "dear old flag" is still there. Let us cherish this beautiful symbol of our National unity, baptized in the blood of heroes for its protection and perpetuity while the Government lasts, and the living millions are shadowed with its folds of stripes and stars.

An appendix lists the names of all those who served in the regiment, the officers first and then the men, company by company. I have read every entry, mentally rejoicing with the families of those who made it back unharmed and commiserating with the ones of those who did not. There were two entries to which I turned first, however. The first of these was:

> Carey, Matthew B., Capt., Company D: mustered out with the regiment June 25, 1865; additional duty, War Department, Washington City, 1865–1866.

And the second was:

> Reed, John T., Col. commanding: killed at Spotsylvania Court House, May 12, 1864; interred at Fredericksburg National Cemetery, Virginia.

Tuesday, October 6th

There is very sad news; four days ago the Judge suffered an apoplectic stroke and is now largely paralyzed on one side. We have only now been informed of this, as for some time his condition was quite precarious and his physician would not allow visitors. Then, too, Julia has been preoccupied with the arrangements for his care. A bed has been set up for him in the family parlor, where he collapsed; two nurses have been engaged to tend to him around the clock; and a strong man who works at the stable has been hired to come by and lift him when necessary. Julia has also been in contact with Reverend Williams.

I was permitted a brief visit this afternoon. Although the Judge appeared to brighten a little when I came into the room, in other respects he seemed frail and confused, his normally penetrating eyes glazed and unfocused. At Julia's suggestion ("just hearing your voice should be soothing to him," she said), I talked to him for a while, recounting the seemingly unimportant events of my life recently. I made a point, however, of mentioning upcoming events of common interest, so as to spark his anticipation and any healing powers that that might furnish. He listened calmly for perhaps five minutes, then closed his eyes and seemed to drift off into sleep, at which point Julia said that perhaps that was enough for today.

She and I spoke briefly as she was seeing me out. She is trying not to be overly optimistic about the Judge's prognosis. In time he may regain some of his functions, but it is unlikely that he will recover completely; both his age and the severity of the attack are working against him in that regard. In any case, there is little that we can do: "What will be, will be; it is in God's hands now. He has lived a long and fruitful life, and there shouldn't be any regrets."

I admire her strength and refusal to entertain illusions; these qualities serve her well. Still, I shall pray for the Judge and hope that life will grant him a few more good years.

Saturday, October 24th

There has been modest improvement in the Judge's condition. Though still largely immobile and unable to speak clearly, he seems much more alert and attuned to his surroundings. His keen eyes followed me closely as I was talking to him this morning, and I had the sense that his mind is as good as ever.

All the same, this incident has caused me to think about death a good deal and to imagine a world without the Judge. His passing would leave me very sad, of course, and life in our village would be the poorer for the loss of his guiding hand. But I would accept it, would see it as part of the order of things and cherish the fact that I had the privilege of knowing him. The world would go on refashioning itself in any case—it may be our alma mater for a time, but ultimately it leaves us by the wayside.

The ability to contemplate death calmly is one of the gifts of age, it seems to me. To a child, death is unspeakably tragic; it tears such a hole in his world that he cannot see how life can possibly go on. When I was seven, for instance, I came across a dead sparrow in the garden and was inconsolable for several days; each time I thought about it there would be fresh tears. Only by taking my mind off it was my mother able to lessen my anguish.

By the time one is my age, however, he will have encountered many deaths, some of which will have touched him quite deeply. But he will then have more perspective on death; it will sadden him, but it will no longer throw him completely off course. In this way, I suspect, life prepares each of us for his own passing.

As it happens, Nature would probably not approve of such somber thoughts just now, as the days this month have been truly heaven sent: pleasantly warm, with clear, deeply blue skies. So vexatious at other times, she now seems to be quietly celebrating the completion of her work. By any measure it is the high point of the year, summoning us to satisfaction and great joy.

Wednesday, November 4th

The Judge has been taken from us. He suffered a second stroke about one this afternoon and expired not long after.

I received the news from a neighbor when I was almost home from the Academy. I took a few moments to settle my things, then closeted myself in my bedchamber. I wept for a while; then, the first wave of grief having passed, I found myself staring vacantly at the objects in the room—the bed, the chest of drawers, the fireplace, the mirror—as if in an attempt to regain possession of the solid world.

Intellectually, of course, I had always acknowledged the possibility that this might happen; but I had never really believed it, less and less so as time went on and the Judge showed signs of recovery. In this I had given myself false comfort, and been brutally disillusioned.

The remedy was action. I went to my desk and penned a short note to Julia; the funeral this Saturday will be fairly elaborate, and there will be many things with which she will require assistance. I then set about straightening up the house and preparing a simple dinner. Matthew, I was sure, would come by when his day's work was finished, and I wanted to have things ready.

Sunday, November 8th

The Judge's funeral was splendid, if one may use that term in connection with so somber an event. The predominant tone was one of celebration, and in giving due honor to this pillar of our community we all received a measure of uplift.

The day did not begin auspiciously. There was heavy rain in the morning, which turned into a light but steady drizzle by noon, when we gathered at the Judge's house for the procession to the church. All of the gentlemen, of course, had their heads uncovered, and only the most elderly and infirm availed themselves of umbrellas; Julia softly but firmly refused the offer of one.

When everyone had gathered, the color guard was called to attention and the Judge's coffin (a simple affair of pine boards stained a dark green and ornamented only by a few late-season wildflowers) was carried out and placed in the hearse. We then formed into our line of march: the color guard first, followed by the hearse, Julia (escorted by the mayor), the Judge's closest friends and associates, and finally other townspeople. All through the procession a drummer beat a slow, steady cadence, a sort of *marche funèbre* accompanied only by the sounds of carriage wheels, horses' harnesses, the slow tramping of many feet, and the rain. It was nearly three-quarters of an hour before we arrived at the church and got settled in our places.

When the room was perfectly silent, Mr. Williams rose and directed us to the service for the dead. I have always found this service to be particularly meaningful. It acknowledges our grief but urges us to look at death in a larger context, affirming the merits of each complicated life and its necessary place in the scheme of things. Above all, it enjoins each of us so to live that, when our own time comes, we can look back with the assurance that we gave full measure, that we were a distinct credit to ourselves and those around us.

The eulogy was one of the finest that I have heard Mr. Williams give. The opening words, in particular, had the quality of an epic poem in the slow, stately way in which he uttered them: "Thomas Sewall Halston was born on the 30th day of December, 1799, at Portsmouth, New Hampshire, into a family of merchants and seafarers long settled in that place."

Much of the Judge's life story was familiar. As a boy he was educated mainly by private tutors, though the most valuable element of his education was unquestionably the reading that he did in his father's extensive library. He early acquired a facility in Latin and with it entrée to the finest writings in that tongue; he was particularly fond of Cicero and Livy, and read them by the hour. He mastered the English classics as well; to the end of his life he sought out Shakespeare and Milton in his more serious hours, Pope and the other Augustans in his lighter ones.

Nor was the practical side of his education neglected. As he grew older he assisted his father in the latter's trading business, immersing himself in the details of shipping and insurance. He later said that the painstaking attention his father gave to contracts first kindled his interest in the law.

His early years, however, were not all work. He played games with other boys his age and was fond of practical jokes. Indeed, his enormous energy and high spirits occasionally got him into trouble. On the whole, however, he was seen as a young man of solid character who had good prospects.

At the age of seventeen he matriculated at Harvard College, where he did well. Early on, his professors recognized in him a rare mental acuity and seriousness of purpose. His probing mind and refusal to take anything merely on their say-so proved to be something of a liability, however; more than one of them was no doubt vexed by his constant challenges. It was probably on this account that he failed to obtain first honors.

Upon being graduated, he took up a clerkship in a law office in Springfield, Massachusetts, which lasted three years. His days were devoted to running various legal errands for the partners, his evenings to reading cases. He once said that those were among the happiest days of his life—how he looked forward to returning to his rooms, lighting his lamp, and opening his law books, to read until late into the night. At each session he peeled back another layer or two of the mystery surrounding the law; little by little it all became clear. The partners took care to guide him in his studies, rewarding him with greater and greater responsibilities as his knowledge grew. In the end, all of these efforts paid handsome dividends: the Judge was admitted to the bar with ease.

He remained with the firm in which he had served his apprenticeship for several more years; then, feeling that he had mastered his craft, he set off on his own. The surfeit of attorneys in the eastern states led him to conclude that he would do better to move west. It was at that time that Westerly was being settled, and there was much hubbub about it in Springfield. The Judge decided to cast his lot with the settlers; he arrived here in the early summer of 1826.

In those days, of course, there wasn't enough legal work to support him. To make ends meet he first kept a school, then used his commercial connections to open a store purveying building materials. This proved to be very successful, netting him a good income until he could devote himself entirely to the practice of law.

Over the next few years he acquired the attributes by which he was best known to us: he married Julia Ward, another early settler whom he had known in Springfield; he built his fine, Federalist house; he became a judge; and in sundry ways he made himself one of the most important and most respected men in the village. The only shadows at this time were the deaths of his two children, both in infancy.

Mr. Williams then turned to the Judge's character. To a great extent, that was rooted in the notions of the last century. He never really adopted the idealism of our age, remaining "charitably skeptical" of man and his proclivities. Chuckling a bit (and apparently departing from his text), Mr. Williams added that he wasn't certain how much of Emerson the Judge had actually read—of modern authors, Dr. Holmes seemed to be his only kindred spirit. He then recounted an anecdote in which he and the Judge were out for a walk early one morning and happened upon a girl of ten or eleven milking a cow in a farm yard. This brought to the Judge's mind a poem in the *Autocrat of the Breakfast Table* in which Dr. Holmes mocks the overuse of Latinate words (and, by extension, the over-intellectualization of the commonplace). In a booming voice the Judge recited the line

Effund thy albid hausts, lactiferous maid!

Both the girl and the cow looked utterly perplexed, but all the same the "milk-bearing maiden" continued to "pour forth" her "white draughts."

On the bench he was known as a paragon of fairness and sound judgment. He viewed the law not as an arbitrary authority to be followed in the most excruciating detail but as an instrument of social harmony. Thus he did not hesitate to intervene when justice seemed to require as much. The best-known instance of this was a very divisive case in which the attorneys for both sides had fanned the flames of suspicion and ill feeling in their presentations of the evidence. Before the closing arguments he summoned them to his chambers and told them in no uncertain terms that he did not know how the jury's verdict would go—"though they would be fully justified in not believing either of you"—but that any one-sided verdict would leave bad blood for years to come. He then proposed a settlement, which his acid gaze compelled them to accept.

He was equally judicious with respect to the great questions of the day. He abhorred slavery and joined an abolitionist society while still in his twenties. It was his hope, however, to remove this scourge through gradual emancipation, as had been done in the Northern states. He was appalled by the depredations of John Brown, and deeply saddened when the country descended into civil war. In his view it would bring much suffering but no true resolution of the issue. Twenty-some years on, his fears seemed to have been all too justified.

In concluding, Mr. Williams observed that in losing the Judge we had lost not only a faithful friend and a trusted counselor but also an important part of our heritage. There were few of the original settlers still with us now. With their passing we were losing our anchor, the spirit of hope and uncompromising integrity that had guided us for so long. Change was inevitable in any case, but it would unquestionably be more difficult without our touchstone.

The rain had stopped and there was a narrow band of clear sky along the western horizon by the time we filed out for the final prayers at the graveside. These concluded, the mourners began to drift away. Julia, however, was reluctant to leave; she kept staring down at the coffin as if recognizing that she would never see even this sober vestige of her husband again in life. She was persuaded to come away only when it became apparent that the grave diggers were anxious to get the grave closed before dark.

It had been arranged that Julia, in company with a few close friends, would have a quiet supper with the Sims afterwards. This proved to be very enjoyable, a more light-hearted counterpoint to the solemn ceremony earlier in the day. We told many stories about the Judge, and laughed as much as we wept. At length, however, Julia grew quite tired and Matthew and I escorted her home.

This morning it is clear and much colder. The rain brought down most of the remaining leaves, and the ground is now littered with wet mats of them. The sky is more open, however, so that there seems to be more light. In a curious way it is as if the drift toward winter has been arrested and we might soon expect the spring.

We know better, however. Whatever solace Nature may seem to extend to us this morning, there is a vacancy in her countenance that hints at our insignificance to her. The world will cycle on with or without the Judge, and we with it, regardless of our vaunted accomplishments and all of our refined sentiments.

V. 1898

Thursday, September 22nd

I have spent an agreeable afternoon on the piazza, reading, answering letters, and simply reflecting on things, mostly small and unimportant ones. The days are still rather warm, such that it tends to be uncomfortable unless one is in the shade. And in any case I am enjoined from strenuous activity by a weak heart.

The change in my health is the only obvious sign of advancing age. My mind remains sharp, and my appearance vigorous and younger than my seventy-three years. Even the condition of my heart is only evident on occasion. Though I tire more easily now, I seldom experience pain or shortness of breath; thus I am able to put it out of my mind much of the time. Still, it has meant significant changes in many aspects of my life: I have given up my position at the Academy and all but a couple of my private pupils; I have greatly curtailed my work in the community, with the result that I am increasingly losing touch with day-to-day life in Westerly; and worst of all, I can no longer indulge in the long walks that I have always found so refreshing.

Thus I am principally an observer of life these days. This is not as great a change for me as it has been for some others, as I have always relished those quiet moments when my only occupation was studying the passing scene. For as long as I can remember, I have made a point of pausing occasionally in my work to take in my surroundings. This, of course, has given me a welcome respite from my task as well as the sensuous delights of, say, the flowers on my table or the dappled sunlight on the lawn. But it has had another salutary effect as well: it has served to *locate* me in my particular setting. In this way I have become aware not only of the letter I was writing but also of myself as the agent behind this, that is, as a woman working at her desk in an attractively furnished room on a sunny afternoon—this being but one of many activities currently going on in the village. For reasons I cannot articulate, such perceptions give me a real sense of comfort, as if without them I could not be certain of the reality of things and of my place within them. If anything, the forced inactivity of recent years has sharpened my powers of observation—in addition to giving me much food for thought.

Not that there are not moments when I am listless and out of sorts, when the world seems shopworn and colorless and I can find little pleasure or even interest it. Although I have experienced such melancholia occasionally throughout my life, it seems to have become more frequent in the last few years. Indeed, I find myself more emotional overall these days, as if a lifetime of assaults on my nerves has worn them down. At the most distressing times, perspective seems to be my strongest ally—I counsel myself that such moments are really an insignificant part of my life, which remains uncommonly rich in most other ways. And although I can no longer counter these moments with vigorous activity, I can still seek distractions from the somber current of my thoughts, and this is often an effective antidote. Yet even so, dark moments remain a persistent facet of my life.

Externally, of course, there have been many changes and this, too, is somewhat unsettling. The village has grown measurably and lost no small part of its small, intimate character. Many of the newcomers are immigrants from abroad whom I do not know, even by sight. One hears half a dozen unfamiliar tongues on the streets now, and there are whole areas of village life of which the original settlers no longer have any cognizance.

To be sure, there are fewer such persons with each passing

year. Julia Halston has died, and George Sims, and Cynthia Edwards. Others are in frail health or have moved away for one reason or another. Though still in reasonable health, Matthew's mother has suffered such deterioration of her mind that she now requires assistance around the clock. This has proved to be difficult for him, the feeling of helplessness especially, as he has always been one to tackle problems head-on. He is trying to be stoical about it, however, and I provide what support and comfort I can.

Of all the changes wrought by time, the retirement of our minister, Mr. Williams, has been the most distressing for me. Though I can well understand his desire to spend his last working years compiling a volume of his best sermons for posterity, in a real sense he was the church for me—the one who guided us through all the difficult years of our great national turmoil. The new man is sincere enough, but he is not in any sense one of "us"; he cannot speak with authority to our generation because he has not been party to our experiences. And, in fact, he seems to address himself mainly to his own generation.

It is said that one's world contracts as he ages, that he becomes more and more absorbed in his own concerns and less and less involved with (or even aware of) things outside himself. If so, this is not due solely to the decline in his powers. At least as great a role is played by the fact that his thoughts and perceptions are no longer seen as relevant in any way. His day has passed; time has brought others to the fore. Though it is seldom spoken of, I imagine that this is the greatest source of unhappiness among older persons.

I must leave this off now, as Marta has summoned me to dinner; she sets it on the table just before leaving for the day. I am fortunate to have a full-time housekeeper again after several years of having to manage without one. She is only seventeen but very diligent; indeed, she has taken charge of the household with a sure hand, more often than not anticipating what needs to be done next before she is told. Her one limitation is her rather poor command of English (she is Czech, the daughter of a new craftsman at the firm). At times I have tried to work little English lessons into the day. She listens politely but seems anxious to get on with her work. In view of her age and inexperience with things in this country, her parents prefer that she continue to live at home for the time being. If all goes well, however, in a year or two she will probably live in.

Sunday, September 25th

An enjoyable day with Matthew. I see him less frequently now that he is president of the firm, but we usually manage to spend Sundays together if nothing else. He is 65 now, but apart from his graying hair shows little sign of his age. Still trim and energetic, he carries himself with quiet confidence. And time has wrought no diminution of his most attractive feature: his keen, intelligent-looking eyes.

We had thought that we might go for a drive in the country this afternoon (in deference to my health, Matthew has acquired a small carriage with which to take me places), but as the day turned out to be rather sultry we elected to remain at home instead. So, after luncheon we settled ourselves on the piazza to peruse the various newspapers to which I subscribe.

Matthew, of course, makes a point of staying up with the business news, and though he often finds the political news exasperating he follows that avidly as well. At one point, after we had been reading for perhaps an hour, he lifted his head from the page and stared off into space as if reflecting on a difficult problem. Then, as he often does when he wishes to share his thoughts, he turned to me with a look that seemed to ask whether he might interrupt.

It turned out that he had been reading about the negotiations with Spain concerning the termination of the recent war, and that there is much debate as to the position the United States should take. There seems to be little question that Cuba is to have complete independence; our strong sympathy with the oppressed people of that island admits of no other outcome. The fate of the Philippines is another matter, however. It is true that after a brief flirtation with the idea of empire most Americans have lost their taste for it. Still, there is a widespread feeling that as an advanced nation the burden of governing the Filipinos naturally falls to us. Then, too, it is highly likely that if we do not take possession of these islands another major power will (the German navy has been dogging our every move in the area since our victory at Manila Bay, and other countries seem to have a serious interest in them as well). To further complicate matters, any foreign power is apt to face an insurrection by the natives, who appear to have little desire to remain a colony under any circumstances.

"I suppose that we should accept responsibility for the Philippines," Matthew said at length and with no small amount of resignation in his voice, "but we may well come to regret getting involved in such adventures to begin with." Of course, we were no longer a relatively insignificant nation with the luxury of distancing ourselves from world affairs; but we had to be careful, for international affairs are both complex and treacherous.

We had a simple supper about half past five, then took a short turn in the orchard. Matthew then went home to prepare for the coming week.

Wednesday, September 28th

This afternoon I received my invitation to the dedication of the monument to the regiment, which is to take place the 22nd of next month. A "place of honor" has been reserved for me in view of my husband's prominent position in the regiment.

I understand that the ceremony itself is to strike a rather solemn note, much like that on Decoration Day. It is also to be fairly brief; there is to be only one principal speaker, a well-respected historian from the state university who saw service during the war, and the only music will be that provided by the regimental bugler. A number of private gatherings have been planned, however, and in the evening there is to be a concert of patriotic music in the town hall, so that the day will have an element of celebration as well.

Naturally, I am pleased that the regiment is to be honored in this way. The Civil War was the central event of the lives of those in my generation, and excepting the Revolution, the most significant event in our country's history. It is only fitting that there be a permanent reminder of it—and the immense suffering and sacrifice it entailed—in the town square. But the erection of this monument occasions some sadness in me as well. For the losses that I and others have incurred; for Cynthia Edwards, who worked tirelessly on behalf of the monument but who did not live to see the full fruits of her efforts; and lastly because, in a real sense, it marks the passing of my generation. For it is only as significant numbers of us are beginning to leave the stage that these monuments are being raised, as if we feared being lost to the memory of those who follow; without question, these granite and bronze structures are our gravestones.

Thursday, October 6th

The temperature dropped into the low forties overnight, the first sign of the impending change of seasons. As the house seemed very chilly when I got up, I lit the fire in the parlor and took my coffee in there, wrapped in a heavy shawl. The sun was just above the horizon when I settled into my chair; I watched enraptured as, little by little, the room became suffused with a soft, roseate-tinged light that not only promised a fine day but also stilled my soul in the way that is unique to natural beauty. I sighed when I heard Marta at the door and realized that this special moment was over, that the "work day" would now begin. Such moments, however, are all the more precious for being so fleeting, and we must take care to give them a secure place in our memory.

The day, in fact, turned out to be quite pleasant and to offer another memorable moment as well. By early afternoon it was comfortably warm, allowing me to do some watercolors on the piazza. My subject was to be the last remaining roses from the bushes along the western edge of the property—the small, pale-cream ones that my grandfather had cultivated with such care—but when I cut them I realized that they were too far gone to make a pleasing picture. Thinking that I could at least salvage some of their scent, I pulled the petals off one by one and arranged them loosely in a small cut-glass bowl. In doing so I discovered how incredibly soft they were—much more so than their blighted appearance would suggest, like pieces of the finest velvet. Over and over I cupped them in my hand, then let them drip through my fingers, luxuriating in the delicate sensation on my skin.

At length I observed that the inner sides of the petals were still quite fresh and that by positioning them in the right way I could produce an attractive composition. Enough of the brown and withered edges would show to set off the perfectly ripe "flesh" of the rest. It took no small effort to capture the many subtle variations in color, texture, and sheen, but in the end I was satisfied with the result. At first glance the composition has a certain abstract quality, as if it were a pure design rather than a representation of actual objects. It is not long, however, before the eye resolves the various curves and scallops into the familiar parts of a flower—though one seen from a highly unusual perspective.

Tuesday, October 11th

The arrangements for the dedication of the monument are proceeding apace, and the general excitement is growing by the day. Though it is the sort of event in which I would once have played a major role, I am content to be merely a spectator; it is time that younger hands take charge of our village rituals.

The mayor has asked if he might read a brief excerpt from one of my husband's letters as part of his opening remarks; the letter in question includes a summary of an address to the regiment shortly before the opening of the 1864 campaign. There was no need for him to ask, as virtually the entire letter was published in the *Clarion* at the time. Still, it is courteous of him, and I shall send a formal note giving my permission.

Wednesday, October 19th

I have resumed my study of Plutarch. I began this several years ago, when Matthew presented me with a deluxe scholarly edition of the complete works in Greek, complete with copious notes. I generally devote two to three mornings a week to it throughout the cooler months, when I am indoors much of the time.

By now I have largely worked my way through the *Parallel Lives*, the sequence of biographies of prominent political and military figures from classical times. To my delight, I have acquired a real facility with this author, reading him almost as easily as I would one in English. Only occasionally do I have to pause to look up a word or tease out the meaning of a difficult passage, and even then it is usually because the idea in question is entirely unfamiliar to me. Of course, it helps that Plutarch writes in a rather easygoing, conversational way, employing numerous anecdotes to make his point. In this he is much more like a popular lecturer than an academic historian whose work will be read only within ivy-covered walls.

Notwithstanding the informality of Plutarch's style, his purpose is entirely serious: to delineate the principles of statecraft and the character of the ideal leader. This is the thread that runs through all fifty of the biographies. Each figure, through his essential traits, contributes to a growing mosaic—be it as an illustration of prudence or impetuosity, endurance or vacillation, faithfulness or self-dealing. Taken as a whole, the *Parallel Lives* is as much a treatise on public morality as a history.

There is, of course, much to lament in the individuals portrayed. One cannot begin to tally the suffering caused by the all-too-common desire for dominance and the willingness to put self above others, even above country. Yet as the *Lives* make clear, societies, too, are subject to willful madness. Witness Athens' reckless attempt to forge a commercial empire in the fifth century (which ultimately led to her defeat by Sparta in the Peloponnesian War) and Sparta's subsequent attempt at dominance (which led to *her* defeat by Thebes and ultimately to the subjugation of all of Greece by Macedonia). Cautionary tales that far transcend their own time and place.

As yet I have spent little time with Plutarch's other great work, the *Moralia*, a collection of philosophical essays on a wide range of subjects in the manner of Cicero and other prominent authors of antiquity. Though some of the subjects now seem dated, I would expect these essays to be as thoughtful and engaging as the *Parallel Lives*. I will gladly consider Plutarch's counsel in these areas, too.

If there is one thing that I have gleaned from my study of ancient Greece—surpassing even the importance of balance—it is the primacy of understanding. For it is only through a genuine understanding of things, one that is firmly rooted in both reason and experience, that we can hope to truly live well. In addition to enabling us to achieve our ends and avoid catastrophes, understanding offers us a certain comfort, a measure of reassurance in the face of difficult situations; even the most horrific events are more tolerable when we have some comprehension of them, when we can fit them into at least a moderately coherent picture of things. Sadly, however, Wisdom—truly the greatest of the Greek goddesses—receives too little worship even now.

Sunday, October 23rd

The dedication of the monument was very fine, but it proved to be more emotional for me than I had anticipated.

Matthew called for me about an hour before the ceremony was to begin, so as to allow time for him to get me settled in my place and take the carriage over to Meredith's (where we were to have dinner afterwards) before the square became too crowded. It was not an ideal day, cool and overcast with a steady wind from the north—the sort of day on which most of us would ordinarily have remained indoors by the fire. I was glad that I had thought to wear a heavy coat, but even then I felt chilled when the wind picked up.

The square, of course, had been nicely done up for the day's events. The monument, naturally, is at the center, facing south. Around it, on three sides, were rows of folding chairs aligned almost as precisely as soldiers in formation. Someone had evidently taken great care to place them in such an exact pattern. A little to the right of the monument was the speakers' platform, to the left the flags of the United States, the state of Ohio, and the regiment itself. Everywhere there was red, white, and blue bunting—on the podium and the railing around the speakers' platform, the lampposts around the square, the doorways and windows of the courthouse and town hall, even many of the storefronts on the surrounding streets.

My early arrival gave me the opportunity to study the monument in detail. It consists of a single figure: a private on patrol, his rifle held crosswise in front of him, his head turned slightly to the left and his eyes alert to some disturbance in the distance. A good deal of thought went into the selection of this design. As one might expect, some on the committee had initially favored a mounted figure or at least one at the height of battle. In the end, however, it was agreed that the best way to honor those who had borne the burden of the war most directly would be to portray an ordinary soldier at a relatively routine task, a task that nonetheless might prove to be fatal and that thus required his utmost diligence and courage. This design has been well received by those who served in the regiment; any number of them have expressed the view that, frightened as they were in the face of known dangers, it was the moments of utter uncertainty that most unnerved them.

The pedestal is a rectangular block about seven feet in height. On the front are three lines of text: the name of the regiment, followed by

WAR OF THE REBELLION, 1861–1865

and then

"FAITHFUL UNTO DEATH."

On the other three sides, in chronological order, are the names of the engagements in which the regiment was involved, ranging from major battles that are so well known as to have become household words to small skirmishes remembered only by those who were actually involved in them. The overall number of engagements was greater than I would have guessed; the regiment was under fire more times than is generally realized.

Although I read each name with care, pausing a moment before moving on to the next one, my eye was instinctively drawn to the place where "Spotsylvania Court House" was entered when I reached the section devoted to the engagements of 1864. I lingered there a few moments, my emotions taking possession of me; not grief of the conventional sort, but an infinite sadness that so much that might have been—that under normal circumstances almost certainly *would* have been—had been precluded forever. Without really intending to, I extended my hand and ran my fingers over the letters, uttering a silent prayer as I did so. Simple as this act was, it served to ground me again, and I calmly resumed reading the names of the engagements. Before taking my seat, however, I glanced once more at that quaint, old-fashioned place name that would have seemed so perfectly charming were it not for the grim reality that it represents.

By this point a large crowd had gathered and the ceremony was set to get under way. The section immediately in front of the monument was reserved for members of the regiment, of whom there were quite a number. Matthew was in the third row, the first two being set aside for those with physical impairments. The civilian guests of honor were seated in the first few rows of the sections on either side of the monument. I was pleased to have a good view, as the crowd was much greater than expected, filling the entire square and spilling over into the streets and onto the far sidewalks.

The ceremony began with the regimental bugler's playing of reveille, the sounds with which the soldier's day starts. He played it somewhat more slowly than usual, so that it had the character of a stately march rather than an urgent summons to duty. Even so, it seemed to stir those who had heard it so many times under vastly different circumstances.

There followed several short speeches, including the mayor's opening remarks and those by our state representative as well as Major Upshaw, the person who became second in command of the regiment when the command passed to Henry Thornton.

These preliminaries concluded, the mayor introduced the principal speaker, Benjamin C. Smith, professor of American history at the state university. He was a rather slight man, though completely erect in his bearing and very neat and precise in his dress. This, and the unchanging gravity of his expression, clearly marked him as a serious scholar. The son of a shopkeeper in Indiana, he had early shown academic promise and entered college at 16, being graduated in the summer of 1861. He immediately enlisted in his local regiment, serving in the Army of the Tennessee for four years and rising to the rank of lieutenant colonel. Following the war, his course seemed quite clear: to refine his knowledge of history and assist his countrymen in understanding the events of their times. After some preliminary studies in Europe, he received an advanced degree from Yale and began his present career. He is now one of our leading historians, having done much to advance American history as a distinct field of study. His work, however, has not been confined to the library and lecture hall; he has sought out numerous occasions, such as the present one, to bring the insights of historians to the public at large.

Indeed, his style was markedly different from that to which we are accustomed on such occasions—more that of a lecture than that of a solemn oration. Simple and direct, it was devoid of the rhetorical flourishes—hollow at best and at worst utterly false—to which many speakers resort to produce an effect on their audience. But by no means did his remarks lack force: his rigorous logic and utter conviction as to the rightness of what he was saying drove every point home.

The first part of the speech was actually relatively conventional. He recounted the history of the regiment at some length, stressing the numerous hardships that soldiers suffer even under the best of circumstances. To this, however, he was able to add one new fact based on a statistical analysis that he had conducted: the regiment had incurred higher numbers of dead and wounded than many other units in similar situations. Thus, our extraordinary devotion and valor were more than a subjective impression— they were fully attested by "the lengthy roster of the dead and wounded."

It was, however, the second part of the speech that was the most memorable and that raised it to the level of true significance. There were, he said, two grave threats to our efforts to create an enduring memorial to the regiment. The first was simply time itself. In as little as fifty years nearly all of the regiment's members would be gone, along with many of those who had known them personally. At that point, the monument (here he paused to study it quietly for a few seconds) would tend to become merely a fixture on the square. Though our descendants would grasp its meaning intellectually, they would have no vital feeling for it—it would carry no more emotional weight than, say, a portrait of Tecumseh or one of the first settlers.

Time, of course, is the great ravager and ultimately cannot be overcome. Still, we had a duty—to those whom we were commemorating today, and even more so to those who would come after us—to resist it as strenuously as possible. Though our nation had been involved in other wars and in all probability would be again, none could have nearly the significance of one of brother against brother. Therefore, each year, as part of our Decoration Day observance, we should make a point of gathering by this monument and "consecrating it anew" as a symbol of the preservation of the union, that is, of our very existence as a nation.

The second threat was more immediate and indeed more insidious, though ironically far less evident. In recent years a real camaraderie had developed among all those who had fought in the war—regardless of the side that they were on—and it was now common for them to hold joint reunions at Gettysburg and the sites of other major battles. To be sure, it was well that the old hatreds be allowed to fade; unfortunately, however, their place was being taken by the belief that all who served, Southern as well as Northern, were part of a single, glorious cause. Not so, he said; not so at all. One side had fought for the liberty of all people, the other against that very principle. It was a crucial difference, one that could not be glossed over no matter how great the fellow-feeling. This, too, we must not forget, however many years were to pass.

With these sobering thoughts he concluded his speech and took his seat. For a time there was complete silence, as if no one were sure what was to come next or wished to disturb the gravity of the moment with ceremonial formalities that could only seem trivial by comparison. At length, however, the mayor rose, expressed the town's great appreciation to Professor Smith for such "compelling" words, and asked the minister to lead us in prayer. The ceremony concluded with the bugler's playing of taps. The slow rising and falling of those simple, three-note sequences have always had a haunting quality for me, particularly at the close, when they seem to usher in a perfect if hard-won peace; inevitably, the final words—"safely rest, … God is nigh"—sounded in my head like an echo from the furthest recesses of the soul. Only then, it seemed to me, had we fully acknowledged the task that Professor Smith had laid before us.

It took some time for me to meet up with Matthew and Meredith, as there was considerable milling about on the part of people anxious to get a closer look at the monument or to greet friends. Finally the square cleared enough for us to make our way to the warmth and comfort of her house, which were most welcome after the rawness and intensity of the afternoon.

Over dinner we discussed the afternoon's events, and particularly the professor's speech. Meredith was of the opinion that "negative elements" had no place in such a speech, that it should have sounded a more uplifting note. From the conversations that she had overheard, many others appeared to feel that way as well. She asked me for my opinion, but sensing that Matthew had something important to say, I deferred to him. Diplomatic as always, he agreed that the professor's remarks would probably seem inappropriate to many. As a veteran of the war, however (and here he thought that he could speak for many of his comrades), he appreciated the professor's honesty and found his words more meaningful than purely conventional ones would have been. The work "so nobly begun" by the regiment was not finished, and in carrying it forward we would honor them more effectively than we ever could by rituals alone.

Meredith acknowledged the point but maintained that Professor Smith might have chosen his words more carefully. Partly to change the subject, I remarked that for me the most poignant moment of the speech was the rather offhand mention of the other wars in which our nation has been involved. This immediately brought to mind the war with Mexico and all that it had represented at the time—the euphoria that most of us had felt as the young, vigorous nation asserted its full power for the first time, defeating the corruption of the old Spanish system and forestalling the designs of several European powers on the western lands. How vividly I recall the wild celebration when word came (in late September, 1847) that our forces had taken the heights of Chapultepec and that the capital would soon fall. It seemed that Divine Providence had indeed laid out a glorious destiny for us and that there were no limits to what the United States might achieve. Ironically, for a time it was even thought that that war would be the signal event of our generation, the one for which all future generations would remember us. Now, I suspect, it will go down in history merely as a prelude to the Civil War, to which it led more or less directly—that is, if it is not eclipsed altogether.

Both Meredith and Matthew were sensibly touched by this thought, that things had turned out so very differently than we expected and that we actually had little control over events. Not surprisingly, it was Matthew, with his deep knowledge of history, who best expressed the enormous irony of the situation: The City of Mexico, he said, had formally surrendered on the 17th of September. Fifteen years later to the day, many of those who were there found themselves on opposite sides at Antietam; *that* day was to become the single bloodiest one in our nation's history.

The three of us left for the town hall immediately after dinner, so as to get to our seats in advance of the large crowd that was expected. An impressive array of musical resources had been assembled for this concert: a brass band, of course, but also a small orchestra with piano and the choirs from several churches as well as the chorus from the Academy. There was considerable variety in the performances as well; though all of the pieces were nominally songs, some were performed without voices, some a cappella, and the others with various combinations of voice and instrument. A good deal of preparation had gone into this concert, I knew; the planning had begun in the spring and rehearsals had commenced well before the end of the summer.

The first half of the concert consisted primarily of soul-stirring marches, such as the "Battle Cry of Freedom" (with which it opened) and "Marching through Georgia." Toward the end, however, most of the instruments fell silent and the choirs sang the old Negro spiritual "We Are Climbing Jacob's Ladder" very softly to the accompaniment of a single violin. Nothing could have conveyed the tragedy of slavery more dramatically—the deep sorrow and constant hope for better days—or more poignantly reminded us why there had been a war. Just as the last sad notes of this piece were dying away, the first, triumphant ones of the "Battle Hymn of the Republic" were heard. Spontaneously, completely unbidden, the entire audience rose and joined in the singing. The hymn gathered force from verse to verse as people's passion mounted, until by the last one the sound was truly thunderous and there could be little doubt that God's truth would prevail against all evils.

Notwithstanding the intensity of the final verses, it is the less dramatic second one that has always touched me the most deeply:

> I have seen Him in the watch-fires of a hundred
> circling camps,

They have builded Him an altar in the evening
    dews and damps,
I can read His righteous sentence by the dim and
    flaring lamps,
His day is marching on.

It bespeaks devotion as well as determination, quiet confidence manifesting itself in action. It is those qualities, I believe, that ultimately carried the day for the North.

Following this there was a brief intermission, during which the three of us stood and stretched our limbs but did not venture far from our seats. The second half of the concert had a more intimate character, with songs about the sorrows and anxieties of individual soldiers and their loved ones at home, such as "Somebody's Darling" and "Was My Brother in the Battle?" These songs touched the deeper emotions of loss and grief and brought many in the audience to the verge of tears, myself included on two especially touching occasions.

The first was during the performance of "Lorena," that sad ballad of impossible love that struck such a chord with the soldiers on both sides. Its sorrowful tones, so affecting in any case, were only heightened by the setting for solo tenor and muted strings. It was the last verse, in which all earthly hope is shattered, that brought tears to my eyes and a feeling of constriction in my throat:

It matters little now, Lorena,
The past is in the eternal past.
Our hearts will soon lie low, Lorena,
Life's tide is ebbing out so fast.

The thought that the past is irrevocable and that death soon puts an end even to our awareness of that injustice was almost more than I could bear.

It was, however, the performance of a song known as "The Vacant Chair" that caused me to weep openly, my head cradled in my hands. This song was written at Thanksgiving-time during the first year of the war in response to the recent death of a Massachusetts soldier at a minor battle at Balls Bluff, in northern

Virginia. It depicts a scene that must have occurred in thousands upon thousands of homes: a family gathering for a holiday dinner with one member missing, one who would not ever be with them again in this life. The melody is tender, and the lyrics attempt to provide comfort:

> We shall meet but we shall miss him;
> There will be one vacant chair.
> We shall linger to caress him
> While we breathe our evening prayer.

Comfort ultimately proves elusive, however. As the closing words seem to recognize, we shall feel his loss as long as we live:

> Sleep today, O early fallen
> In thy green and narrow bed.
> Dirges from the pine and cypress
> Mingle with the tears we shed.

When the spasm of grief began, Meredith immediately put her arm around my shoulder and drew me to her. Matthew refrained from touching me but looked utterly aggrieved that there was so little he could do to comfort me. With some effort I soon righted myself, however, helped by the release of emotion from the first onslaught and the desire not to cause my companions any further distress. Still, I felt rather hollow and a bit shaken for the remainder of the program, of which I am sure they were aware.

The program closed with "The Star-Spangled Banner," as if to remind us why all of our sacrifices had been necessary. We all rose and listened in silence, with pride and gratitude, perhaps, but not jubilation—the reminders of our personal losses had affected us too deeply for that. There was, however, lengthy applause at the end.

It was much colder when we left the hall. Meredith had earlier invited me to spend the night with her rather than going home to a house that would have been unheated for hours, and I was only too glad to accept. Matthew would come in the morning to reclaim his carriage and take us to church.

I have been thinking about John a good deal the last several days, and this afternoon I found myself going through some of my mementoes of him: photographs, letters, a few of his smaller possessions. In the process I came across an item that I'd largely forgotten about, namely, the official notification of his interment in the national cemetery at Fredericksburg.

I have visited his grave only once, about eight years ago. For a long time I was reluctant to venture into Virginia owing to the ill feelings that lingered from the war, though no doubt I was also anxious about the pain that it might cause me. Time, however, had allayed both of those concerns, and I began to recognize that it was my clear duty to do this. Though summer would have been the most logical time, I settled on early spring, both because travel would be more comfortable then and because I felt that I would be in a calmer frame of mind. This required me to obtain a brief leave of absence from the Academy, but the headmistress was entirely agreeable to that.

Matthew accompanied me as far as Washington, where he had business. Early the next morning I boarded a train that would take me the fifty or so miles to Fredericksburg. I had a vague but pronounced sense of unease as, shortly after our leaving the station, the engine lumbered up onto a bridge crossing the Potomac River: as greatly as the South had figured in our lives, I had never actually been in any Southern state and could only envision them as utterly alien. This illusion was soon dispelled, however. The terrain south of the river is virtually indistinguishable from that north of it (gently undulating with numerous small streams), and below Alexandria the country has a very quiet, peaceful character. Then, too, the landscape wore the agreeable dress of April, a mist of small green leaves punctuated here and there with the almost iridescent colors of dogwood and redbud blossoms. Far from being in an alien setting, I was in a pleasantly reassuring one.

As we traveled further south, however, I began to notice more and more "scars" from the war: burned-out buildings, bridges reduced to a few stone pillars, trenches and breastworks slowly being reclaimed by forest. Still more prominent were the signs of the economic stagnation into which much of the South had fallen after the war. I saw any number of abandoned farms, the buildings collapsing and the fields a tangle of invading shrubs and trees. Even in places that were still inhabited there were clear signs of decay: peeling paint, gaps in fences where pickets had rotted away, and fallen porches, among others. Here and there one might see a bit of new construction, but for the most part the small hamlets through which I passed were tired reflections of the architecture of many years ago. Fredericksburg itself had a less dejected appearance; though it had suffered a great deal of damage during the war, the prosperity that it enjoyed as a result of its being a regional trade center had enabled it to put on a fresh face. Still, from time to time one could see pockmarks caused by shot and shell.

From the station I took a carriage up the long rise to Mar-ye's Heights, where the cemetery is located. It was on this slope, of course, that so many Union soldiers fell in a futile attempt to dislodge Longstreet's seasoned, well-entrenched troops during the Battle of Fredericksburg in December 1862. Some elements of the Fifth Corps, I knew, had been engaged here along with others from the Center Grand Division; thankfully, however, the regiment was held in reserve well to the east of the town and saw no action. Today, the ascent of the ridge makes for a pleasant drive with fine views.

Near the top was a little lane leading to an attractive Greek Revival mansion in red brick. Once the focal point of a large plantation, it seemed the perfect emblem of the Old South that was no more. As I had arranged my visit in advance, I was met in front of the small superintendent's lodge by the assistant superintendent, a Colonel Randolph. The colonel was a distinguished-looking man of about my age with the highly refined manners of the Virginia gentry. I was particularly taken by his accent—a soft drawl that gave a poetic quality to his every word and that I found very soothing. In response to my unspoken question, he quietly mentioned that he had "worn the gray."

The initial courtesies concluded, he led me down a brick path that leads to the cemetery proper not many steps distant. The setting was as lovely as I could have imagined, the landscaping reminding me of the extensive parks at country estates in England

on which the architect had no doubt modeled it. The cemetery itself was exceptionally well maintained—no grass or leaves around
the headstones, the paths free of twigs and other debris—a sign
of respect for those interred there and a real comfort to those
visiting them.

As we walked, Colonel Randolph gave me various particulars
about the cemetery, including the fact that there were two types
of headstones. The familiar arched ones were for persons whose
identities were known, the small square ones with pairs of numbers for those whose identities were not (the latter graves were in
fact mass ones, the first number denoting the plot and the second
the number interred within it). It was obvious from the stones that
the vast majority of those buried in the cemetery were unknown,
a fact that Colonel Randolph confirmed.

At length he paused and gestured toward a headstone
by which a small flag had been placed; a folding chair had also
thoughtfully been provided. "This is Colonel Reed," he said gently.
The sight of the headstone gave me a momentary shock. I may
have been lulled by the loveliness of the day and the setting or the
pleasant conversation with the colonel, or assumed that I would
have more advance warning; in any case I was quite unprepared
for this sight and was grateful for Colonel Randolph's assistance
in locating the chair and sitting down. He waited until I had recov-
ered, then quietly took his leave. He did, however, ask that I stop
by the lodge before departing.

I listened to his retreating footsteps as if grasping at a lifeline,
apprehensive about surrendering this last human contact. They
soon fell silent, however, and I was quite alone. The moment having come, I centered my concentration on the headstone and read
the few lines there: my husband's name, his rank and regiment, and
the years his life had spanned. The barest of details, like entries in
a ledger. They gave no indication of his superlative character, the
fine things that he had done with his life, or the enormous grief
that his untimely death had caused. I felt the beginnings of anger
and resentment welling up in me.

After a time, however, my mind began to fill with memories
of him and our life together. My anxieties were dispelled, replaced
by an overwhelming sense of calm, even joy. In silence I spoke

to him as if he were right before me, much as I might have over dinner when we had been parted only nine or ten hours. I recalled some of our most delightful moments as well as some amusing ones that I knew would bring a smile to his lips. I told him about my subsequent life and the richness it had brought me (not excepting my friendship with Matthew, of which I felt certain he would understand and approve). I reminded him of my enduring love for him and my hope, if there is indeed life beyond the grave, of being reunited with him soon. I wept a little at this last thought, but the catharsis of my conversation with him was soon complete. I stood, and bidding him a heartfelt farewell, turned toward the lodge. I looked back several times, the last when I could no longer distinctly see the headstone and could only tell its location by virtue of the chair placed there for me. Here I offered my final adieu, knowing that in all probability I would never be here again.

As I drew near the lodge, Colonel Randolph appeared on the lawn and asked if I would like to have some tea before departing. It was a very kind gesture, and I readily accepted. He ushered me onto a small porch where a table had been set with two places.

Our conversation, naturally, was a little awkward at first. With consummate grace, however, Colonel Randolph then turned it in a more congenial direction by asking me whether I had found the conditions at the cemetery "entirely to my satisfaction." I replied (quite truthfully) that I had, adding that it was a real comfort to see the grounds so well cared for. He thanked me, noting that those responsible for them regarded their charge as a sacred trust. After a brief pause, he added that it was an "honor" to have my husband in their keeping, as most officers of his rank had been sent home for burial.

I wasn't certain how to respond to this. I had known that I could have had John's remains brought home, but somehow it seemed sacrilegious to disturb them further. I felt, too, that he would prefer to lie near where he had fallen in the service of so noble a cause, that he would want to be close to those still engaged in the struggle. I told Colonel Randolph simply that, being in military service, he would consider it a duty to remain with his comrades, even if that meant that his last resting place was far from home.

The colonel then inquired whether he had been a professional soldier. To that, of course, I replied no, that such a course was far less common in the North than it was in the South; he had simply answered the call to arms when it had come. In response the colonel merely nodded, as if he found that all perfectly understandable. Sensing a bit of a strain in the conversation, I went on to give him a more complete portrait of my husband, stressing his human qualities as well as his strong character. The colonel listened appreciatively, concluding that John must have been "a remarkable person."

By way of lightening the conversation, I then remarked that Randolph was a famous name in Virginia and that he must have some illustrious forebears. To this he smiled broadly, almost laughing, his honesty not allowing him to claim a distinction it did not deserve. It was, he said, a large family, and he was only distantly related to those who had made the family name. His own father had been a small planter, comfortable enough but not in any sense wealthy. He himself was sent to a military academy, his father figuring that a sound education would be his only real legacy. He had spent a number of years in the army, his profession (and a respectable marriage) having given him wide entrée to Virginia society. But then, "the South is not what it was."

There was such a note of despondency in this last remark that I longed to press him on it. Did he regret the course of secession and war that the South had chosen? Did he view it as an impetuous act that a little more thought would have forestalled? Or was his sorrow more personal, occasioned by the natural changes in the world one has known as time goes by? It would have been impertinent of me to ask, especially under those circumstances, so I said no more and we allowed the topic to drop. Not long after, he said that he really should be returning to his work; I might remain on the grounds if I wished, or he would summon a carriage for me. Though the train back to Washington would not be leaving for several hours, I thought it best not to linger at the cemetery. I thanked him profusely for his kindness, which was truly extraordinary, and wishing him well took my leave. In response he was most gracious, telling me to return as often as I wished.

I had a simple luncheon at a restaurant near the station, then walked around the town a little. My thoughts, of course, were very full. The only unsettling ones, however, were those about the colonel—in a situation calling for a profound human connection, we had seemed to interact only in the most formal of ways. But perhaps that was for the best, perhaps a deeper connection would have left both of us more disturbed than we were. Perhaps, too, he had gone beyond his customary bounds in dealing with visitors, perhaps he had shown me something of his true emotions. It could not have been particularly easy for him in any case, I had to remember that.

My heart, of course, was very full during the return trip, my sense of loss awakened as it had not been for years. Almost in desperation, I found myself asking a lot of what-ifs. What if there had been no war or John had survived it, what if we had been allowed to enjoy our perfect life together into old age, as we fully expected to? Why had life been so terribly cruel? The sheer senselessness of such questions only intensified my pain, however, and, being alone in the car, I sobbed uncontrollably for some time. When I managed to recover my composure, I felt utterly drained and even drifted off to sleep for a brief while, awakening just as we were once again crossing the Potomac River. As it happened, Matthew had managed to conclude his business early enough to meet me at the station, which was a great relief to me.

We spent two more days in Washington, which I found very trying. Despite its wealth and its appearance of refinement, it is a thoroughly vulgar place. Its raison d'être is the exercise of power, that is the sole goal toward which every muscle strains. In their private conversations, at least, our politicians are very open about this—there is not the slightest pretense of their serving any nobler end. It is altogether a very sad monument to those who gave their lives for this republic. I filled the days as best I could by visiting galleries and such, but was only too glad when the hour of departure came.

Friday, October 28th

I did not sleep well last night, lying awake for over three hours, my mind beset with thoughts of death. Such thoughts are rare for me; like most of humanity, I have an intellectual awareness of death but shy away from imagining its actually touching me. This is an illusion, of course, but a necessary one: without it, we might be too fearful or dispirited to carry on with the demands of living. It becomes increasingly difficult to maintain this illusion as one ages, however, and certainly the memories that have surfaced over the last few days would serve to dispel it.

I would not say that I actually fear death; I increasingly lean to the view that it is like an endless sleep in which we have neither feeling nor consciousness. But it saddens me immensely to imagine a world in which I have no part or even awareness. It is as if I am somehow instrumental to it all, that the affairs of this house, the village, even the nation would be in less secure hands without my involvement in them. Absurd as this may be, it is more than mere vanity: the power that we seem to exert appears to be central to our being, and its dissolution in death strikes us as an unbearable loss.

Indeed, the merest hint of the impermanence of things is profoundly unsettling to us. We resist change even within our relatively short lives, blinding ourselves to the fact that the world will surely be very different in fifty years—to say nothing of a thousand. Worse still, if the astronomers are correct, our solar system has a finite term, and we with it. Nor is there any reason to suppose that evolution will continue to favor humanity that long; well before then it may eliminate us or transform us into other beings altogether. Our possession of the earth is clearly just a life tenancy.

Though many take comfort in the prospect of immortality, I cannot do so. A state of eternal bliss, it seems to me, would be so far removed from our earthly existence that we would in any real sense cease to be ourselves entirely. Does not the greatest part of our happiness lie in overcoming difficulties, of experiencing release from the tensions that have been building up within us? Would moments of peace be as welcome if they were not preceded by moments of turmoil? Constant tranquility, it seems to me, would lead to an unbearable ennui unless we are to become very different beings than we are now—which I, for one, am quite loathe to do. Better oblivion than consuming such lotus blossoms.

If no longer being alive holds no real terrors for me, it is quite otherwise with the act of dying itself. Indeed, the thought of prolonged suffering, attended by increasing pain and finally a moment of crisis (the stopping of my heart, say, or suffocation because I cannot draw adequate breath) weighs on me enormously. This may be the reason many people hope that they will simply die in their sleep and be totally unaware of their passing. It is not so with me, however: I harbor the notion of being conscious during my last moments, of being able (however briefly) to "appreciate" them. Sometimes, when I go to bed, I experience a twinge of fear that I will not live through the night, that my life will end without a final acknowledgment from me.

Needless to say, death will choose its own time and place, and I will have little if any say in the matter. I would do well simply to accept it whenever and however it comes and allow myself to be ushered into the hereafter gracefully. And yet my soul protests and insists upon what it imagines as its rights.

Toward dawn I fell into a drugged sleep, from which I awoke several hours later feeling groggy and listless. The day, it seemed, was in complete sympathy with me: damp and cold, with occasional gusts of wind that blew the fallen leaves about in no set direction.

Sunday, October 30th

This afternoon Matthew and I went for a long drive in the country, as we are particularly fond of doing in the autumn. The day could not have been better; after several days of rain, we were again blessed with the warmth and radiance of Indian summer—to my mind the high point of the entire year. It was the peak of color as well, the rich reds and yellows of the leaves positively luminescent in the brilliant sunlight. Even in falling they provided a feast for the eye, dancing and twirling in the air before finally clattering to the ground. I cannot get enough of such enchanted spectacles.

The day offered another delight as well, in that it seemed almost praeternaturally quiet, as if the earth itself were drawing a deep breath. I say "delight" because this stillness is soothing in its own right as well as offering us a vision of a universe that is, for the moment at least, perfectly at peace with itself. It has another side, however, reminding us that the year is dying and that Nature is preparing herself for a long absence. This is always an anxious moment for us, however much we may trust in her return. It is an especially poignant moment for those of us who are older, as we do not know which such days will be the last ones we shall ever see.

Wednesday, November 2nd

I spent the afternoon running errands downtown. I rarely do this anymore, leaving most such things to Marta, but these particular tasks (meeting with the president of the bank about my investments and purchasing a gift) were not ones that I could delegate to her. A neighbor returning to his office after luncheon was kind enough to take me; afterwards, Matthew would meet me at the hotel and bring me home.

As I had about an hour to fill after completing my errands, I decided to have tea at the little tea-room in the hotel. This is a pleasure in which I often indulged in the past, but one that has grown increasingly rare as I have become more housebound. To my delight, it was quiet in the room just then and I was given a table right by the window, overlooking the square.

The hotel, as it happened, had undergone an extensive renovation since my last visit. Its relatively simple mid-century décor had given way to a markedly richer and more ornate one, replete with dark walnut wainscoting surmounted by textured wallpaper with a floral design, heavy drapes in a rich ruby color, thick oriental carpets, and highly polished brass sconces. The table at which I sat consisted of a disk of gleaming white marble supported by a frame of slender iron rods, gracefully curved; the matching chair had a plush, heavily upholstered seat. The overall effect was one of luxury, but more than that: a luxury in which we are quite secure, one that is entirely natural to us and not to be swept away by the next turn of fortune. Sitting there I had a real sense of reassurance, even though I generally prefer lighter tones. In this, however, I had an ally in the afternoon sun, which had bathed the room in a soft, almost ethereal light.

My close attention to the room must have heightened my visual sense, for when my tea was poured I was especially taken with its appearance: its agreeable reddish-brown tint, its transparency against the white porcelain cup, the ghostly wisps of steam rising from its slightly disturbed surface, its almost blinding reflection of the sunlight when held at the right angle. My artist's eye, of course, would naturally be drawn to such details, but it seemed to go deeper than that. For as long as I can remember, I have taken a peculiar pleasure in immersing myself in the subtlest elements of sensory experience. It is this, more than anything, that gives such experiences meaning to me; a more cursory engagement would leave me cold and even ill at ease, as if I had failed in some obvious duty.

It is not just the small details that attract my attention, however; I also have an extraordinary sense for things in the large. Indeed, I often picture the village as if it were a diorama, its streets and buildings in miniature, each of its diminutive human forms busy with its own task (a teamster urging his horses on in order to complete his delivery on time, a well-to-do woman entering a dressmaker's shop to order a new gown for an upcoming ball, a businessman pausing to speak to an acquaintance on the sidewalk). Here the myriad details are overshadowed by the larger whole, here we perceive a pattern and harmony not apparent to the individual figures, each preoccupied with his own concerns. It is perhaps natural that we take a parochial view of things, but what joy, what comfort there is in relinquishing it from time to time—at least, I have always found it so.

Toward the end of my visit to the tea-room I was accorded yet another angle of vision: myself, in a mirror that had until then been obstructed by other guests. Here was revealed an older woman, prim but not severe in her appearance, sitting erect in her chair and taking her tea with a certain grace and refinement. It was an image that pleased me immensely. Though I am not vain and seldom give much thought to how I appear to others, this is how I would wish to be seen—as self-possessed but modest, taking an intelligent interest in the world around me. Such a portrait, I flatter myself to think, would be my best and truest one.

That moment, I realize now, was another of Wordsworth's "spots of time," a rare moment of especial happiness and revelation. I shall cherish it, as such moments come more and more infrequently now.

Monday, November 7th

If some of our moments are truly sublime, others are the exact opposite of that. I experienced one of the latter this morning, and it has greatly saddened me.

A little after ten I spotted a young woman coming up the street who occasionally does laundry for one of my neighbors; she had her three young children with her and was apparently coming just to collect her wages. As always, she was rather shabbily dressed and her hair was disheveled. Although she is quite pretty, her looks were marred by an expression of anger coupled with despair. Her husband, I believe, has no regular work but simply does odd jobs around town when he can find them. I do not know where they are from or in what part of Westerly they live.

As they were passing my house, the smallest child (whom I would put at about three years of age) started to fuss and was sharply upbraided by his mother. When he then began to cry, she cuffed him hard several times, threatening much worse if he did not stop. She then grabbed his arm and yanked him along, his little feet barely able to keep contact with the ground, sobbing and rubbing his eyes with his free hand but not daring to cry openly.

This was not the first time that I have witnessed an angry outburst, of course. I believe that it affected me so greatly for two reasons: it was directed toward a young child who could not possibly comprehend his offense (indeed, he was not the source of his mother's anger but only a convenient outlet for it), and it epitomized the utter hopelessness of the family's situation. A life with no comfort or security—to say nothing of joy—how could it be anything but degrading? How could any but the most resolute souls manage to turn such a life around?

Many would no doubt judge this woman harshly. Others, more charitable, would recognize the role of contingency and thank Heaven that they had been spared such grinding circumstances. For my part, I am increasingly out of sympathy with both of these sentiments. Our task, it seems to me, is to render assistance to such people, if only for the children's sake. Perhaps we could secure some warmer clothes for them before winter fully comes on. Perhaps we could give them some books and even a few toys. Perhaps, in time, the firm could even take them on in some capacity. There is no end of possibilities, given the will to actually *do* something.

Thursday, November 17th

I spent the afternoon superintending the men raking up the last of the leaves from the grounds. This is one of our final preparations for winter that we only seem to get to the week before Thanksgiving.

The day, in fact, was quite wintry, with a leaden sky and a damp, cold wind out of the north. The raking was not finished until after dark, and by then I was thoroughly chilled. I say "chilled," but it was actually a more complex sensation—the feeling of being cold alternating with that of being flushed from exertion and exposure to the wind. It is a sensation that I have experienced only in late autumn, and it seems endemic to this time of year. And even though it is not serious it is very discomfiting, a sort of false fever that presages the real ones that will attend our illnesses in the winter.

When we were at last finished and I was able to get inside, I planted myself by the stove in the front parlor, alternately wrapping myself in a large shawl to warm myself and opening it when I felt too warm. It took the better part of an hour for me to recover my equilibrium. Marta, thankfully, stayed until I did so, even though it was past time for her to leave.

Saturday, November 26th

I devoted yesterday afternoon to reading the essay about the Puritans that has received so much attention in educated circles. It actually appeared in the September issue of the *Prospect*, but only now have I felt that I had the time to do it justice. Then, too, it seems fitting that I read it on the day after Thanksgiving, as that is the one holiday we owe entirely to them.

The author of the essay is what one might call a cultural critic. He regularly contributes reviews of books, plays, art exhibitions, and so forth, along with original essays on the state of the arts in America. His concern, however, goes beyond the purely aesthetic aspects of these works to their social significance: the fundamental attitudes and anxieties that they reveal—the state of our soul, as it were. He was the first to observe, for instance, that the paintings of the West now being turned out in such profusion reflect an unconscious desire for simpler times and clearer moral choices. After all, fifty years ago acquisitiveness required no defense and "primitive" peoples might be pushed out of the way with complete impunity.

The essay had its origins in his observation that our current view of the Puritans reflects a fundamental shift in our national character. Nowadays our references to them are almost always derogatory. When we call someone an "old Puritan," we mean that he is so obsessed with rectitude that he can find no joy in life at all, that the soul about which he manifests so much concern is in fact a dry and withered husk. We can find nothing admirable in such a person; he is merely ridiculous, and we treat him with the contempt that he deserves.

If this stereotype were true, however, we would immediately be faced with a major conundrum: how could such a crabbed, moralistic view of the world have given rise to a nation as flourishing as ours? After all, it was the descendants of those first Puritans who spearheaded the Revolution, made the United States a nation of industry and trade, and gave us a literature and philosophy uniquely our own. Then, too, no small number of today's progressives—those pressing for the adoption of more liberal views in society, government, religion, and many other areas—trace their roots to the first settlers of New England.

The way out of this difficulty, of course, lies in amending our view of the Puritans themselves. As it happens, the stern rigidity that we associate with them lasted only a generation or two; later generations had much more liberal views. Even within the earliest generations, however, we find positive attributes that were to have an enormous influence in the years to come. It was these attributes that formed the crux of the essay.

The first, naturally enough, was the Puritans' strict piety in all things. Such a worldview, of course, appeals to some persons in every age, but it was particularly likely to arise in the Puritans' own time. In the first instance, their era was an intensely religious one. People in general took their faith much more seriously in the sixteenth and early seventeenth centuries than they have subsequently; it was literally a life-or-death matter for them to a degree that is difficult for us to imagine. In the second instance, the dominance of an established church (dissent, we must remember, was at times tantamount to treason and punished severely) had given rise to a vast array of arcane rituals and official corruption. Thus, the Puritans' quarrel with the Church of England did not stem from doctrinal differences alone. To them, the Church had become an unholy institution that not only stood in the way of the individual's communion with God but also made a mockery of Christianity itself. It would therefore be a grievous sin to give it their allegiance; rather, it was their *duty* to purify the Church from root to branch.

The same principle—the obligation to assert right against authority when authority is in the wrong—would manifest itself very dramatically nearly two centuries later, in the War for Independence. Later still, it would sustain the North's long campaign against slavery. Two events of enormous significance that had their origins in the resistance of a small sect to spiritual domination in a distant, almost unimaginable era. Then, too, it is to one of the earliest Puritan settlers, a man called Roger Williams, that we owe one of the most cherished principles of American government—the separation of church and state. In one sense this is ironic, as such tolerance had little place in the world of that time and was certainly anathema to the authorities in early Massachusetts. In another sense, however, it is a natural outgrowth of the Puritans' belief in freedom of conscience—a principle that would find fertile ground in the more enlightened days after the Revolution.

In truth, there was a mundane element at work in the Puritans' strict moral sense as well. The Puritans were mostly burghers—that is, middle-class merchants and artisans whose well-being hinged on forming prudent judgments and, above all, on maintaining the utmost diligence in their work. They naturally viewed the idleness, frivolity, and vice of the upper class in England with suspicion and contempt. Curiously, this has an echo in the conflict between North and South in our own times. One reason Northerners were so appalled at Southern ways is that there seemed to be no deep purpose to their lives, that they appeared to be governed largely by earthly pleasures.

For the Puritans' overwhelming emphasis on rectitude stemmed from their view that, while life may have its joys, it is not simply a lark: it is a very serious business that imposes numerous obligations on us, toward which we must constantly direct our best efforts. Clearly, this present age could do with more of such sentiments—there is ample evidence to that effect.

An excess of piety would ordinarily lead to a certain withdrawal from the world, a turning away from earthly things. But this was not the case with the Puritans. Their religious views went hand in hand with a vigorous entrepreneurial spirit—so much so that worldly success came to be seen as a sign of divine favor. To them, the day was not for prayer and contemplation alone; the largest part of it had to be spent at the loom, the anvil, or the shop counter.

This coupling of commercial and religious motives shaped the lives of the Puritans in other ways as well. At a time when literacy was by far the exception, it was widespread among them. Rare was the person who could not read the Scriptures to at least some extent or make sense of ordinary commercial documents. The education of their ministers went far beyond that, of course. Colleges were founded early on for this purpose, and the typical Puritan divine was a fairly learned man. The best of them produced works of scholarship equal to those emanating from the universities in Europe, even if they were confined to religious subjects. It should thus come as no surprise that many of the leading lights of our own era have the blood of the old Puritans in their veins. What we admire in Emerson's essays—his great intellect, his passion for truth, the forthright nature of his words—we find in sermon after sermon from the previous two centuries. There is a direct line between them: Emerson is but a modern incarnation of the Puritan mind.

The Puritans' devotion to their religious studies does not mean that they had no regard for secular knowledge. On the contrary, as a commercial people they had a natural interest in discovering new products and improved means of production. At times their efforts even took on a scientific character, as witness the opening up of mines and the development of a metal-working industry in Connecticut in the seventeenth century. Of course, the unfamiliarity of their surroundings virtually compelled them to explore and experiment—an impulse that is now deeply rooted in the American character.

One area in which the Puritans definitely differed from us is their aesthetic sense. They produced virtually nothing in the way of art or music and relatively little in the way of literature (and their most celebrated writers were largely preoccupied with theological themes). They excluded the arts from their worship on the grounds that they were at best distractions and at worst idolatrous. They excluded them from their day-to-day lives on the same grounds as well as their association of the arts with the vanity and frivolity of the aristocrats. It is only in certain domestic arts, such as lace making and embroidery, that we find a true artistic hand. It may be that such arts were tolerated because they were relatively understated or increased the value of the goods that were their principal store of wealth. In any case, this demonstrates that even a people as severe as the Puritans had some instinct for beauty, as all humans do.

Nor would it be right to assume, as many seem to do, that the Puritans were "cold fish" in regard to their emotional lives. True, the age in which they lived was much less sentimental than ours, and their sober view of life probably discouraged effusions of feelings. But we must not suppose that they cherished their loved ones any less than we do ours or grieved the loss of them any less intensely. In fact, the documents that have come down to us—letters, journals, poems, and even sermons—reveal a depth of feeling that is all the more touching for not being overstated.

Perhaps the finest illustration of the Puritans' ability to integrate emotion with piety lies in the writings of Anne Bradstreet. Born into a prosperous and cultured family in England in 1612, she, together with her parents and husband, was among the first settlers of the Massachusetts Bay Colony in 1630. Throughout her life, she recorded her spiritual journey and day-to-day events in poems and meditations intended primarily for her own family. Many of these celebrate commonplace but still significant occurrences, such as her recovery from an illness or the safe return of her husband or sons from a voyage. Though not of the highest literary quality, they nonetheless have an innocence and sincerity that render them thoroughly delightful.

If there is one overarching theme in her work, it is her trust in the goodness of God. In keeping with Puritan doctrine, she gracefully—even gratefully—accepts misfortunes as divine "corrections" that serve to return her to the right path. Thus, in passing the shell of her home in Andover that had recently burnt to the ground, she says

> Under thy roof no guest shall sit,
> Nor at thy table eat a bit.
> No pleasant tale shall e'er be told,
> Nor things recounted done of old.
> No candle e'er shall shine in thee,
> Nor bridegroom's voice e'er heard shall be.
> In silence ever shall thou lie,
> Adieu, adieu, all's vanity.
> Then straight I 'gin my heart to chide,
> And did thy wealth on earth abide?
> Didst fix thy hope on mold'ring dust?
> The arm of flesh didst make thy trust?

It is not that she is insensitive to the many joys that her house brought her, it is simply that she can accept its loss as having a higher purpose, namely, to caution her against too great an attachment to earthly things. The same theme, even more poignantly, is sounded in "In Memory of My Dear Grandchild Elizabeth Bradstreet, Who Deceased August, 1665, Being a Year and a Half Old":

> By nature trees do rot when they are grown,
> And plums and apples thoroughly ripe do fall,
> And corn and grass are in their season mown,
> And time brings down what is both strong and tall.
> But plants new set to be eradicate,
> And buds new blown to have so short a date,

Is by His hand alone that guides nature and fate.

Her best-loved poem, however, is without question the familiar "To My Dear and Loving Husband," which opens with the tender couplet

> If ever two were one, then surely we,
> If ever man were loved by wife, then thee;

and closes with the sweet, timeless injunction

> Then while we live, in love let's so persevere
> That when we live no more, we may live ever.

Thus, we are forced to conclude that although Anne Bradstreet was a devoutly religious woman, she possessed the full range of human emotions; and while she was undoubtedly exceptional in her ability to give voice to her innermost thoughts and feelings, she cannot have been alone in having such thoughts and feelings.

The last topic with which the essay dealt—the Puritans' relations with the native inhabitants of New England—is in many ways the most surprising and the most revealing of their character, for they saw themselves not so much as the natives' masters but as their benefactors. It became their mission to extend the benefits of civilization and Christianity to the natives by settling them in "praying towns" where they would live much as the Puritans did but largely under their own governance. And nothing symbolizes their attitude toward the natives better than the fact that one of the Puritan divines, a man called John Eliot, translated the entire Bible into Algonquian, the principal native language of the region. It would have been far more natural for him to teach the natives to read English, but he felt that they could not truly grasp the meaning of the Scriptures in any tongue but their own. A small number of the praying towns exist to this day; the Eliot Bible has recently gone out of use, but well-worn copies of it are still to be found in churches throughout the area originally settled by the Puritans.

Of course, one could argue that it was naïve to imagine that the natives would adopt European ways without resistance, and so it proved. In the mid-1670s the simmering tensions between them and the English settlers boiled over into a bloody war, at the conclusion of which the supremacy of the settlers was firmly established. From then on, the future of New England would be shaped by them alone. Still, the policy that they initially tried to pursue was remarkable in its humanity. It stands in marked contrast to the enslavement, exile, and outright extermination that were the norm virtually everywhere else in the New World—including the greater part of the United States.

Thus, in the Puritans we have a people who, like most others, were complex and not without their flaws but who also possessed extraordinary virtues. It is those virtues that loom largest today, it is in the shade of the Puritans' "lengthened shadow" that we find no small measure of our current freedom and material comfort.

I have seldom given any thought to my distant ancestors or to the principles by which they lived. I see now, however, that I am their true descendant, that their finest qualities have shaped both me and, perhaps more importantly, the age in which I came to adulthood. Like them, I am serious but unprepossessing; like them, I have a passion for justice. Above all, I share their conviction, not that life can be made perfect but that it can be well lived and, in some measure, become a lasting achievement. If someone were to attempt to wrap me in the mantle of Puritanism, I would accept it with little hesitation.

Friday, December 2nd

This afternoon's mail brought a welcome letter from Lucy Thornton with the proposal that she come stay with me for a few weeks after Christmas, "so that we can while away the dull, dead time of the year together."

Of course, I shall be delighted, as she is my dearest friend and we have not seen each other for several years. But there is another reason as well: of all the people whom I know, she is the one who most exudes a sense of real joy. Not wild rapture, but a quiet, deeply rooted delight in things that bespeaks a confidence that all is surely right with the world. Even the immense sorrow that she has experienced has not diminished this to any great extent.

Such pure joy seems to have only a small place in American

life. We have our amusements, to be sure, but these are often as frenetic as our work, as if all of our pleasures had to be crammed into the few hours that we can spare from more remunerative pursuits. There is no time to linger over particularly fine lines of poetry, or observe the splendor of a sunrise in its entirety, or bring our best thoughts to complete fruition. We must always be on the move, always "improving" the day. I suppose that this trait, too, we owe largely to the Puritans, but if so, it is certainly no virtue; this is one area, in fact, in which we need to steal a march on our heritage.

In this I myself have had only partial success. Though my life has in many ways been blessed—and I have made a point of cultivating as many moments of joy as seemed possible—a truly carefree spirit has not been granted me. Still, I am content; such fruit as I have is sufficient.

Thursday, December 8th

The last few days have turned into an extended meditation on the times … and time itself. Such events are becoming increasingly common for me as I get older; more and more, I feel the need for a summing up, for articulating the lessons that I have learned from life and what it has all meant to me. This, it seems, is now my principal task—to settle my accounts, as it were.

This particular meditation was prompted by a sudden, seemingly spontaneous memory from many years ago. I was standing by the window in the front parlor, when there came to me an image of that scene as it was right after my grandfather and I moved into this house. The street had been newly cut through and was still quite rough, and although a couple of other lots had been cleared, they were filled with slash and stumps and showed no real signs of impending construction. For all practical purposes, it was still virgin forest. In time, of course, the hand of man would soften and refine this landscape, giving it the settled, agreeable appearance that it has today. The transformation, in fact, has been so complete that I doubt that anyone who had not seen the area as it was originally would even be able to imagine it in its primal state.

Thus the present tends to efface the past, at least as far as our day-to-day experience is concerned. In some ways, however, the past unquestionably lives on in us. We are shaped by past events in our own lives, of course, as well as by our forebears' circumstances; we are also affected by events on the larger stage in the years and even decades before our birth. How different my life would have been, for instance, if I had not been born into a relatively well-to-do family that cherished education and the arts. How vastly different it would have been if there had been no war. Such chains of causation are endless, of course, and any number of contingencies might well have altered them. Still, we remain in thrall to past events, whatever their nature.

There is another, more subtle sense in which the past continues in us, one of which we are seldom even aware. These words that I write: they were forged in the smithy of daily use over many centuries, with many a workman taking his turn at the anvil. We can trace the English language back to a certain Germanic dialect—a distantly related tongue that took shape in the dark forests of northern Europe many eons ago. Its true origins, however, lie much further back—in the unrecorded evolution of that dialect, and ultimately in the first appearance of human speech itself. I, however, have inherited the English of today as a precision instrument ready for immediate use. It is the same with countless other things, from the most practical ones to the most abstract; without these "bequests," our lives would be much the poorer and more difficult.

In a profound way, the past also grounds us spiritually; we derive real comfort from the realization that those who came before us also faced great difficulties that they managed to surmount. How many times during the war, for instance, when fortune had turned against the North, were we reminded of the setbacks experienced by the colonists during the Revolution? How many times were we urged to persevere as they had, trusting that we would prevail in the end? We could multiply such examples endlessly.

My own most memorable reception of a blessing from past times was more intimate. It occurred in Germany, when I was en route to Rome to take up my art studies. I had gone into a very old stone church, as much to escape the heat of the afternoon as from interest in the site itself. Inside it was cool and still; a few votive candles flickered near the altar, and I could make out the indistinct shapes of several persons kneeling in prayer. Almost without conscious intention, I immediately knelt as well and silently uttered the words of a short prayer in Latin that I knew. Despite my being from an altogether different time and place and possessing a much more liberal faith, the Middle Ages actually breathed through me at that moment; to a degree, I acquired the soul of a simple peasant from some centuries ago. This only lasted a few minutes, of course, nor would I have wanted it to continue much longer; but I was grateful for this rare moment of transcending my own time and experiencing a degree of reverence that is almost unimaginable now.

If the past clearly resides in us, in a certain sense the future does as well. This is particularly the case for Americans, with our constant focus on commercial prospects: next quarter's income statement, say, or the returns that we will realize from our investments in a year's time. Even outside of the material realm, we are a people of projects and anticipations. The verb tense that is most natural to us is the future perfect.

Ironically, though, our ability to envision the future in any detail is very limited. In envisioning the past we have artifacts and images upon which we can draw; we can readily conjure up convincing tableaux, even for fairly distant times. With the future, however, it is largely an empty canvas. Developments such as the telegraph and electric lighting invariably take us by surprise.

Notwithstanding our connections to the past and the future, in the most literal sense we live only in the present moment. It is our immediate concerns—answering the knock at the door, preparing a cup of tea, or writing these lines—that most occupy us, often to the exclusion of all others. Emerson seems to recognize this when he says that "our office is with moments" and therefore urges us to "husband them."

We do not perceive individual moments as completely isolated events, however. Rather, they succeed one another so effortlessly that for the most part we sense only continuity. Indeed, without this sense of continuity, we would be utterly lost; if the world were entirely new each moment, it would be nothing but chaos. Thus, it is memory—not conscious memory but a sort of intrinsic recollection of which we are barely even aware—that really holds things together.

In this respect, our experience of time resembles the mosaics from Roman times. Taken individually or in small clusters, the different tiles have little meaning; taken together, however, they form a coherent, often arresting whole. Nor are any of the tiles necessarily less significant than the others. Though our eye may be drawn to the most colorful ones or those that form the central image, this reflex is crucially dependent on the contrast provided by the duller, less conspicuous tiles. It is ultimately the entire pattern that matters. And so it is with our lives: the individual events have, if not a design, at least a recognizable pattern. They array themselves in a familiar way, the exact form depending on our circumstances and our character; in the end, they form the true portrait of ourselves.

There is another lesson in this as well, one of which I am constantly in need of reminding myself: not to disparage my seemingly unsuccessful moments. There have been times, for instance, when I have struggled to conceive a drawing in my mind, unable to settle on the exact placement of the figures, the angle of the light, or some other crucial detail. Numerous preliminary sketches were to no avail: it simply would not come, and I was ultimately compelled to give up in frustration. Yet the next time that I took up the problem, everything seemed to fall into place effortlessly—I had unconsciously been framing the solution in my mind in the interim. The seeds that I had previously sown, to all appearances so barren and lifeless, had sprouted into vigorous young shoots. The moment that I had cursed was in fact a blessed one. For all our failures and false starts, many things do in fact come right in the end.

Thus my thoughts on time. As for the times, this is a subject on which I have had numerous occasions to remark in recent years. It is a changed world that we live in now, one that bears little resemblance to that of my youth. The obvious changes are large enough in themselves: we now do things on a scale and at a pace that would have been unimaginable fifty years ago, and virtually everything is more complex, so that it is really impossible for anyone to take complete charge of his destiny or even to fully comprehend the forces that govern his life.

These outward changes, of course, have been accompanied

by an almost seismic shift in the prevailing view of things. I believe that I can best sum it up by saying that we no longer live in an age of idealism—in either the philosophical or the ordinary sense of that term.

The philosophy of my youth had an almost religious character, proffering us a vision of a more perfect world and summoning us to our highest selves. That of the present seems more in the nature of a science. Its principal purpose is to explain, as objectively as it can, the ways in which our minds function; it may offer us a certain practical counsel, but it cannot satisfy our innermost longings, cannot give us the reassurance that we so urgently need or prompt us to great deeds.

Nor does idealism play much of a role in day-to-day life any longer. We lack the fundamental optimism and energy of the 1840s, when all things seemed possible. The confident, forthright actions of that era have given way to a sort of nervous clutching; we constantly cast our eyes about us for ways to take advantage of others or forestall them from taking advantage of us. We are always on our guard. The great issues of the day seem so intractable that we despair of resolving them. As a result, we take refuge in a safe harbor—indulgence in luxuries, say, or in a sterile aesthetics. In all these ways, life is much diminished from what it was.

In many quarters, of course, idealism now seems to be a relic of a more naïve time, a faith that was bound to succumb to the horrors of the war and its aftermath. Without question, extreme idealism has done immense and lasting harm—our history amply attests to that. Then, too, even in the best of times life counsels a certain stoicism, repeatedly reminding us to prepare ourselves for disappointment. Still, in the most fundamental sense there is no one who is not an idealist, no one whose guiding principles do not aim at some sort of good, however he may conceive of it. "A person will worship something, have no doubt about that," Emerson assures us. The only question is what the object of his worship will be, and there I appeal to the virtues of my own time rather than those of the current age. One of our writers, lamenting the rabid quest for profit underlying the country's settlement of the West, has best expressed the impoverished spirit of the present age: "It is not illuminated by a thought," he says, "it is not warmed by a sentiment."

None of this would seem to bode well for the legacy that my generation will leave. And, in a literal sense, we *have* failed, having left virtually no mark on the rising generation. Perhaps it was unrealistic to expect otherwise: no generation willingly bends the knee to its predecessor, and each confronts its own unique challenges, to which it must devise solutions never even envisioned until that time. And we may yet leave a greater mark than we have thus far, for time is long and it tends to preserve only the truest things. Thus, the generation now supplanting ours will, in a few short years, find itself being supplanted in turn. Many of the arbiters of the current age, so supremely confident in their power over things, may well seem mean and paltry to future generations—if they are remembered at all. The river, it is said, has its bend, beyond which every generation disappears; only over the longest distances is its course straight.

Then, too, I am convinced that there are times in human history when the pulse of life quickens, when people's souls are stirred to a degree unimaginable at other times and they simply brush aside the barriers that have long held them back. Shakespeare alludes to this in one of his plays:

> There is a tide in the affairs of men,
> Which, taken at the flood, leads on to fortune.

The 1770s were one such time—the events of those years forever changed the meaning of liberty. And I believe that the middle years of this century will come to be seen in a similar light. The Civil War, of course, will cast a very long shadow. Of more significance, however, is the uncompromising moral vision with which our generation faced the challenges before it. Though we may be eclipsed for a long while (perhaps even decades), there will surely come a time when that vision will answer to the needs of the people then living. Facing similar challenges, they will draw on it to sustain them in their struggle. Wherever there is an impulse to live life more abundantly, to overturn the falsehoods of convention, and above all, to ensure justice, we will have a place. Such is my faith—a small voice barely audible above the wind, perhaps, but one, I am convinced, that can never be stilled completely.

Tuesday, December 20th

Thirty-eight years ago today, South Carolina seceded from the Union, setting in motion a chain of events that forever altered the course of history. My memories of that winter are so fresh that it does not seem possible that so much time has passed—and that in another few years the intensity of the secession crisis may well slip from the general consciousness altogether. Certainly, for most of those now living in the United States it is merely a tale that they have heard and not a vital memory.

We do not, of course, mark this anniversary in the usual way, with public or private ceremony, but few of us who were there can let it pass without deep reflection. Many of us would no doubt have preferred that this signal event had never occurred, that we had been allowed to live out our lives without disturbance and had then passed into a quiet obscurity. This might well have been the case if the Southern states had simply accepted the election of President Lincoln and remained in the Union. There would then have been no great cataclysm in our national life, and in time it might have been possible to negotiate a gradual emancipation of the slaves, as occurred in the Northern states in the years following the Revolution. It is an attractive vision, perhaps, but it was not our fate. *Our* fate was to be roused from our ignoble slumbers and thrust, however reluctantly, into a struggle for the very life of our nation—and ultimately into a measure of true greatness.

Ironically, it is a very dull day, cool and overcast with periods of rain. Not a day conducive to profound thoughts or anything more than attending to the mundane matters that crowd most of our days. And yet it is different. It reminds us that, for all of life's banality, there is a significance to things—and evils that we must confront, in good times and bad.

— The End —

Author's note

This novel was inspired by a song from the Civil War period called "The Vacant Chair," two verses of which are included in the last chapter. This song portrays a family gathered for a festive holiday meal, perhaps Thanksgiving or Christmas, in the first year of the war. One place at the table, however, is empty—that of a father, brother, or son who was recently killed in battle. Although the family tries to be stoical and to console itself through its honoring of its loved one, its sense of loss is immense. Clearly, grief will be a prominent note in the family circle for as long as any of those who remember him are still around.

As I was listening to this song, I began to imagine a woman in a similar situation, that is, a woman in early middle age who had lost her husband in the war and who was now faced with the prospect of living out the rest of her life alone. Grief, of course, would be a constant element of that life, and all the more so in that in addition to her feelings of loss she would be expected to honor her husband's memory for the rest of her days, to maintain a sort of shrine for him in her heart. But she would face other challenges as well: those of simply living each day, her own aging, and the vast and disturbing changes that were then taking place in the United States.

It is difficult to overstate the extent of the transformation that occurred in late nineteenth-century America. The America of 1900 would probably seem a bit quaint to us, but its essential features would be familiar: we would find it to be highly urbanized, industrial, multi-ethnic, fast-paced, and generally fairly complex. The America of 1860 was altogether different. Most people then lived on farms or in small towns, communities were tightly knit and largely self-sustaining, and life in general was simpler and slower paced. This is not to say that life in 1860 was idyllic or that none of the changes were beneficial; it does, however, highlight the enormous transition experienced by people after the Civil War.

Included in this transition were profound social changes. Life became a great deal more impersonal, with the result that there was an erosion of trust between people. Corruption was also rampant at virtually all levels. Overall, there was a sense that individuals had largely lost control over their lives, that they were now entirely in the grip of powerful corporations and corrupt governments. In this, of course, there are distinct parallels with our own times.

I have cast the narrative in the form of entries in the main character's journal for two main reasons. First, keeping a journal was a common practice in the nineteenth century; more so than people at other times, people in that era were concerned to record the many details of their lives as they unfolded day by day. To judge by the ones that have come down to us, these journals were taken very seriously. Often the handwriting is very neat and the entries are carefully composed, as if the journals were seen as important records of lives well lived. Keeping a journal, of course, is essentially an attempt to derive a larger meaning from the events of ordinary life, and that was especially true in the nineteenth century.

The second, and perhaps more important, reason for adopting the journal form is to create real intimacy between Ellen and the reader. We see virtually everything through her eyes, as if we were reading over her shoulder as she records her thoughts and experiences.

As befits the main character's temperament, *Gathering Years* is largely quiet in tone. Although there are a few dramatic incidents in it, for the most part it is simply an account of a thoughtful woman's experiences and her reactions to them. As is common in the journals of the period, in many entries Ellen attempts to draw the "moral" from an incident or experience. In others she simply records quiet joys, such as watching a sunset. In a sense, then, many of the entries in this journal have the character of little meditations—a reflection of the belief that life should be lived deliberately and with an awareness of its larger significance.

Acknowledgments

A number of people read all or portions of *Gathering Years* in draft form and gave me valuable comments on it, including Ruth Bell, Chancy Bittner, Kathy Cooper, Fred Eastman, Carrie Meyer, Chuck Nicholson, Kim Nicholson, and Chuck Smith. I am especially grateful to my wife Karen, who has lived almost as closely with the main characters as I have and whose counsel on many matters was invaluable; to Pat Winters, whose overwhelming enthusiasm for the novel gave me needed encouragement; to Kathy Eastman, Pam Petrusso, and Deb Wender, whose keen editorial eyes both spared me some errors and helped me sharpen the focus at certain points; and to Linda Lovell, who assisted me in crafting a proposal for it. Although I did not take all of the suggestions that were offered, I did consider all of them carefully. Certainly, having different perspectives on my story and the way in which I was telling it was a huge asset.

I am also very grateful to John Hennessy, the chief historian and chief of interpretation at Fredericksburg and Spotsylvania National Military Park in Virginia, for providing me information about Fredericksburg National Cemetery.

Finally, I would like to express my appreciation to Marj Charlier of Sunacumen Press, without whose support *Gathering Years* would never have found its way into the wider world.

Sources

This novel reflects my reading and other sources of information—lectures, television programs, visits to historic sites, and so forth—over many years. As a certain amount of this information now resides almost unconsciously in my mind, it is not really possible to acknowledge all of the sources that I drew on for the novel. The ones listed below were consulted specifically for it.

All of the historical incidents in the novel took place substantially as I have portrayed them. I have, however, taken several liberties that I should acknowledge. First, the new-style cemetery in Springfield, Massachusetts, in which Ellen's parents were buried in 1834, was not in fact laid out until 1841. Second, the labor strike mentioned in Chapter III is based on a strike that occurred in the coalfields of the Hocking Valley in 1874 (see Gutman 1970), one year before it does in the novel. And third, the prominent painter mentioned in Chapter IV is closely modeled on William Merritt Chase (1849–1916), who was based in New York and had a summer home on Long Island (see Pisano 1983); my principal adaptation was to place him in a Midwestern setting. With only a few exceptions, the paintings that the central character views in the fictional painter's studio are actual paintings by Chase.

Although most of the central themes of the novel are my

own, in some cases I (may) have silently purloined ideas or interpretations of events from others. One source in particular that deserves mention is Morison (1930), on which I drew heavily for the fictional essay on Puritanism that appears in Chapter V. In all cases, however, the sources are included in the list of references that follows, and I trust that each author (and/or his or her publisher) will be content with this indirect acknowledgment. I have also borrowed some of the settings of the songs featured on the disk by Sony Music Enterprises (1991) in my account of the concert portrayed in Chapter V.

At various points in the narrative there are quotations from well-known authors, most of whom are identified. In some instances, however, the quotations are simply attributed to "one of our writers." In every instance, the source is Henry David Thoreau. I chose not to name him explicitly for two reasons: he was not overly well known during the period in which the novel is set, and some of his writings (particularly his journal) were not published until long after his death in 1862. Thus, although his thoughts are true to the times and the milieu in which the central character lived, she would probably not have known of them.

Finally, in the regimental history mentioned in Chapter IV, I have taken the two quotations directly from an actual regimental history (that of the 126th Ohio Volunteer Infantry; see Gilson 1883). They just seemed perfect to me, and I hope that in some small way this honors the memory of those who actually endured the enormous cataclysm of the Civil War.

Byron, M. Christine, and Thomas R. Wilson. *Vintage Views of Leelanau County.* Chelsea, MI: Sleeping Bear Press, 2002.

Carlson, Peter. "130 Years Ago, Parallels Up to a Boiling Point." *Washington Post,* December 13, 1998.

Clark, Kenneth. *The Nude: A Study in Ideal Form.* Princeton, NJ: Princeton University Press, 1956.

Durant, Will. *The Story of Philosophy: The Lives and Opinions of the Greater Philosophers.* New York: Simon & Schuster, 1926.

Durant, Will. *The Life of Greece.* New York: Simon & Schuster, 1939.

Engerman, Stanley L., and Robert E. Gallman, editors. *The Cambridge Economic History of the United States.* Vol. II, *The Long Nineteenth Century.* Cambridge, UK: Cambridge

University Press, 2000.

Foner, Eric. *A Short History of Reconstruction, 1863–1877.* New York: Harper & Row, 1990.

Franklin, John Hope. *Reconstruction: After the Civil War.* Chicago: University of Chicago Press, 1961.

Frisch, Michael H. *Town into City: Springfield, Massachusetts, and the Meaning of Community, 1840–1880.* Cambridge, MA: Harvard University Press, 1972.

Gilson, John H. *History of the 126th Ohio Volunteer Infantry.* Huntington, WV: Blue Acorn Press, new edition of book first published 1883.

Gottlieb, Anthony. *The Dream of Reason: A History of Philosophy from the Greeks to the Renaissance.* New York: W. W. Norton, 2000.

Greene, A. Wilson, and Gary W. Gallagher. *National Geographic Guide to the Civil War National Battlefield Parks.* Washington, DC: National Geographic Society, 1992.

Gutman, Herbert G. "The Workers' Search for Power." In H. Wayne Morgan, editor. *The Gilded Age,* revised edition.

Hamilton, Edith. *The Greek Way.* New York: W. W. Norton, 1930.

Hensley, Jeannine, editor. *The Works of Anne Bradstreet.* Cambridge, MA: Belknap Press, 1967.

Howat, John K. *The Hudson River and Its Painters.* New York: American Legacy Press, 1972.

Littell, Edmund M. *One Hundred Plus Years in Leelanau: A History of Leelanau County, Michigan.* LeelanauCounty, MI: Leelanau County Prospectors Club, 2007.

McPherson, James M. *Crossroads of Freedom: Antietam.* New York: Oxford University Press, 2002.

Menand, Louis. *The Metaphysical Club: A Story of Ideas in America.* New York: Farrar, Straus and Giroux, 2001.

Morgan, H. Wayne, editor. *The Gilded Age,* revised edition. Syracuse, NY: Syracuse University Press, 1970.

Morison, Samuel Eliot. *Builders of the Bay Colony.* Boston: Houghton Mifflin, 1930.

Morison, Samuel Eliot. *The Oxford History of the American People,* vols. 2–3. New York: New American Library, 1972.

Nevins, Allan, and Henry Steele Commager. *A Pocket History of the United States.* New York: Washington Square Press, 1967.

Nugent, Walter T. K. "Money, Politics, and Society: The Currency Question." In H. Wayne Morgan, editor. *The Gilded Age,* revised edition.

Parker, Francis H. *The Story of Western Philosophy.* Bloomington,
    IN: Indiana University Press, 1967.
Perret, Geoffrey. *Ulysses S. Grant: Soldier and President.* New York:
    Random House, 1997.
Perry, Mark. *Grant and Twain: The Story of a Friendship that Changed
    America.* New York: Random House, 2004.
Pisano, Ronald G. *A Leading Spirit in American Art: William Merritt
    Chase, 1849–1916.* Seattle, WA: Henry Gallery Association, 1983.
Rhea, Gordon C. *The Battles for Spotsylvania Court House and the Road
    to Yellow Tavern, May 7–12, 1864.* Baton Rouge, LA: Louisiana
    State University Press, 1997.
Robertson, Ross M., and Gary M. Walton. *History of the American
    Economy,* 4th edition. New York: Harcourt Brace Jovanovich, 1979.
Roseboom, Eugene H., and Francis P. Weisenburger. *A History of
    Ohio,* 2nd edition. Columbus, OH: Ohio Historical Society, 1967.
Santmyer, Helen Hooven. "… *and Ladies of the Club.*" New York:
    Berkley Publishing Group, 1985.
Smith, Gene. *High Crimes and Misdemeanors: The Impeachment and
    Trial of Andrew Johnson.* New York: William Morrow and
    Company, 1977.
Smith, Martin Ferguson, editor. *Lucretius: De Rerum Natura,* revised
    edition. Cambridge, MA: Harvard University Press, 1975.
Sony Music Enterprises. *Songs of the Civil War.* Compact disc. New
    York: Sony Music Enterprises, 1991.
Stewart, David O. *Impeached: The Trial of President Andrew Johnson
    and the Fight for Lincoln's Legacy.* New York: Simon & Schuster,
    2009.
Sutherland, Daniel E. *The Expansion of Everyday Life, 1860–1876.* New
    York: Harper & Row, 1989.
Time-Life Records. Listener's Guide to "The Age of Revolution" in *The
    Story of Great Music.* New York: Time-Life Records, 1968.
Tipple, John. "Big Businessmen." In, H. Wayne Morgan, editor. *The
    Gilded Age,* revised edition.
Traxel, David. *1898: The Birth of the American Century.* New York:
    Vintage Books, 1998.
Turner, Gerard L. *Scientific Instruments, 1500–1900: An Introduction.*
    Berkeley, CA: University of California Press, 1998.
Vidal, Gore. *1876.* New York: Random House, 1976.
Waterfield, Robin, translator. *Plutarch: Greek Lives.* Oxford, UK:
    Oxford University Press, 1998.
Waterfield, Robin, translator. *Plutarch: Roman Lives.* Oxford, UK:

Oxford University Press, 1999.

Withuhn, William L., editor. *Rails across America: A History of Railroads in North America.* New York: Smithmark Publishers, 1993.

Made in USA - Kendallville, IN
1083574_9781734564303
04.21.2020 1258